How I Made $436,797 In One Year Selling Other People's Stuff Online

I Do It, and YOU Can Too!

The Super Affiliate Handbook

by Rosalind Gardner

Copyright Notice

Library and Archives Canada Cataloguing in Publication

Gardner, Rosalind, 1959-
        The super affiliate handbook: how I made $436,797 in one year selling other people's stuff online / by Rosalind Gardner.

ISBN 0-9733287-4-6

        1. Affiliate programs (World Wide Web)
        2. 2. Internet marketing.
I. Title.

HF5438.35.G37 2005   658.8'4   C2005-901295-1

Legal Notices and Disclaimer

As much as I'd love to think that every reader of the "Super Affiliate Handbook" (SAH) will follow its advice and become fabulously wealthy by result, the truth is that I can't promise that will happen for you.

I can't guarantee that you will actually read the book, follow my suggestions or that you will write copy that entices your visitors to buy vast amounts of your merchant partners' products.

I wish I could, but I can't.

So here's the nitty gritty legal statement.

THE FOLLOWING TERMS AND CONDITIONS APPLY:

While all attempts have been made to verify information provided, neither I, nor any ancillary party, assumes any responsibility for errors, omissions, or contradictory interpretation of the subject matter herein.

Any perceived slights of specific people or organizations are unintentional.

To the fullest extent permitted by applicable laws, in no event shall SAH, agents or suppliers be liable for damages of any kind or character, including without limitation any compensatory, incidental, direct, indirect, special, punitive, or consequential damages, loss of use, loss of data, loss of income or profit, loss of or damage to property, claims of third parties, or other losses of any kind or character, even if SAH has been advised of the possibility of such damages or losses, arising out of or in connection with the use of the SAH or any web site with which it is linked.

Some of the URL's in this book are affiliate links, which means that I may earn a commission if you buy a product through a particular link. This is an example of affiliate marketing in action - and the subject of this book.

Acknowledgements

I am enormously grateful to both the late Corey Rudl of the Internet Marketing Center and Allan Gardyne of AssociatePrograms.com.

Corey profiled my affiliate business success story on his "Secrets to Their Success" site, and Allan published information about that interview.

By result, I received hundreds of emails from aspiring netpreneurs who were interested in affiliate marketing. Their questions helped me realize that I had valuable information to share, and each and every question asked was another good reason to write "The Super Affiliate Handbook".

I therefore am thankful to everyone who ever asked me a question about doing business as an affiliate marketer.

Last, but not least, I am grateful to you, Dear Reader, for making time to read this book. I hope it proves enormously beneficial to you in all of your online moneymaking ventures!

With Best Wishes for YOUR Success,

Rosalind

Table of Contents

Table of Figures

Please Read This First

Thank you for buying the "*Super Affiliate Handbook*," and congratulations for taking a positive step towards your future as an affiliate marketer. You will find the "*Super Affiliate Handbook*" a valuable resource that you return to again and again as you build your own affiliate marketing business.

Before reading any further, sign up at http://NetProfitsToday.com to receive the '*Net Profits Today [NPT]*' free newsletter to stay current on Internet and Affiliate marketing changes and developments.

If you are reading the **soft cover version**, and would like a discounted copy of the ebook, please contact us through the Support Desk at http://www.netprofitstoday.com/support/.

How to Get the Most from the "HandBook"

You are reading the 'Super Affiliate Handbook' because you want to learn how to make money with affiliate programs, and you want to do that without reading an encyclopedia or spending a lot of money. So, I've kept things simple and concise.

In order to get the most out of the Handbook, take these steps:

1. **Stay Connected to the Internet** - There are many links to useful resources in the Handbook. To take advantage of them, you'll have to be connected to the Internet when you read the book. If you'd rather read "*The Super Affiliate Handbook*" while relaxing on your couch, that's OK too! Simply take note of links in the book that you want to visit later.

2. **Read the Book from Cover to Cover** - I know that the prospect of starting your own business is really exciting. But before you open an HTML editor or sign up for a bunch of affiliate programs, read "The Super Affiliate Handbook" in its entirety. By doing so, you will avoid the possibility of missing essential information and wasting both your time and money.

3. **Take Action** - A goal without a deadline is nothing more than a wish. To achieve success, you must set highly specific goals with target completion dates, and develop a plan to meet those goals and then put the plan into action. Read the Handbook completely, and then act on your plan! By approaching your work in bite-sized chunks as described in the manual, you'll find that your project becomes easily manageable.

4. **Keep Learning** - Change is happening faster and faster all the time. This is especially true where technology and the Internet are concerned. Successful Internet marketing entrepreneurs realize that they need to stay abreast of the industry, or get left in the dust. This entails reading relevant newsletters, keeping an eye on your competitors and making regular investments in educational materials.

Once you finish reading the 'Super Affiliate Handbook,' you will have all the information you need to start your own profitable affiliate marketing business quickly, easily and inexpensively.

CHANGES & IMPROVEMENTS SINCE 2003

The 'Super Affiliate Handbook' was originally published in June 2003 under the title "*The Super Affiliate Handbook: How I Made $436,797 Last Year Selling Other People's Stuff Online*." Since then, the book has undergone numerous revisions to introduce and explain new technology, software and working processes.

Topics such as blogging, RSS and how to use foreign currency rates to your advantage are now included. Most notably, I have simplified the niche selection / market research process considerably. My original and basic business strategies remain unchanged however because they still WORK extraordinarily well.

Because I want YOU to succeed over the long term, you will learn strategies that I and other Super Affiliates use to build *sustainable* and *highly successful* businesses. Here are 6 ways in which my strategies differ from the 'Gray Hat' approach to affiliate marketing.

1. **Profit from What You Know** – Putting profit potential first is a sure recipe for failure, especially for those starting their first business. I advocate building your business around a topic that you enjoy and either know well or are willing to learn about, *and* has huge profit potential. The added benefit is that you will have more fun during the business-building process.

2. **Build Sites for People not Search Engines** – Successful affiliates build sites for people, not search engines. To satisfy your customers' needs and wants, you will learn how to build sites with real content such as product endorsements, articles and reviews – NOT Gray or Black Hat tricks that will kill your business in the wink of an eye.

3. **Build Fewer Sites with Better Content** – Building site after little site is more like a job than a business and is also more costly. You will therefore learn how to build a lucrative affiliate business around just one or two large content sites.

4. **Use Multiple Marketing Methods** – Affiliates using my prescribed marketing methods do not have to worry that their traffic or income will suddenly disappear, as happened to many who bought into false promises about building an affiliate business using only search engine marketing. I teach a variety of ways to market your site which guarantees that your site will always receive a flow of traffic. If one method of traffic delivery slows down temporarily, many more are in place to sustain, or even boost, your income.

5. **Build Community** – Super Affiliates build community to interact with their visitors through newsletters, blogs and forums. As your visitors get to know you, your visitor-to-customer conversion rate increases – as will your income.

6. **Brand Yourself** – Community interaction 'brands' you as a trusted source of valuable information. Your income increases even more when new and repeat visitors as surfers recognize you as an expert in your chosen topic.

In other words, you make money by using sustainable business strategies and by having fun. I urge you to start having fun as soon as possible. ☺

Happy reading!

Introduction to Internet Marketing

Anyone who sells or resells a product online, is an Internet marketer. That includes affiliate marketers, online merchants, dropshippers and online auction sellers just to name a few.

In this section about Internet marketing, we'll look at some of the biggest myths about doing business online and the opportunity for online sellers as it exists now.

You will also learn how affiliate marketing works, how affiliate marketers make money and get a general overview of the business building process.

Let's start with those myths...

Online Business: The 6 Biggest Myths BUSTED

Tales of fame, fortune and financial disaster abound in the world of online marketing. Most of those tales are completely mythical. So in this section I debunk the most prevalent myths about Internet marketing.

1. **You can "get rich quick" online**. Lottery wins and large inheritances aside, there is no way to 'get rich quick' online or off. However, you can build and grow an online business more quickly than you can a brick and mortar business.

2. **Internet marketing is easy**. The person who never gets off the couch will not succeed online. Nor will the individual who reads every online business manual ever published yet fails to act on a viable plan. Success in any endeavor takes time and effort.

3. **Affiliates marketers have it particularly easy**. Although few opportunities are as quick, easy and inexpensive to implement as an affiliate marketing business, success as an affiliate still requires an investment of time, effort and resources.

4. **Doing business online is free.** Just as offline businesses pay rent, telephone and advertising bills every month; online businesses pay Internet connection, hosting fees and other service charges to their suppliers. Compared to running an offline store however, operating costs for Internet businesses are relatively low.

5. **It's too late to start an Internet business.** No marketplace is easier to reach than the Internet and growth is forecasted to continue for years to come. For some encouragement, read "*Online Sales Report Spell Opportunity*" which discusses consumer online spending forecasts for 2007.

6. **Only big companies make *big* money online.** A completely ridiculous statement. Read '*Examples of Successful Internet and Affiliate Marketers*' to be inspired by sole proprietors in the affiliate space... and those are just a few of the many successful affiliate marketers I know personally --- some of whom have started businesses within the last year or two.

Although the Internet is rife with tales of fortune and failure in mythical proportions, the reality is that thousands of ordinary people (like you and me) are earning good livings online from the comfort of their own homes.

Online Sales Report Spells OPPORTUNITY

A May 14, 2007 press release based on a study conducted by Forrester Research, reported that online sales rose 25 percent in 2006 and are forecasted to soar again in 2007. I've included the full report below. Take special note of merchandise categories that are hot. Are you interested in selling products in those categories? ☺

WASHINGTON, May 14 /PRNewswire-USNewswire/ -- As the Internet grows up, computers have moved over to make room for clothing at the top of the sales list. According to the first part of The State of Retailing Online 2007, the tenth annual Shop.org study conducted by Forrester Research, Inc. of 170 retailers, Americans last year spent more online on clothing than they did on computers for the first time in history. The report found the apparel, accessories and footwear category reached $18.3 billion in 2006 and is expected to hit $22.1 billion in 2007. This year, 10 percent of all clothing sales are expected to occur online.

"Apparel retailers have overcome a number of hurdles to encourage shoppers to buy clothing and accessories online," said Scott Silverman, executive director of Shop.org. "Retailers are doing such a great job online that in some cases it's easier to find and buy clothing on the web than it is in a store."

The report suggests that the apparel and accessories category has experienced strong sales because of an influx of new companies and liberal shipping policies such as free shipping on returns and exchanges. Additionally, apparel and accessories retailers are integrating new technologies onto their sites including rich imaging, where customers can zoom and rotate merchandise or see the item in different colors before buying, all of which eases the mind of a customer who is hesitant to purchase apparel online.

Computer hardware and software, long the frontrunner for non-travel online sales, moved into second place in 2006 at $17.2 billion, followed by sales of autos and auto parts ($16.7 billion) and home furnishings ($10 billion).

Online Sales to Soar Again this Year

According to the report, 2007 online sales (including travel) are expected to rise 18 percent to $259.1 billion. Sales excluding travel will reach $174.5 billion. This strong growth will come off of an impressive performance in 2006. Online sales last year rose 25 percent to $219.9 billion. Excluding travel, online retail sales rose 29 percent to $146.5 billion, representing six percent of total retail sales in 2006.*

"As consumers flood the web to purchase merchandise and research products, online retail is moving full speed ahead," said Sucharita Mulpuru, Forrester Research senior analyst and lead author of the report. "This strong growth is an indicator that online retail is years away from reaching a point of saturation."

Another sign that e-commerce has come of age is that profitability throughout the sector has stabilized. Eighty-three percent of respondents to the survey reported profitability and 78 percent said they were more profitable than 2005. Profit as a percentage of revenue did not change, the report notes, because revenue and expenses grew as well.

The second part of the study, which will examine tactics that online retailers found most successful and site features that resonated most with online consumers, will be released in September at Shop.org's Annual Summit.

About Forrester Research

Forrester Research, Inc. is an independent technology and market research company that provides pragmatic and forward-thinking advice to global leaders in business and technology. For more than 23 years, Forrester has been making leaders successful every day through its proprietary research, consulting, events and peer-to-peer executive programs. For more information, visit http://www.forrester.com/.

About Shop.org

Shop.org is the network for retailers online. Its 600 members include the 10 largest retailers in the U.S. and 70 percent of the Internet Retailer Top 100 E-Retailers. It's where the best retail minds come together to gain the insight, knowledge, and intelligence to make smarter, more informed decisions in the evolving world of the Internet and multi-channel retailing. Founded in 1996, Shop.org became a division of the National Retail Federation in January 2001. Shop.org programs and activities include benchmarking research, events and networking communities.

* "Retail Sales" exclude travel and include the following categories: apparel, accessories, and footwear; computer hardware and software; autos and auto parts; home furnishings; consumer electronics; music and video; appliances and tools; office supplies; sporting goods and apparel; books; toys and video games; gift cards and gift certificates; event and movie tickets; food, beverage, and grocery; jewelry; flowers and cards; over-the-counter medicines and personal care; computer peripherals; baby products; cosmetics and fragrances; and pet supplies. These are not the same categories that the National Retail Federation tracks; therefore, the numbers are not comparable.

Source: National Retail Federation

Affiliate Marketing Basics

I feel like I 'lucked out' when I discovered affiliate marketing as a way to do business online, and chose to pursue it ahead of other options such as auction selling, drop-shipping, MLM or selling my own products as a merchant.

At the time, I knew nothing of the benefits of working as an affiliate, nor did I consider them. In retrospect however, I'm thrilled that I chose the affiliate marketing path primarily because of the benefits.

In this section, you'll learn about 17 of those benefits and some of the 100's of market categories in which you can sell products. For inspiration, you'll see examples of highly successful affiliates and then we'll get down to the nitty-gritty of how affiliate marketing works and the 6 basic ways affiliates earn commissions. Wrapping up the section, you'll see the 7-step outline from which you will be working to build your own affiliate business.

First, let's find out why affiliates love affiliate marketing.

17 Benefits of Working as an Affiliate

1. **No Production Costs** - The cost to develop and produce a new product is prohibitive for almost anyone who wants to start a home-based business. With affiliate programs, production costs aren't an issue. The product has been developed and proven - all on the merchant's nickel.

2. **Low Cost Set-up** - Compared with building a store offline, becoming an Internet marketer is cheap. You probably already have a desk, Internet-connected computer and word-processing software, which is all the equipment you may need.

3. **No Fees or Licenses** - I often compare doing business as an affiliate, with distributing a line of products in the real world. The biggest difference is that the distributor must often pay for a license to distribute products within a limited geographic region. Affiliate programs, on the other hand, are usually free to join, and geographic market reach is limited only by the affiliate's ability to promote his web site.

4. **Sell Almost Anything** - What isn't sold online? That list must be shorter than the one describing all that IS sold online. There are thousands and thousands of affiliate programs selling every product under the sun. That makes it easy to find products related to your current or planned web site.

5. **No Sales Experience Required** - When I started my affiliate business, I had absolutely no sales experience. That wasn't a problem, however. The companies I affiliated with provided excellent marketing material. Using their sales copy, I was able to get my first affiliate site up in less than a day.

6. **No Employees** - Employee salaries are the biggest business expense. Although you may need or want someone to work for you on occasion, you'll never have to worry about hiring full or part-time employees while working as an affiliate marketer. When you have a project you want to hire out, it is easy to find specialists in every computer-related field who can work for you from the comfort of THEIR own homes. You pay only for the project, and never have to worry about ongoing employee-related benefits and deductions.

7. **No Merchant Accounts** - Setting up a merchant account is time-consuming and costly. However, affiliate marketers don't need merchant account. Merchants bear all the costs for payment processing. As an affiliate, you'll never lose sleep over chargebacks, fraud or losing your merchant account.

8. **No Inventory** - As an affiliate marketer, you can sell large items without storage concerns, even if you live in a small one-bedroom apartment.

9. **No Order-Processing** - Forget the problems associated with collecting and storing names, addresses, credit card numbers, etc. The merchant does all that!

10. **No Shipping** - The cost and hassle to prepare and ship products to customers worldwide could be staggering. Affiliates never have to worry about packaging supplies or postal rates.

11. **No Customer Service** - Do you hate the prospect of dealing with nasty people or customer complaints? Don't worry about it! The merchant handles the snivelers.

12. **Make Money While You Sleep** - What other business allows you as a sole proprietor to keep your doors open and keep making money even when you take breaks or after you go home for the night?

13. **Worldwide Marketplace** - The Internet is the world's largest marketplace. You can drive more visitors to your online store in a day, than a small-town merchant will see in his or her brick and mortar business in a year.

14. **Work from Home** – Working from home is considered the best advantage to having an online business by those who despised a long commute to work or prefer to work in their pajamas. Parents, in particular, value having more time to spend with their children.

15. **Work Anywhere in the World** – An online business is perfect for those who love to travel. I've used my laptop to maintain my affiliate business throughout North America as well as from remote locations in South America and China.

16. **Minimal Risk** - The product you chose isn't making money? Dump it. Take down your links and promote another! It's that easy. There are no long-term contracts binding you to products that don't sell.

17. **High Income Potential** - If you have a job, your salary or hourly wage is probably pre-determined. Maybe there's not much, other than working overtime, that you can do to increase your income. With your own affiliate business on the Internet your income potential is limited only by your desire, effort and imagination.

That's why affiliates LOVE affiliate marketing.

With my almost insatiable wanderlust, my favorite thing about affiliate marketing is the ability to work anywhere I am in the world.

What will yours be?

100'S OF MARKETS, 1000'S OF MERCHANTS & MILLIONS OF PRODUCTS

There is almost no end to the types of products and services that you can sell online as an affiliate. Shown below is a generic list of products and services sold in various categories by merchants that are part of Commission Junction (CJ.com), the largest affiliate network.

Scan the list to get some ideas about what you might like to sell online. A little later I will help you brainstorm your best topic through some simple market research.

CATEGORY	PRODUCTS & SERVICES SOLD
Accessories	Cosmetics/Fragrance, Handbags, Jewelry - Shoes
Art/Photo/Music	Art, Music, Photo
Automotive	Cars & Trucks, Motorcycles, Parts & Accessories, Rentals, Tools and Supplies
Books/Media	Audio Books, Books, Magazines, News, Television, Videos/Movies
Business	Business-To-Business, Marketing, Office, Productivity Tools, Travel
Careers	Employment, Military
Clothing/Apparel	Children's, Malls, Men's, Women's
Commerce	Auction, Classifieds, E-commerce solutions/providers, New/Used Goods, Telephone services, Utilities
Computer & Electronics	Computer HW, Computer Support, Computer SW, Consumer Electronics, Peripherals
Education	Children, College, Languages, Professional
Entertainment	Memorabilia
Family	Babies, Children, Entertainment, Teens, Weddings
Financial services	Banking/Trading, Credit Cards, Investment, Loans, Real Estate Services
Food & Drinks	Gourmet, Groceries, Restaurants, Tobacco, Wine & Spirits
Games & Toys	Electronic Toys, Games, Toys
Gifts & Flowers	Care Packages, Collectibles, Flowers, Gifts, Greeting Cards
Health & Beauty	Bath & Body, Cosmetics, Health Food, Nutritional Supplements, Pharmaceuticals, Self Help, Vision Care, Wellness
Home & Garden	Bed & Bath, Construction, Furniture, Garden, Home Appliances, Kitchen, Pets, Real Estate, Utilities
Insurance	Commercial, Personal Insurance
Legal	Services
Marketing	Business-to-Business, Network Marketing
Medical	Equipment
Phonecard Services	Online/Wireless
Recreation & Leisure	Astrology, Betting/Gaming, Communities, Events, Matchmaking, New Age, Outdoors, Party Goods
Sports & Fitness	Exercise & Health, Professional Sports Organizations, Sports, WaterSports
Travel	Accessories, Air, Car, Hotel, Luggage, Vacation
Web Services	Advice, Banner ads, Domain Registrations, Email Marketing, Internet Service Providers, Intranets, Search Engine, Web Design, Web Hosting/Servers, Web Tools

To give you even *more incentive* and motivation to start your affiliate marketing business as soon as possible, I've included examples of high-earning affiliate marketers in the following section.

EXAMPLES OF SUCCESSFUL AFFILIATE MARKETERS

We've all heard about the huge successes that companies such as Amazon and eBay have achieved online. But what about the 'Mom and Pop' work-at-home businesses? How much do they make?

Well, with a winning combination of desire, faith and positive action, online business success as a sole operator is entirely possible, as shown in the following examples.

1. **eBay Affiliates** – eBay reported that their top affiliate earned $1,400,000 in February '04 commissions, $1,300,000 in January '04, and $1,000,000 in December '03! That's OVER 1 MILLION dollars per month, folks!

2. **Dating Service Affiliates** – Friendfinder pays out more than $1,000,000.00 in commissions to its affiliates every month and as of October 2007, Cashring reports having paid $19,763,645.60 to its affiliates since 1996 and its top affiliate earns approximately $20,000/month from their program alone!

3. **Matt Haller, Deborah Casey and Jim Cockrum** - Matt Haller earns $10,000/month with a hip-hop affiliate site and Deborah Casey earns $15,000/month as an affiliate. Jim Cockrum made $1000 in one day selling the 'Super Affiliate Handbook' as an affiliate.

4. **Jeremy Palmer** – Earned 1.4 million dollars as an affiliate in 2006, over 800K of which was pure profit.

5. **Yours truly, Rosalind Gardner** - I was earning between thirty and fifty thousand dollars per month in affiliate commissions in 2002, and my earnings for 2007 will be just under the million mark (600K+ profits)... but, I don't work nearly as hard as my friend Jeremy (see above). ☺

No other business is so inexpensive to start yet offers such high profit potential without investing years of work on your part.

How Do Affiliate Programs Work?

Also known as associate, referral and bounty programs, an affiliate program is a partnership with an online merchant in which the affiliate earns a commission for referring sales and/or leads to the merchant's online store.

Simply put, affiliate marketing is commission selling on the Internet. Commissions may be based on the purchase amount (Pay per Sale), a set value for each visit (Pay-per-click), or action such as regisitration or download (Pay per Lead).

Tens of thousands of merchants from sole proprietors and Mom-and-Pop operations to major corporations such as Sony and Dell have their own affiliate programs.

From a merchant's perspective, partnering with affiliates is an inexpensive marketing strategy to increase sales, drive traffic, generate qualified leads and extend brand reach.

From an affiliate's perspective, few other businesses online or off are as relatively inexpensive and simple to start and maintain.

Here is a 4-point overview of how affiliate marketing works.

1. You join an affiliate program and are given a unique affiliate identification and access to your special links.

2. You place your affiliate links on your web site, or in your newsletter.

3. A visitor on your site clicks that link and buys a product, service or fills out a form at the merchant's site.

4. You earn a commission for sales and/or leads generated through your links.

Pretty basic, eh? ☺

Commission Schemes: 6 Ways Affiliates Earn

The most common types of commission schemes are described and listed below according to my personal preference for working with affiliate programs.

1. PAY-PER-SALE & PERCENTAGE PROGRAMS

Also known as 'Partnership,' 'Percentage' and 'Percentage Partners' programs, these programs pay either a fixed dollar amount or a percentage of sales generated by your links.

eHarmony.com is a highly popular Internet dating service available for signup through the *Commission Junction* (CJ.com) affiliate network. They pay their affiliates a percentage of the sale of each membership as shown in the table to the right.

Membership Period	Commission Percentage
1 month	40%
3 months	35%
6 months	25%
1 year	30%

For each 1-month $59.95 membership sold, the affiliate earns 40%, or $23.98. The year-long membership costs $251.40, and affiliates who sell this membership are paid $75.42, or 30% of the total cost to the member.

eHarmony also offers a *pay-per-sale* commission option, which is a flat fee on sales of their gift certificates.

You will learn more about product endorsements and how to achieve high conversion rates in a later section of the handbook.

Membership Period	Flat Fee
1 month	$20.00
3 months	$35.00
6 months	$40.00
1 year	$75.00

2. PAY-PER-LEAD, PAY-PER-ACTION AND PAY-PER-SIGNUP

Pay-Per-Lead, Pay-Per-Action and Pay-Per-Signup schemes are very similar. With Pay-per-lead, affiliates earn a set amount whenever a visitor from their site provides a merchant with their contact information, e.g. name, address and email.

A Pay-Per-Action commission scheme pays out a commission when a visitor from your site completes a required action by the merchant, such as downloading free trial software or signing up for a free trial membership. As such, the visitor is also providing name and address information, and is thus providing a 'lead' for the merchant.

Entire networks known as CPA networks have been created to promote merchants programs, the prime objective of which is lead generation.

These schemes tend to see better conversions than pay-per-sale campaigns, as the visitor doesn't have to open his or her wallet to take advantage of the merchant's offer. However, commissions paid per lead are often quite low, which means that the affiliate must send large amounts of traffic to the merchant's site to make promoting the offer worthwhile.

An exception to the 'low commission' generality are commissions paid by merchants in the Financial Services category, such as credit card, loans, insurance and mortgage providers.

For example, LowerMyBills.com pays $32.00 for completed home refinance loan applications and inquiries related to home equity loans.

In both cases, LowerMyBills.com offers a 'performance incentive' to increase the affiliate's commission by 25% if they generate 50 or more 'actions'.

Have you seen the Crush Calculator shown here to the right?

I run the offer on Sage-Hearts and it pays $4.00 per lead.

FIGURE 1 CPA EXAMPLE

3. PAY-PER-CLICK PROGRAMS

Pay-Per-Click affiliate programs are similar to Pay-Per-Lead. Essentially you are paid a set amount each time one of your visitors clicks on your affiliate link and lands on the merchant's site.

For example, Cashring.com, a company that sells dating service memberships through IWantU.com pays *up to $1.00* for every unique visitor sent to their site --- provided you meet specific traffic criteria.

Placing *Google Adsense* or other contextual advertising on your site is another way that you can earn 'per click' revenue. Affiliates can enroll in this program to run text, image and/or video ads on their sites. The ads generate revenue on either a per-click or per-thousand-impressions (CPM) basis.

The 'Cancun and Mayan Rivera' link shown on the right is how Google Adsense appears in the right navigation bar at Roamsters.com, my travel blog.

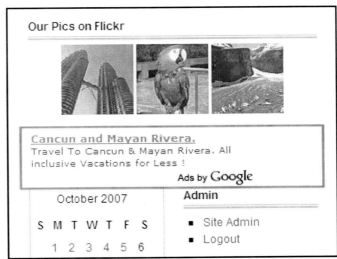

If you visit the site, you will see another instance of Google Adsense near the bottom of the page with 4 separate ads.

Contextual advertising is discussed in the *Join Contextual Advertising Networks* section of the 'Monetize Your Site' chapter.

FIGURE 2 GOOGLE ADSENSE EXAMPLE

4. PAY-PER-CALL

Pay-per-call is a compensation model similar to pay-per-click, except that it drives phone leads to a business' phone, rather than clicks to a merchant's website.

The merchant pays the affiliate a fixed amount for telephone calls received from potential customers and sophisticated call-tracking technology identifies which affiliate referred the caller to the merchant.

5. PAY-PER-POST

The pay-per-post model pays affiliates (primarily bloggers) to write reviews about products, services and websites for advertisers that post 'opportunities' on services such as ReviewMe.com and PayPerPost.com.

FIGURE 3 PAY PER POST

The downside to this model is that you are paid only once for the review, and are not allowed to post affiliate links for the advertiser within the review.

Writing a product review for placement on your site or blog that contains affiliate links from a pay-per-sale or percentage program is preferable to the pay-per-post scheme, as you can generate multiple referrals and earn on-going commissions from a single review.

6. BROKER PROGRAMS

Also known as '2-tier' or 'webmaster referral programs,' broker programs pay affiliates for referring other webmasters to the affiliate program. Some pay a percentage of the referred affiliate's earnings forever, whereas others pay a bounty or one-time fee.

Cashring, for example, pays 5% of all the referred affiliate's earnings.

Of the 6 different commission schemes discussed above, I look first for pay-per-sale and percentage programs, which are particularly lucrative for affiliates who can attain high conversion rates through well-written product reviews. The art of endorsing and reviewing products is covered in the '<u>Add Your Content</u>' section of the book.

Let's now look at an overview of the affiliate business building process.

Overview of the Business-Building Process

It's always easier to tackle a big project, when you break it down into manageable steps. Taken step-by-step, you'll soon find that you're making money on the Web! Here are the 7 basic steps involved in building an affiliate business.

1. **Market Research** - What will your site be about? First you'll brainstorm a number of possible topics for your site. Then you'll assess demand, supply and the potential for profit in your chosen topic with easy-to-use tools.

2. **Building Your Site** – Once you've found a potentially profitable topic, you're ready to register a domain name, arrange for web hosting and start building your site.

3. **Add Content to Your Site** – Content is king. You'll learn about two types of essential affiliate site content and look at 3 different ways to develop your content – from writing it yourself, to buying existing content and outsourcing your articles.

4. **Monetize Your Site** – Next, you'll find merchants with affiliate programs; and review products and programs to determine those with the highest quality.

5. **Market Your Site** – Now it's time to bring visitors to your site. Choose from 25+ marketing methods to get a flood of traffic to your site and start making money, honey!

6. **Manage Your Business** – Managing your business is easy with defined daily, weekly, monthly and yearly tasks and routine.

7. **Grow Your Business** – Ask for higher commission rates, use fluctuating currency rates and other 'tricks of the trade' to increase your conversions and sales.

After your visitors buy copious amounts of your affiliate products and services, you'll deposit numerous large checks into your checking account. You will then repeat the process all over again with one of the other topics you chose in step number one.

Those are the basic steps to building your own lucrative affiliate business.

Now it's time to check out the basic software, services and knowledge that you will need to start your affiliate business.

Basic Services, Software & Know-How

Affiliate marketing on the Internet is NOT rocket science.

You don't need an MBA or other degree to succeed in an online business. If you know how to access the Web, as well as send and receive email, you've already mastered the two activities you'll perform most frequently. Now we'll look at a few services, software and some basic knowledge that will help simplify and speed up your work.

Basic Services

GOOGLE ACCOUNT

Google is much more than just a great search engine. As an Internet and affiliate marketer, I use its services extensively, including Gmail, Gtalk, the Google Calendar, Google's webmaster tools, Google Adwords, Adsense, Google Docs and more.

As you begin doing business online as an affiliate marketer, you too will use Google's services – most likely Google Adwords and Adsense – so I recommend that you sign up for a Google account (https://www.google.com/accounts/NewAccount) sooner than later.

PAYPAL ACCOUNT

Many merchants with affiliate programs pay their affiliates using PayPal and you will be asked to provide your PayPal email address when you sign up for their program. PayPal is an account-based system that lets anyone with an email address securely send and receive online payments using their credit card or bank account.

I suggest that you sign up for a PayPal account now at Paypal.com.

Basic Software

In this section you will learn about software that allows you to surf the web more easily, do research, help you with communication and accounting. The good news is that most of it is FREE!

GOOGLE TOOLBAR

To make the research process easier and faster, I suggest that you install the free Google Toolbar which allows you to search the web from any website, without having to return to Google's homepage to start another search. It takes only seconds to install and is available in a variety of languages, including 'Elmer Fudd' and 'Pig Latin.' The Google Toolbar appears in your browser window like this:

FIGURE 4 BASIC SOFTWARE: GOOGLE TOOLBAR

You can download the Google Toolbar at http://toolbar.google.com/ If you prefer not to install the toolbar, go to http://Google.com to do your research.

TEXT EDITOR

Using a text editor eliminates many of the 'formatting characters' that are embedded by more sophisticated word-processing programs such as *Microsoft Word*. These 'formatting characters' can cause havoc with the appearance of email messages, so using a simple text editor eliminates the potential for messages that look like a bunch of gobbledy-gook.

NotePad is an easy-to-use text editor, and is probably already installed on your computer if you are running Windows. I now use UltraEdit-32, which you can download for a free 45-day trial at http://www.ultraedit.com.

COMPRESSION/EXTRACTION UTILITY

If you are reading the digital (ebook) version of the Super Affiliate Handbook, you are already familiar with how to download and extract ZIP files, and may continue to the next section, *File Transfer Software*.

If on the other hand, you've never downloaded a 'zipped' file from the Internet, please keep reading. Zipped files are files that are compressed to take up less space and bandwidth. An 'extraction utility' is used to extract zipped files.

WINZIP FOR WINDOWS USERS

WinZip (for Windows users) is one of the most popular extraction utilities. WinZip compresses and decompresses files using the zip format. This is the most common format used on the Internet for compressing Windows files. Files compressed in this way are identified with the extension .zip.

WinZip can be downloaded FREE from any of the following Web sites:

http://www.tucows.com
http://www.shareware.com
http://www.download.com

STUFFIT EXPANDER FOR MAC USERS

Stuffit Expander, (for Mac users) is a utility that will decode and extract Macintosh files downloaded from the Internet.

Unlike Windows downloads, which must be decompressed, Macintosh downloads must be decompressed and decoded before they can be used. Fortunately, Stuffit Expander combines both these steps. Stuffit Expander can be downloaded at:

http://www.stuffit.com/expander/index.html

FILE TRANSFER SOFTWARE

Although you can use your web host's facilities to transfer files to your site, an easier way to transfer files fast is to use FTP (File Transfer Protocol) software.

If you run Windows, I recommend that you download and install FileZilla, which is available for free at http://sourceforge.net/projects/filezilla/

Mac users may use Cyberduck, which is an open source FTP and SFTP (SSH Secure File Transfer) browser licenced under the GPL (General Public Licence). CyberDuck is available at http://cyberduck.ch/

Now let's cover some of the basic knowledge that you'll need to run your affiliate business.

Basic Knowledge

Do you know how to copy and paste text from one document into another? Do you know how to download a file from the Internet to your computer and find it again easily? If not, learning some basic computer skills including a few computer codes and some file management techniques will save you time in the long run.

COMPUTER CODES AND MACROS

A macro is a way to automate a task that you perform repeatedly or on a regular basis. The following macros or computer codes are common across most Windows platforms and are worth memorizing for the time they can save during your daily tasks.

Ctrl-A	Select All	Ctrl-N	New Document
Ctrl-B	Bold	Ctrl-O	Open Document
Ctrl-C	Copy	Ctrl-P	Print
Ctrl-D	Fill Down	Ctrl-R	Right Justify
Ctrl-E	Center	Ctrl-S	Save
Ctrl-F	Find	Ctrl-T	Tab
Ctrl-G	Goto	Ctrl-U	Underline
Ctrl-H	Replace	Ctrl-V	Paste
Ctrl-I	Italicize	Ctrl-W	Close Document
Ctrl-J	Full Justify	Ctrl-X	Cut
Ctrl-K	Hyperlink	Ctrl-Y	Redo/Repeat Last Action
Ctrl-M	Increase Indent	Ctrl-Z	Undo

FIGURE 5 COMPUTER CODES/MACROS

LEARN EFFECTIVE SEARCH TECHNIQUES

Did you know that you can limit your Google search results to only pages that contain your search query within the title by typing "intitle:" (without the quotes) followed by your search phrase in quotes?

For example, the query *intitle:"sony digital camera review"* will return just those pages with Sony Digital Camera Review in their title.

There are numerous searching tricks and techniques that help you find what you are looking for faster, and getting *fast* results helps tremendously as you research potential niche markets, existing competition and affiliate programs. In other words, it pays to learn proper search techniques from the outset.

Google provides Basic & Advance search tips and techniques at :
http://www.google.com/support/bin/static.py?page=searchguides.html&ctx=basics
http://www.google.com/support/bin/static.py?page=searchguides.html&ctx=advanced.
Take some time to review those pages and master searching techniques.

How to Keep Your Affiliate Business Organized

I know a webmaster who bookmarks every 'great' site he sees, without organizing his bookmarks into categorized folders. It can take 5 minutes and longer for him to find just one of those sites amongst the hundreds of bookmarks he has stored.

Basically, he wastes valuable time every day looking for bookmarks, files and other records essential to his web business. UGH! Do you want to spend your time (life) like that?

Starting your business with good organization techniques and practices in place is critical to your success. Moreover, you'll save time – time that you can spend concentrating on marketing and making more money or, better yet, having fun.

In this section you'll learn about keeping your bookmarks, email, computer and affiliate business organized.

BOOKMARKS & COMPUTER FILES

The (partial) screenshot below shows you how I organize my bookmarks for easy access to my sites, affiliate commission information, software and sites that I use for research.

FIGURE 6 ORGANIZED BOOKMARKS

To save time on basic tasks, I recommend that you establish categories within your bookmarks, email program and computer file folders that contain documents relevant to your web business. Examples of categories include:

- Accounting / Financial
- Merchant Partners / Affiliate Programs
- Correspondence
- Newsletters
- Web Sites

Top-level categories are then broken down into more specific categories.

I store all my web pages in folders named for their domains, i.e. Sage-Hearts.com, Roamsters.com, 101Date.com and NetProfitsToday.com.

Look at the screenshot to the right to see how my site files are named and organized within the 'My Documents' folder on my computer.

All files belonging to those domains are stored in the corresponding folder.

Save time and keep your sanity – keep your bookmarks, email and computer files organized right from the start.

FIGURE 7 ORGANIZED COMPUTER FILES

SET-UP FILTERS IN YOUR EMAIL SOFTWARE

I receive about 500 emails a day – most of which are junk.

But many are notices sent by merchant partners that include information about important updates to their programs or new product offers.

Missing those offers could mean missing possible commissions --- something we don't want to do!

So, to make sure I see email that is important, I set up mail boxes, folders and filters in my email software, Eudora.

Actually, the ability to apply filters easily is the reason I use Eudora. I tried switching to Microsoft Outlook in early 2007, but found that Outlook's filter setup was clunky compared to Eudora's.

The 'Dating' mailbox contains folders for each major program that I promote in that category.

When mail is filtered into a folder, that folder's name is bolded, which alerts me to new mail. Certain folders, such as 'Program News' and 'Sales Notices' folders get priority attention.

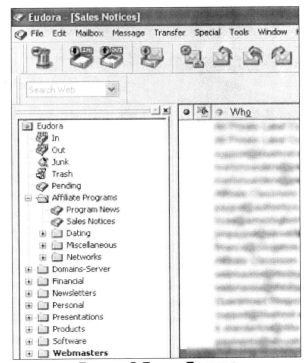

FIGURE 8 EMAIL FILTERS

Filters are also useful for directing unwanted or superfluous notices to the Trash.

ORGANIZE AFFILIATE DATA

You may end up with one site with 5 affiliate programs, or 10 sites and 50 affiliations. You will have different login information for many of the programs that you join. If you've got a good memory you could memorize all that data, but the rest of us usually need assistance.

Here are 2 ways to keep track of your affiliate information.

USE A SPREADSHEET

A spreadsheet is basically a computerized ledger, and the best way to keep track of many aspects of your Internet business.

I use *Microsoft Excel*. If you don't have *Microsoft Office* or spreadsheet software installed on your computer, check out *EasyOffice, a* complete office suite that includes *EasySpreadsheet*. *EasyOffice* is a popular shareware program available at <u>Tucows.com</u>.

'Shareware' is software distributed on the basis of an honor system. Most shareware is free of charge, but the author usually requests that you pay a small fee if you like the program and use it regularly. By paying the fee, you can register your ownership of the software and in turn receive service assistance and updates.

You may use a spreadsheet to organize your data in a way that makes sense to you.

Add a column, delete a column or widen and narrow the columns. Add as many parameters as you like. Make the fonts any size and color that you see fit. Link your affiliate information spreadsheet to your conversion rate information spreadsheet and access either with a single click.

The *'Affiliate Data Spreadsheet'* screenshot shows a portion of the spreadsheet that lists my dating programs.

62	Dating Programs	Acct#	Password	Affiliate Link
63	2ofaKind			http://www.2ofakind.com/ma
64	A Pretty Woman			http://aprettywoman.com/a.c
65	Antopia			http://www.mpwh.net/?CA37
66	Cherry Blossoms			http://www.cherry-blossoms
67	DoubleYourDating			http://affiliate.doubleyourdatin
68	Foreign Affair			http://www.loveme.com/go?r
69	Friendfinder			http://friendfinder.com/go/g95
70				
71		https://secure.friendfinder.com/p/partners/ main.cgi?site=ff&action=login		
72				
73				

FIGURE 9 AFFILIATE DATA SPREADSHEET

Although only 4 columns are shown in the graphic above, you can create as many columns as you like to display as much information about each program as you find necessary. I keep a link to this spreadsheet on my desktop and access it several times a day.

Here are some suggestions for items to place on your own affiliate information spreadsheet.

- Program/Company Name – Linked to the affiliate interface login page
- Username
- Password
- Affiliate Links
- Broker links - Used to refer other affiliates to the program.
- Affiliate Manager's contact name, email address and phone number.
- Commission Info
- Remarks

USE SPECIALIZED SOFTWARE

Alternatively, **Affiliate Organizer** (http://OrganizedAffiliate.com) software, developed by Jon Mills lets you to store all your most important data from your day-to-day business.

This software is easy to install and an icon appears in the bottom right-hand corner (the system tray) of your desktop making the program simple to access.

The software is simple to use. You just fill in the blanks then hit "Save."

Your data can also be backed up and restored at the click of a button.

So, there's no chance that you'll lose data, which is a major relief for anyone who's ever lost data before. ☺

Here is a list of the types of information you can input into Affiliate Organizer:

• Hosting	• Projects and Ideas	• Services
• Websites	• Keyword Lists	• Training
• Advertising	• Domain Registrars	• Resources
• Merchants	• Forums	• Software
• Outsourced Work	• Link Partners	• Autoresponder
• Adsense	• Blogs	• Memberships
• Tasks/Alerts	• Year Plan	• Contacts

Regardless of which method you choose to organize your affiliate business, remember to enter new data into your spreadsheet or "*Affiliate Organizer*" software as soon as possible.

After you forget to make a few entries and have to search your email program for the information, entering it immediately will start to become a habit.

Now that you have the basics, it's time to get to work! We'll start by finding a profitable niche market and topic around which you will build your business.

Find Your Niche

The word 'niche' originates from French and is pronounced "nitch" by Americans while Canadians stick with the French pronunciation "neesh." Regardless of how you say it, a niche market is a focused portion of a targetable market.

For example, cooking is *not* a niche as the audience and competition are both too big to target effectively --- especially for a Mom and Pop affiliate site. As competition online steadily increases, it is best to carve out a *niche within a niche*, i.e. create a site about desserts. Better still, one could slice the dessert niche finer still into a site about pies and pie-making. ☺

The most successful niche sites usually target a combination of two and even three large markets such as "job opportunities for stay-at-home moms," "internet dating for Jewish singles" or "small breed dog training."

However, before you start working on a site about '*The Care and Nurturing of Red Maple Trees in Western Canada*'; you will need to research the market to determine whether there is sufficient demand, yet not too much competition. You will also want to confirm that the niche is profitable.

You will learn how to assess demand, competition and potential profitability in this section.

Work through the sections and recommended actions in order, and by the end of this chapter you will have found YOUR best niche topic and will be ready to start building your website.

And, just in case you are considering a site that consists of a variety of vastly different topics, or building several sites around the same topic, I've included a strong caution against using that approach in the *Forget the Mall: Build a Theme Park!* section.

Consider Your Hobbies and Interests FIRST

Many new webmasters try to market products they know nothing about to people about whom they also know nothing. Although it may be tempting to 'chase the money,' there are 2 good reasons why it makes no sense to build a site around a topic in which you have no interest or knowledge.

1. It is extremely difficult to discuss a topic one knows nothing about, which makes it impossible to make honest, in-depth product recommendations and surfers do not buy from sites where lack of knowledge and experience is obvious.

2. It takes time and energy to create a content-rich site that is popular and is trusted by visitors. If you can't fathom writing about a particular topic in a year from now, you should consider choosing another topic.

Every highly successful businessperson I know started their business in a niche about which they were interested, knowledgeable and even passionate. They know what works in their industry, what does not work, and why.

When you build a site around a topic about which you are knowledgeable and have credibility - *or about which you are willing to learn* - the result is improved conversion rates, increased sales and ultimately, success.

BECOMING AN 'EXPERT' IS EASIER THAN YOU THINK

Don't let the fact that you aren't an expert or passionate about any particular topic dissuade you from becoming an affiliate.

Jim Edwards, my friend and co-producer of the AffiliateBusinessBlueprint.com audio project, teaches a 3-step formula for becoming an expert in virtually any topic, which I've condensed for you below.

1.   Buy a book or ebook on the subject by an expert and read it from cover to cover.

2.   Visit Amazon.com and read the table of contents of at least 5 more books on the subject.

3.   Make a list of the 10 main problems faced by people interested in that topic and the techniques used to solve them.

Jim suggests that by doing that exercise you will know more about the topic 'than 90 percent of the people on this planet.' You will also have all the expertise you'll need to start writing articles and recommending products that help people solve those problems.

TRUE STORY: HOW JIM DID HIS HOMEWORK

The following section is transcribed from the Affiliate Business Blueprint audio tutorial.

In it Jim explains how he took ten minutes one afternoon and used his 3-step process to learn about a topic he knew nothing about.

"Let's say I wanted to go sell in the market of online gambling and I don't know anything about online gambling. What gave me the idea for this is I just got back from Las Vegas.

So I literally — and my hand on a bible — this is the truth — I gave myself ten minutes this afternoon to find as much info as I could. I wanted to know some of the top keyword phrases and get an idea how big the keyword universe is. I also wanted to know the five top issues facing online gamblers, and — that would make an excellent article — I wanted to know the five main forms of online gambling.

So the first thing I did was I went and did a search for "gambling," but I realized real quick that it's not called online gambling, it's called 'online betting' and 'online gaming,' which I guess makes it sound more socially acceptable.

It's important to know that distinction when you're looking at your keywords.

So I went to Amazon and I looked up what the best books were and I found an 'Idiot's Guide.' And your best books to learn to become an expert quickly are the 'Idiot's Guides' and the 'Dummie's' books.

So I looked at the 'Complete Idiot's Guide to Online Gambling.' Cost seventeen bucks. But I'm not going to buy it because I don't need to. Because they let me read the first two chapters online, they let me look at the whole table of contents, and they let me look through the entire index in the back.

That gave me all the keywords I needed and it gave me all the issues I needed.

Some of the keywords I saw that were new to me that I never would have thought of were 'online gaming;' that has 50,000 searches.

Something called 'chuck-o-luck,' which I've never heard of. That had 191 searches and I didn't see anybody bidding on it.

'Daygo Mania,' 'Online Sports Book,' 'Videotino' and another one that killed me here was 'Let it Ride Poker.' It had over 1,500 searches and so from just that quick searching, I could tell that there were a million or more searches a month going on for online gambling. So that's a good one.

And the five main problems or issues I saw them facing — there were actually six — that I thought of would make good article topics.

Number one was how to get started in online gambling, major pitfalls faced by online gamblers and how to avoid them, how to compare one online casino against another, legal aspects of online gambling and betting, unusual online betting opportunities and the hottest online betting craze, which apparently right now is bingo, which I did not know.

So — and also the five main forms of online gambling which are traditional casino favorites like slots, video poker, and then regular poker, then horseracing, and then sports book like football and lotteries and raffles and bingo and stuff.

The point of that is I now know enough to go find either articles or be able to find enough information where I can create my own articles to generate web site content and then be able to get the keywords I'd need to drive traffic and I'm going to let Rosalind cover that.

But just in ten minutes, I became an instant expert as far as being affiliate to market online gambling and online gaming, excuse me."

START BRAINSTORMING IDEAS FOR YOUR TOPIC

Consider the following questions and suggestions carefully to generate a list of possible topics for your site.

- Do you feel especially passionate about any subject in particular?
- Are you an expert in anything?
- Do you have hobbies or interests that you pursue regularly?
- Are you active in a sport?
- Ask your friends and family what they think you might be especially good at doing.

- What have you learned from your jobs, hobbies and general life experience? Do a skills and knowledge assessment.
- What problems have you solved in the past?

Make a list of topics in which you are most interested. Don't worry about whether or not there is a market for your topic yet. You will learn how to research demand for your topic in '*Do "Keyword" Research to Assess Market Demand*.'

Here is an example of my 'short list' of potential topics:

singles and dating	making	golf
camcorders / online	running	motivational methods
video / vblogging	shoes	teddy bears
beer and beer	cats	shawls & wraps
	Vietnamese cooking	yoga

Is *your* list ready? Good! However, before we find out how many people are surfin' the 'Net for information, products and/or services related to the topics in your list, here are 2 more important things to consider before you choose your site's final topic.

FORGET THE MALL: BUILD A THEME PARK!

How and why do you surf the 'Net? Do you turn on your computer, open your browser, then scratch your head and think to yourself, "**Hmm... wonder what I should look for today?**" I would bet your approach to surfing the 'Net isn't so haphazard. If you are like most Internet users, you know exactly what you want before you start surfing.

For example, when you started looking for ways to make money online, you probably went to Google.com and typed in phrases such as 'make money,' 'make money online' and 'affiliate programs.'

Now think about the sites that you found. Were they 'mall sites,' consisting of a mish-mash of unrelated subjects? Probably not! The results returned were highly relevant, which saved you time, effort and frustration during your research.

Your site visitors will be no different. They too want to save their time and effort and get highly relevant results when they are looking for specific information.

Yet, many newbies still persist in building a site that covers too many different topics. Perhaps they think that a mall saves their visitors time by giving them a one-stop shopping experience. That, unfortunately, is a pipe dream.

To build a mall site with universal appeal and umpteen hundred categories, requires umpteen hundred pages each about a specific topic. That takes time - lots and LOTS of time.

Customer satisfaction must be the first goal of *any* business, including an affiliate marketing business. When you focus on your customers first and foremost, the few extra dollars you spend on building individual theme sites, will be more than offset when happy customers support your site(s) with their dollars.

ONE TOPIC: MULTIPLE DOMAINS?

Building a plethora of sites, all around the same theme or topic is also a waste of time, effort and money.

First of all, when you use pay-per-click advertising services, you may advertise a keyword or keyword phrase only once with the same service. For example, if you have 10 sites focused around dating service affiliate programs, you may advertise the keyword 'dating' only once. So, to which site would you send your traffic?

Secondly, you'll have to work harder to get multiple sites listed with the search engines. Concentrate your efforts on getting traffic to a main site focused on a single theme, and you will be rewarded with higher listings in the engines.

The only time multiple sites with a similar theme works is when you make some clear distinction between the products offered or the site topics. For example, I have three domains offering three different categories of service with my dating service review sites. They are categorized as mild, medium, and hot - or in other words, non-adult, mixed, and mature. It's then easier to make keyword distinctions among sites that offer similar services within different categories.

On the other hand, building 3 different sites to sell the same products on each site doesn't make sense and is much more trouble than it's worth.

Now that you've been spared the agony of building a mall site or a number of useless sites, let's fine tune and hone your niche.

Do Keyword Research to Assess Market Demand

While you may think that the North Atlantic Gannet is the most extraordinary sea bird on the planet, you shouldn't start building a site around the topic until you know that *enough* others share your interest. In other words, you need to assess market *demand* and you do that with *keyword research*.

The term that surfers type into the search box at Google or another search engine is called a 'keyword' or 'keyword phrase.' For example, if you want to find a site that sells or has information about Barbie dolls you would enter the *keyword phrase* 'Barbie dolls' in the search box at Google.com.

As Internet marketers, we want to find out *which* keywords surfers search for and *how often* those keywords are searched. To do this, I use a service called Wordtracker, available at http://Worktracker.com (http://Wordtracker.com), which will be used for demonstration purposes throughout this section.

IS THERE SUFFICIENT DEMAND?

I started my dating service review site for singles back in 1998 – but does that topic still attract enough interest to warrant its consideration as a site topic today?

To find out, I typed the word 'singles' into the Wordtracker interface as shown in *Figure 10 1st Keyword Search* shown to the right.

As single people represent a *very* large market, we will research several niche categories within the market in order to target profitable segments of that market.

A number of keywords related to "singles" was returned by Wordtracker and displayed on the left side of the page, as shown in *Figure 11 Review Related Terms* screenshot to the right.

The benefit of having related keywords show up in the results is that you may get ideas for site topics and sub-topics that you may not come up with on your own – making Wordtracker a very effective tool for brainstorming.

NOTE: Using the trial version produces only 15 related keywords, however the full version of Wordtracker returned 285 keywords related to the term 'singles.'

To find out how many searches are estimated for the term 'singles' today, I clicked on the linked word 'singles.'

FIGURE 10 1ST KEYWORD SEARCH

FIGURE 11 REVIEW RELATED TERMS

The following screenshot, *Figure 12 How Results Appear,* shows how results appear on the right side of the page.

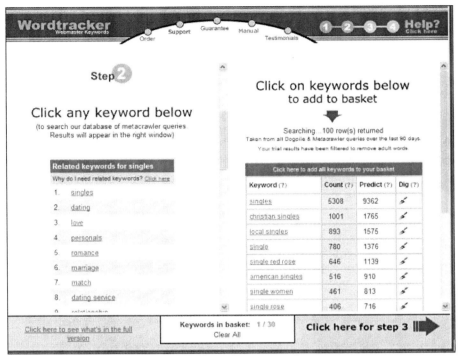

FIGURE 12 HOW RESULTS APPEAR

Here is an enlarged view of the right side of the expanded results.

Note that under the term 'singles,' a list of phrases that also include the term 'singles' appears.

In this case, the term singles appears in the Wordtracker database 5308 times. At the time of writing, the Wordtracker database held 366,061,205 words.

More relevant to our research are the numbers in the column labeled 'Predict.'

This number represents the maximum total predicted traffic for all of the major search engines, pay-per-click search engines and directories for the current 24-hour period.

Statmarket supplies Wordtracker's database with reports from Google, Yahoo!, MSN, AOL, Ask, Altavista, Excite and Lycos.

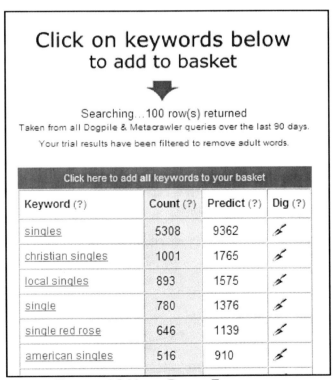

FIGURE 13 VIEW DAILY ESTIMATES

These engines represent 72.7% of the total search engine queries per day; therefore, 27.3% of the queries are left out of the results. You can therefore assume that there will actually be more searches for your keyword than predicted by Wordtracker.

In this example, the number of predicted searches for the term 'singles' is **9362.**

I then checked results for the other related terms that were returned in Step 1, including 'dating,' 'personals,' 'love,' 'romance' and 'online dating' and noted specific niche segments that arose within the topic including geographic, ethnic and religious affiliations such as "Canadian", "Latin" and "Jewish."

So, was there enough demand to warrant building a site for singles?

Absolutely!

If Wordtracker generates an estimate of 20,000 searches per day from a *combination of generic and more specific terms* related to that market – I consider that a niche market with *more than ample demand.*

RESEARCH SPECIFIC PRODUCTS, BRANDS AND MODEL NUMBERS

Far fewer daily searches are necessary to warrant *building a sub-category page* of a topic or specific brand name products, i.e. Christian dating or Yahoo! Personals, which returned 1291 and 4166 searches respectively. Let's look at another example.

Imagine that you are interested in video production and are considering a camcorder review site. To determine the most popular brands and model numbers that people are searching for, you would search for 'camcorder' at Wordtracker.

Again, when you click on the word 'camcorder' in the left pane of the Wordtracker interface, the top terms that include that keyword are returned in the right pane as shown in the screenshot shown here to the right.

The 7th and 8th terms returned are 'Sony camcorder' and 'Sony camcorders,' respectively. The 12th term is 'JVC camcorder.'

Once you determine that there are a sufficient number of searches for a specific brand name product, you can dig deeper to find out whether people are searching for specific model numbers under that brand name.

Click here to add all keywords to your basket			
Keyword (?)	Count (?)	Predict (?)	Dig (?)
camcorder	867	1529	✎
camcorders	506	892	✎
camcorder reviews	493	869	✎
digital camcorders	219	386	✎
digital camcorder	194	342	✎
camcorder batteries	190	335	✎
sony camcorder	186	328	✎
sony camcorders	184	325	✎
digital camcorder reviews	165	291	✎
dvd camcorder	155	273	✎
camcorder review	143	252	✎
jvc camcorder	122	215	✎

FIGURE 14 PRODUCT RESEARCH

To do that, click on the little shovel graphic in the 'Dig' column.

The screenshot to the right shows the results returned when I 'dug' for more terms under the keyword 'Sony camcorder.'

As you can see, 'Sony hd camcorder' showed up in the 4th row of returns with 125 searches predicted for that day.

When I saw 111 searches predicted for 'sony mini dv camcorder laptop battery' in the 8th row, I wondered how many people might be searching for 'sony mini dv' camcorders.

So, I clicked that link and the results of that search are shown below and to the right in the *Figure 16 Model Research* graphic.

Click here to add all keywords to your basket			
Keyword (?)	Count (?)	Predict (?)	Dig (?)
sony camcorder	186	328	
sony camcorders	184	325	
battery charger aa sony digital camcorder	76	134	
sony hd camcorder	71	125	
batteries camcorder sony	65	115	
inkjet lexmark printer sony digital camcorder	65	115	
sony digital camcorders	63	111	
sony mini dv camcorder laptop battery	63	111	
digital camera lens sony digital camcorder	61	108	

FIGURE 15 BRAND RESEARCH

At this point you can see that people are searching for specific models of Sony mini dv camcorders.

Indeed, nearly 100 daily searches are estimated for the **Sony DCR-HC19 Mini DV Camcorder** alone!

4350815 sony mini dv camcorder	57	101	
camcorder dv hc19 mini sony	56	99	
camcorder dv mini sony laptop battery	55	97	
sony dcrhc42 mini dv handycam camcorder	54	95	

FIGURE 16 MODEL RESEARCH

Furthermore, because surfers may misspell 'mini dv,' I also search for 'minidv'… and indeed many more searches for the term showed up as shown in the screenshot *Figure 17 Search for Misspellings* to the right.

Keyword (?)	Count (?)	Predict (?)	Dig (?)
Click here to add all keywords to your basket			
minidv camcorder review	57	101	✎
10 camcorder canon minidv optura	48	85	✎
dvd camcorder or minidv	48	85	✎
camcorder d22u digital gr jvc minidv	47	83	✎
minidv digital camcorder jvc	47	83	✎

FIGURE 17 SEARCH FOR MISSPELLINGS

In summary, researching specific products, brand names and model numbers will give you significant clues as to where to put your efforts when you build your site.

EVALUATE MARKET TRENDS

You don't want to find out that interest in the product or service you are trying to sell is rapidly decreasing *after* you've built your site. To evaluate and stay current on trends in the market, read the newspaper, magazines and do online research.

Let's look at how **online dating services** have performed over the years and in which direction the industry is headed.

According to the '**2003** Paid Online Content U.S. Market Spending Report' (http://www.online-publishers.org/?pg=press&dt=051104) conducted by the Online Publishers Association (OPA) and comScore Networks, personals/dating category was the largest, making up almost 30 percent of total online content spending by U.S. consumers. Spending on online personal ads and dating Web sites in 2003 reached $449.5 million, up 49 percent from 2002.

Just one year later, in their '**2004** Paid Online Content U.S. Market Spending Report' (http://www.online-publishers.org/?pg=press&dt=031005) the OPA stated:

Online Personals/Dating remained the leading paid content category in 2004, with spending at an all-time high of $469.5 million for the year, up 4% over 2003. However, spending on Entertainment/Lifestyles grew a remarkable 90%, from $217.6 million in 2003 to $413.5 million in 2004, while spending on Business/Investment content declined 6% over that same time period. As a result, Entertainment/Lifestyles overtook Business/Investment content as the No. 2 paid content category and is on track assume the top position should its current rate of growth continue.

Sure enough, in the '**2005** Paid Online Content U.S. Market Spending Report' (http://www.online-publishers.org/?pg=press&dt=031406), released in March 2006, the Online Publishers Association reported:

> Consumer spending on Entertainment/Lifestyles content, spurred by sales of music online, reached $264.8 million in H1 2005, surpassing the Personals/Dating category to rank first amongst all paid content categories.
>
> Personals/Dating remained a strong second-highest revenue producer, with online content sales of 245.2 million in H1 2005.

Some marketers would interpret that news negatively and quit right there. Other marketers would keep researching the topic.

I chose to do the latter and searched for '*online spending*' and '*dating*' and '*2006*' at Google which led me to an article called "Online Dating Gets Tough" published by eMarketer on February 14th, 2006 – Valentine's Day – go figure.

Mr. Belcher, eMarketer senior analyst and author of the report says that 'online dating is a mature market' and contends that free sites like MySpace and Friendster may pose a competitive threat. Mr. Belcher, however *also* said:

> 'Free online dating sites, be they social networking or other, are not after the same customers as subscription-based online dating sites. Free sites are pursuing advertisers. Subscription-based online dating sites, on the other hand, are pursuing serious paying online daters.
>
> The fact that serious online dating sites are not only surviving, but in some cases are charging higher fees, reveals that those who want such services will seek them out, and at a price.'

Would an affiliate marketer let these reports dissuade them from starting an Internet dating service review site?

That depends on the affiliate.

An affiliate who can present a strong enough case to his or her site single visitors about the benefits of joining a dating service, as opposed to trying to find a partner on a free site, would evaluate this niche as a good option.

That affiliate would especially appreciate the figures released in March 2006 by Internet research firm ComScore that indicated that the UK online dating market grew 30.9%, representing 9,495,000 unique users across the industry in the month of February alone compared with only 7,254,000 in December. ☺

On the other hand, an affiliate who had '**camcorders /online video / vlogging**' as an item on their potential topic list would appreciate this October 15th, 2006 press release from Comscore, and continue to research *that* topic further.

RESTON, VA, October 13, 2005 – comScore Media Metrix today released the first publicly available analysis of consumer usage of online streaming video content, based on the comScore Media Metrix Online Video Ratings service.   In June 2005, more than 94 million people in the U.S., or 56 percent of the domestic Internet population, viewed a streaming video online. Over the three months ending June 2005, the average consumer viewed 73 minutes of streaming video content per month.

"Online video is uniquely positioned to break through clutter, changing media preferences, and other obstacles facing advertisers today," noted Mr. Daboll.

The point is to do your homework and evaluate trends in your potential market thoroughly *before* you make a decision.

Your first choice may not be your best choice. Alternatively, you may end up with more ideas and options for potentially profitable topics.

Review the Competition

Once you've concluded that there is sufficient demand for your chosen topic, it's time to research the competition. To analyze our competition, we'll evaluate both the paid search engine listings and the natural or 'organic' search results.

RESEARCH THE PAID SEARCH LISTINGS

To find out who qualifies as your *real* competition, we'll evaluate sites that use pay-per-click (PPC) to promote their sites. **I call this *real* competition because *real* businesses pay to advertise their products and services.**

Pay-per-click (PPC) advertising is a type of search marketing where advertisers bid for placement in the search results and pay each and every time their ad is clicked. Yahoo! Search Marketing and Google Adwords are just two examples of companies that offer pay-per-click advertising. PPC will be discussed in more detail in a later chapter.

In the meantime, we will use Google to find out how much competition there is relevant to your site's topic, categories and brands.

Google's Sponsored Listings are located at the top of the search results page, while Google Adwords, are on the right side of each results page.

FIGURE 18 GOOGLE ADVERTISERS

You get a good idea of how many Google Adwords advertisers are bidding on individual keywords and keyword phrases by clicking on 'More Sponsored Links' at the bottom of the Adwords column.

I found 14 additional pages of advertisers, including actual dating services such as Match.com, affiliate sites and some sites that were completely irrelevant to dating.

As there are 8 advertisers on the first page of results and 10 advertisers on each additional page, there are a total of 148 sites bidding on the term "dating service."

However, when I 'honed' my search to a category that showed high demand, the results were much rosier.

FIGURE 19 HOW MANY ADVERTISERS?

A search for "seniors dating service" resulted in 42 advertisers, the majority of which were irrelevant listings that linked to very generic dating service review sites.

Indeed, only 4 of the 8 advertisers on the first page of results were linking to dating services for seniors or reviews of seniors' dating sites. These results bode very well for this particular category, as it demonstrates that competing against the irrelevant advertisers with well-worded highly relevant PPC ads will be quite simple.

We will cover advertising and ad writing in the *4 Primary Marketing Methods* section. In the meantime, let's "look inside" Google Adwords to check your potential competition. You may do this by using Google's Keyword Tool at:
https://adwords.google.com/select/KeywordToolExternal

The Keyword Tool generates potential keywords and reports their Google statistics, including search performance and seasonal trends. Cost and ad position estimates may also be displayed.

In the example below, I used the Keyword Tool to check competition for the term "dating service." To display those results, I selected "Keyword Search Volume" from the drop-down box beside "Choose data to display."

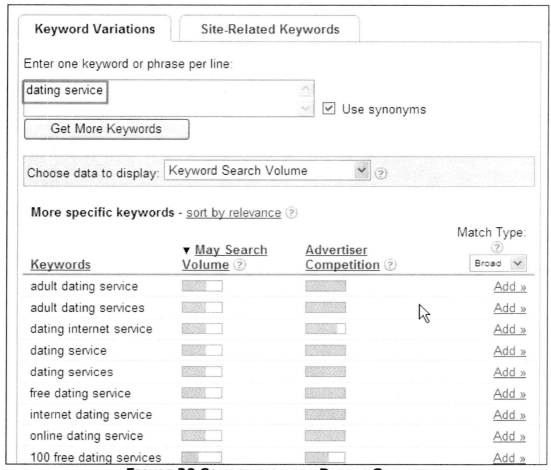

FIGURE 20 COMPETITION FOR DATING SERVICE

I sorted the results by search volume by clicking on the linked titled, "May Search Volume."

In the *Figure 20 Competition for Dating Service* screenshot above, notice how the green bars below the title "Advertiser Competition" are almost all solid green, indicating *very high advertiser competition* for the resulting terms.

I scrolled down the page to look for terms with average to high search volume and low advertiser competition, but as 'dating service' is such a generic keyword phrase with a lot of competition, there were none to be found.

The task at this point is to review the categories and sub-categories that you developed earlier and find those with the highest search volume and the lowest amount of competition. The *Figure 21 Keyword Disabled Dating* screenshot on the next page shows results for dating services for disabled people, a category that had shown promising demand in my earlier research.

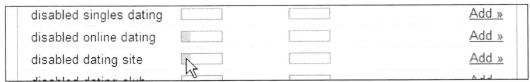

FIGURE 21 KEYWORD "DISABLED DATING"

Although the search volume in the example above is low, competition for those keyword phrases is *very low*, which represents a potentially profitable opportunity, as even 'low search volume' phrases may have *thousands* of searches per month.

HOW MUCH ARE ADVERTISERS WILLING TO PAY?

The amount that advertisers are willing to pay-per-click for keywords related to their industry is perhaps the best indicator of profitability in that niche. To see estimates of what advertisers are paying, we use the Google Keywords Tool again at: https://adwords.google.com/select/KeywordToolExternal

This time, enter your keyword, select 'Cost and Ad Position Estimates' from the drop-down box, choose a currency to display and enter a dollar amount beside 'How much would you be willing to pay-per-click (Max CPC)' as shown in the screen shot to the right.

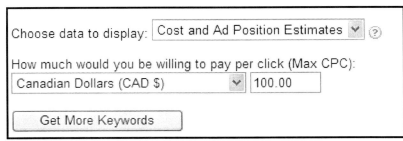

FIGURE 22 COST AND AD POSITION ESTIMATES

Tip: Enter a high dollar amount (e.g. $100.00) as shown above to see all the results.

Results for 'dating service' are shown here to the right.

At an estimated cost per click of $19.30, gay dating is obviously a valuable and profitable niche market!

Keywords	Estimated Avg. CPC	Estimated Ad Position	Match Type: Broad
free dating service	$4.12	1 - 3	Add »
online dating service	$7.93	1 - 3	Add »
dating service	$5.67	1 - 3	Add »
match dating service	$11.78	1 - 3	Add »
gay dating service	$19.30	1 - 3	Add »
adult dating service	$1.75	1 - 3	Add »

FIGURE 23 ESTIMATED AD PRICES

ORGANIC SEARCH ENGINE RESULTS

Continuing with my research into the 'dating/personals' category, I typed the word "dating" into the search box and the results appear as shown in the graphic below. 'Organic' results are those with the titles, "Welcome to dating.com" and "Dating – washingtonpost.com" in the graphic below.

FIGURE 24 ORGANIC SEARCH RESULTS

Yikes!

There were more than *205 million* results for the word 'dating' and the prospect for this topic doesn't seem to get any better…

- **65,000,000** for the keyword "personals"
- **118,000,000** for "singles"
- **1,210,000** for "internet dating"

When you see HUGE numbers like that returned it would be easy to conclude that there is *no way* you'll ever be able to compete in that particular topic.

DON'T be intimidated however by large numbers of organic search engine results, as the number of 'organic' or 'natural' search results for a particular keyword or keyword phrase is a poor indicator of actual competition for the following 4 reasons.

- **Organic results may be irrelevant**. "Dating" is a very generic keyword. Some of those pages may actually be about 'carbon dating.' Many of those pages are likely on the sites of teenage girls who are writing about their two favorite topics – boys and 'dating.'

- **Organic results are dynamic.** As Google changes which pages qualify to rank near the top of their listings, sites that were in the 'top spot' yesterday, may suddenly be in the twentieth spot, or are completely removed from the results. Therefore, a site that looks like a 'stiff' competitor may be no competition at all.

- **Organic results may be outdated**. Because it appears that Google gives precedence to pages that first mentioned a particular topic, you'll often find that the information on that page is out-of-date.

- **Lastly, but perhaps most importantly**, no one in their right mind would sift page-by-page through 228+ million results to find what they want. Most people click a link on the first or second page of Google returns, which basically makes the other 227,999,980 sites irrelevant. Only the sites on the first two pages of returns may qualify as competition.

The best use of organic results is to see how others in the industry promote their products and to get some idea of how you can do it better!

FIND COMPETING AFFILIATE SITES

What we *really* want to know, however, is whether affiliates are advertising within a particular niche – as that proves profitability within a niche.

To find affiliate advertisers, add the words 'guide,' 'review' or 'comparison' to your basic search term.

For example, I searched for 'cell phone review' and 'cell phone comparison' which were both average search volume keyword terms with low competition. Sadly, or fortunately, as per your viewpoint, the majority of affiliate sites appeared as shown in the following screenshot --- essentially 'affiliate arbitrage' sites that provide no information at all (despite promising a review in their Google ad!) that make money listing Yahoo! search marketing ads.

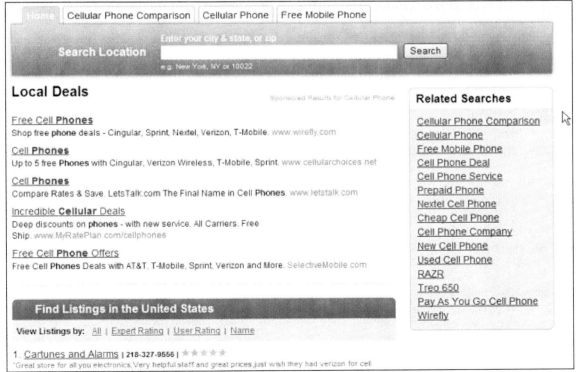

FIGURE 25 CELL PHONE REVIEW AFFILIATE SITE

Although these sites are prevalent throughout the 'net and are a complete waste of time for surfers, if you've never seen one before, here is how you can tell that the site monetizes by displaying Yahoo!'s advertisers' ads.

Just cursor over a link and right-click to copy it.

The "Free Cell Phones" link in the example above had the following as a portion of the link:

```
http://www.thebadaffiliatesite.org/redirect.php?r=http%3A%2F%2Frc12.overture.
com%2Fd%2Fsr%2F%3Fxargs%3D15KPjg149Sk5amwraocLjBSuWDx14axca59chqB5F7HsMPrH9uW
eV8aKrBktMpEOFv7wjVy%255FSR%252DaQVLvr5mvyKGg%252DMUwLXFOH634XEzo04ZpmUBtxCjr
MoxeJJr7ZTfHIEYG6xb4P%
```

The 'overture.com' portion in bold confirms my suspicions.

Regardless of our disdain for sites that waste our time in this manner, this bodes well for affiliates that intend to produce real information (cell phone reviews in this case) for their visitors.

We can assume that the surfer who clicked on the Google ad to get to the bad site, will hit his or her "Back" button and click on the next sponsored listing to get to a real "cell phone review" site. With luck, that site will be your site! ☺

Instead of earning pennies per click, you — the smarter affiliate — will offer well-written product endorsements for phone sales and plans merchants.

LetsTalk.com pays $45.00 per phone sale, and offers to increase commissions by 40% when sales equal or exceed 30 in any given month.

I have been both surprised and delighted on several occasions to discover that sites paying the most to advertise were poorly designed or didn't offer a very wide range of products relevant to my topic.

A Note about Irrelevant Paid Listings

You may completely disregard irrelevant, non-competing sites found through natural search. Simply be glad that they're not competition. However, if you discover a completely irrelevant site in the paid listings, please take the time to drop the editors at Google Adwords, Yahoo! Search Marketing or other PPC a note about your findings, since sites that pay to advertise under irrelevant terms push bid prices up unfairly.

Here's an example.

Let's say that the first advertiser under the keyword 'wine bag' is bidding 15 cents to hold that spot. If you plan to sell wine bags and wanted to advertise on Yahoo! Search Marketing, you'd have to pay 16 cents to claim the top listing. However, if that site doesn't sell wine bags, other advertisers should not have to compete with them.

Yahoo! Search Marketing's advertiser guidelines are very stringent about relevancy, and you'll have no problem getting this site removed from the sponsored listings. Not only will you save money by writing that note to Yahoo! Search Marketing, but you will also save Yahoo! Search Marketing 's users time when they don't have to visit useless sites.

In those cases, if you build a well-designed Web site that gives the surfer exactly what they want, your site should be successful, even if you don't list it in a top spot on the pay-per-click search engines.

In other cases, you will find examples of excellent affiliate sites from which you can garner good ideas for your own site.

Don't overlook competition research in your affiliate business-building process. You'll be surprised how much you will learn by researching the competition. In many cases you will be pleased to see how little competition there is, and how much room the market holds - just for you.

Build a Keyword List as You Research

As you research your topic, start building a list of keywords relevant to your topic. Your keyword list will be used to create focused content and to drive traffic to your site through natural and paid search engines.

Wordtracker makes it easy to build a list of keywords.

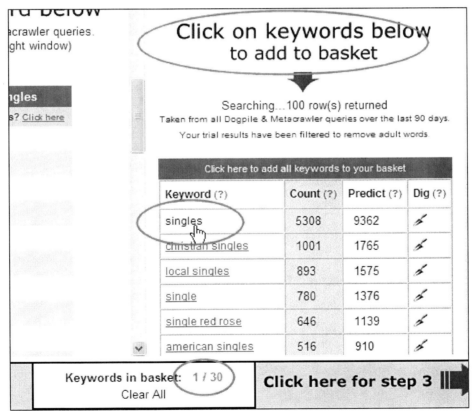

FIGURE 26 SELECT YOUR KEYWORDS

As shown in the graphic above, you simply click on a keyword to add it to your basket.

This allows you to eliminate irrelevant keywords such as 'single red rose,' which was returned in the 5th row of results under a search for singles.

Going through the related keywords such as 'dating,' 'personals' and 'romance,' I selected 20 keywords using Wordtracker's free trial and then clicked through to Step 3, as shown in the next graphic.

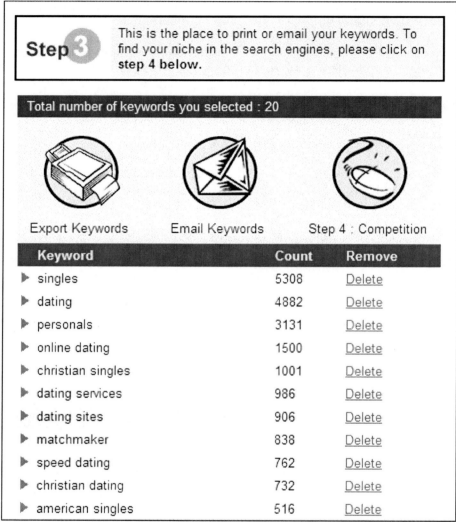

FIGURE 27 BUILD YOUR KEYWORD LIST

When the list of keywords is returned, I click on 'Export Keywords' and then 'Click here to get TAB delimited output' which produces the list shown in the following graphic.

1	5308	9361	singles
2	4882	8610	dating
3	3131	5522	personals
4	1500	2645	online dating
5	1001	1765	christian singles
6	986	1738	dating services
7	906	1597	dating sites
8	838	1477	matchmaker
9	762	1343	speed dating
10	732	1291	christian dating
11	516	910	american singles
12	464	818	personal ads
13	461	813	single women
14	344	606	interracial dating
15	341	601	dating service
16	224	395	singles dating
17	216	380	single russian women
18	213	375	online dating service
19	41	72	online dating personals
20	19	33	alternative matchmaker

FIGURE 28 BUILD A TAB-DELIMITED LIST OF KEYWORDS

As you can see, the counts and predicted searches are built into the list of keywords, and ordered from highest to lowest 'count.' This is useful information when you want to decide which specific topics you should start working on first.

Looking at the list above, I might concentrate my efforts on building a page about 'christian singles' before tackling the topic of 'single Russian women' because there are more searches for – and therefore more interest in - the former subject.

Do NOT make that determination until after you do competition research (covered later in this chapter) as you may discover that a sub-topic with fewer searches may have considerably less competition and is therefore more profitable.

ORGANIZE YOUR CATEGORIES AND SUB-CATEGORIES

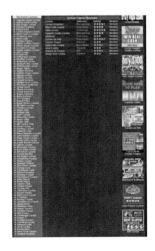

In their excitement to get online and start making money, new webmasters often omit the planning process as time-wasting, unnecessary work. Unfortunately, they don't establish a clear picture of how their site will be arranged, and the lack of focus and planning is sadly evident. For example, you've probably seen sites that list 40 or more items in the navigation bar, which is simply too many to expect visitors to scroll through on every page.

The small picture to the left shows a truly ridiculous navigation bar.

You however won't fall into that trap, because as you do your research, you'll develop a manageable list of site categories and sub-categories.

As you research, you will come up with ideas for site categories and sub-categories to use in your site's navigation.

After working through the terms related to singles and online dating, my list of topics for Sage-Hearts.com looked something like this:

Adult	Chinese	Gifts	Muslim
Age-related	Chocolate	Greeting Cards	Parents
Alternative	Christian	Hispanic	Regional
American	Disabled Singles	Indian	Regional/Ethnic
Asian	Ethnic	Italian	Religious
Black	Fiancée Visas	Japanese	Romance Tours
Books	Flowers	Jewish	Russian
Canadian	French	Korean	Sexual Orientation
Candy	Gay	Lesbian	Speed Dating
Chat	German	Mail-Order Brides	Single Parents

With 38 items, that's a pretty sizeable and unwieldy list, and far too large for a navigation bar. On closer examination however, you can see that that single people who are interested in online dating are searching according to geographic region, ethnicity, sexual orientation, types of online dating (i.e. chat) and religion. They are also looking for gifts.

To shorten the navigation list, I developed a list of top-level categories and eventually got the list down to 17 lines as shown in the screenshot to the right. In some cases, I was able to place 2 'related' topics (i.e. 'Gay' and 'Lesbian') on a single line. Notice that the list is ordered **alphabetically** for ease-of-use.

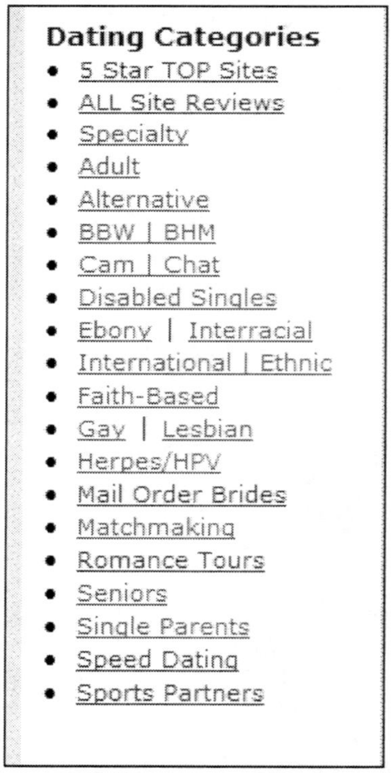

Note that '5-Star Dating Sites' and 'All Dating Site Reviews' are additional categories that were placed in the navigation after the reviews were complete. They are intended to simplify navigation to individual pages.

BREAK-OUT 2ND TIER CATEGORIES

Because I didn't want to list every ethnicity and religion on the homepage in our navigation bar, our topic list needs to be broken out into categories and sub-categories, or 1st and 2nd level tiers.

So, instead of putting 'Jewish' and 'Christian' in the navigation bar, I listed 'Faith-based' as a top-level category.

Dating Categories
- 5 Star TOP Sites
- ALL Site Reviews
- Specialty
- Adult
- Alternative
- BBW | BHM
- Cam | Chat
- Disabled Singles
- Ebony | Interracial
- International | Ethnic
- Faith-Based
- Gay | Lesbian
- Herpes/HPV
- Mail Order Brides
- Matchmaking
- Romance Tours
- Seniors
- Single Parents
- Speed Dating
- Sports Partners

FIGURE 29 BUILDING NAVIGATION

As I can reasonably assume that there are singles of all religious faiths seeking partners, I built a 'sub-category' for each religion.

I ended up with the following 2nd tier categories, as I found dating services for each of those religions for which I could write product reviews.

- Adventist
- Christian
- Catholic
- Jewish
- Mormon / LDS
- Muslim

BUILD SEPARATE KEYWORD LISTS ACCORDING TO CATEGORIES

When using Wordtracker to build my keyword lists, I prefer to separate and export keywords according to their category or sub-category.

For example, rather than building a huge list that contains all the keywords related to 'singles,' I will create separate keyword lists around such topics as 'dating russian women,' 'interracial dating' and 'Christian singles' and copy the lists into separate pages on an Excel spreadsheet.

Here is an example of a list that I built around the term 'Christian singles.' Note that the entire list of keywords would be contained within one column, not two as shown in the screenshot.

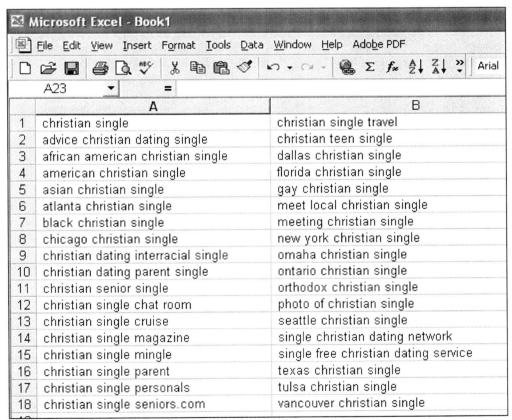

FIGURE 30 KEYWORD SPREADSHEET

What's interesting about this list is that it demonstrates that Christian singles are looking for other Christians according to geographic region, sexual orientation and ethnicity as shown by terms such as 'Texas,' 'gay' and 'african american'.

Single Christians are also looking for chat rooms, cruises, magazines and specific dating services such as Christian Single Mingle, which is now called Relationships.com. I use that information to look for products and services that I can offer to my site's customers.

If enough searches occur for any particular sub-topic, I would consider building a separate landing page on my site to serve that specific market or to promote a specific product.

More importantly, I try to build a HUGE list of keywords, each containing the term 'Christian singles' to use in my pay-per-click advertising campaigns, a topic covered in a later section of the book.

IMPORTANT NOTE ABOUT KEYWORD LIST BUILDING

In order to get more traffic through natural and paid search engines, your goal is to create a HUGE keyword list that includes generic topic terms, categories, sub-categories, brand names, product names and model numbers.

The free trial version of Wordtracker is quite limited when it comes to building large lists of keywords, as it allows only 15 words in each of the lateral search (related terms) and the number of keywords returned per search.

On the other hand, the paid version permits 300 and 500 terms, respectively. More importantly, the full version allows you to put 5000 keywords in your basket, unlike the trial version which only allows 30!

The paid version of Wordtracker is therefore a very worthwhile investment. You may upgrade to the full version at http://Worktracker.com.

It's Time to Choose Your Niche

Having gone through the process of assessing demand and reviewing the competition, you should now be ready to choose a topic for your site.

Don't wait until you find the 'perfect topic.' It doesn't exist. There will *always* be some little problem or weakness with whatever niche you choose.

Choose the best of those you have researched, or continue researching until you find something that you can work with.

Remember too, as you gain experience, your site will grow and evolve into something likely much larger and better than you ever hoped or expected.

Be patient and give it time... but don't spend too much time analyzing (over over-analyzing) the niche research portion of the process ... or your project may take much longer to get off the ground. So... do it now!

Build Your Site

Now that you've chosen your niche, it's time to start building your web site.

Domain Registration and Web Hosting

First you will have to choose a domain name to register and then arrange for web site hosting.

6 KEYS TO CHOOSING THE RIGHT DOMAIN NAME

Your domain name is your business name on the web. It represents both you and your business – therefore it is extremely important that you choose your domain name carefully.

Here are 6 key things to consider when choosing your domain name.

1. **Make it DOT COM** - Although there are a number of domain name extensions to choose from, including .com, .net, and .biz amongst many others, choose .COM. Dot Com comes to mind first when people think of web addresses, so go with it. You wouldn't want your potential customers to head off to 'thepuppytrainer.com' if your site is registered as 'thepuppytrainer.net,' would you?

2. **Make it Relevant** - The next rule of thumb is to include at least one, preferably two, of your important 'keywords' in your name. Let's assume that your site is about dog training. So which keywords work best? Dog, puppy, pooch? Train, training or trainer? One way to decide is to find out which of those keywords or keyword combinations is searched for most often. To find that out visit WordTracker.com. You can use their free trial to establish which of your keywords is the most popular. Using the keywords we chose above, WordTracker shows us that the keyword 'dogs' outstrips the word 'puppy' by about 34,000 searches in a period of 60 days. Knowing that should make your decision just a little easier.

3. **Make it Memorable** - Which of the following names will you remember a week from now? DogTraining.com, DoggyU.com or DogCollege.com? Shorter names are also easier to remember.

4. **Avoid Hyphens** - One of the bigger mistakes I made when registering my first domain, was to hyphenate the name. Sometime later I discovered a site using the non-hyphenated (hmm... that LOOKS like an oxymoron) version of my domain name - and he was promoting the same products as I had on my site. This webmaster is STILL capitalizing on my oversight and selling to my visitors who forget the hyphen in my domain name.

   Make it Easy to Spell - My old site 'byebye925.com' is a good example of a bad domain name. When you hear it spoken, you could guess that is spelled 'bybynine2five.com,' 'byebyeninetofive.com' or a number of other ways. For that reason, I had to spell it out each and every time I said it. Adding numbers into the fray adds to the inconvenience. Imagine having to say, '*B-Y-E-B-Y-E, number 9, number 2, number 5 DOT COM*' several times a day.

5. **Beware of Trademark Infringement** - A trademark is a name or symbol officially registered to a third party, and unless otherwise specified, the trademark owner is the only party that can legally make use of a trademarked name. When purchasing a domain name, be forewarned that buying a domain containing a trademarked name could result in a legal battle and the registrar will likely side with the trademark owner. VeriSign's dispute policy, for example, reads: "It is your responsibility to determine whether your domain name registration infringes or violates someone else's rights." A court order could have your site shut down quickly. So before registering a name, do some research to make sure you won't run into trouble later. Trademark research and information can be obtained at Nameprotect (http://nameprotect.com) and The Trademark Association (http://www.inta.org).

Have fun!

Get out your dictionary and thesaurus and play with words. Brainstorm a long list of possibilities and come up with something that is uniquely your own.

CHOOSING A WEB HOST MADE EASY

A Web host is a service that stores, or hosts, your Web site pages on its servers (computers) so others on the Web can access your material 24/7.

Choosing a web host service is usually the most confusing thing a webmaster has to do when setting up a new site. So, I'm going to make this usually difficult choice VERY easy for you, however.

Get a cPanel host with Fantastico because the cPanel interface is easy to use, and Fantastico is FANTASTIC! (I regret that I didn't switch to cPanel sooner than I did.)

With just a couple clicks of your mouse, and entering a few pieces of data, you can set up a blog, content management system or dozens of other applications in a minute, or even less!

I'll take you through the Wordpress blog installation process step-by-step later in the book, and you will be amazed at how easy it is!

RECOMMENDED CPANEL HOSTING SERVICES

BlueHost (http://BlueHost.com) - Offers Fantastico-enabled cPanel hosting at very reasonable prices and gives first-rate 24/7 support.

iPowerWeb (http://iPowerWeb.com) - $7.95 per month includes 500 Megs of space, stats, CGI, PHP, SSI, FrontPage, SSL, manager console, free setup and more.

RECOMMENDED (NON-CPANEL) HOSTS

Third Sphere Hosting (http://thirdsphere.com/) - Total ecommerce solution includes affiliate management, complete customer relationship management features, and everything else you need to build & manage your web site. Recommended by Internet marketing 'powerhouses' such as Mark Joyner, Michel Fortin and Terry Dean.

HOW TO ASSESS A HOSTING SERVICE

If you prefer to choose a hosting service other than one I've suggested above, here are a number of key features, descriptions and questions to consider.

- **Interface or Control Panel** - Is the account managed through an easy-to-use administrative interface? I fought with every hosting service interface until I got a hosting service with cPanel, which is my control panel dream-come-true. I've included a graphic image of the interface in the next section.

- **File Storage** - How many Gigabytes (GB's) of storage space are offered to house your Web site files? Files include pages, images, sound and video clips. The larger your site, the more storage you will require. Most basic plans offer between 3 and 5 Gigs to start you out.

- **Data Transfer** - How many gigabytes (GB's) of data transfer are allowed? Fast-loading pages with few graphics don't take up much bandwidth, but if you are posting videos on your site, you'll want to look for a plan that offers a lot of data transfer. For example, BluehHost offers 15,000 GIGS of Transfer per month, about twice as much as HostGator.

- **POP3 email accounts** - How many do you get? I recommend that you choose a host that allows an unlimited number of POP3 email accounts. That way you can create a different email address for different programs that you join, ie. cj@mysite.com and linkshare@mysite.com. It's a tactic I use to keep the spammers at bay.

- **Browser Based Email** - Allows access to your email accounts through your Web browser from anywhere, as long as you have Internet access.

- **Forwarders and Autoresponders** – Send all email from one account to another email account with a forwarder. Set up an autoresponder if you want the sender of an email to receive a message back from you as soon as they send you an email to a specific address.

- **WebStats** - Can you access your Web site's log files and server statistics?

- **Site Builders and Design Tools** – Some hosting services offer their own WYSIWYG online design tools and/or site builders. Look for 'FrontPage extensions' if you use Frontpage to design your sites. Some examples of services that offer site builders include SBI and Yahoo! Web Hosting.

- **Scripting and Database Tools** – Look for Perl, PHP, MySQL and Server Site Includes (SSI). Perl and PHP are programming languages that require host support if you plan to run those scripts. MySQL is necessary if you plan to run a database, and SSI allows you to dynamically include data in your Web pages.

- **Stated 'Uptime'** – The percentage of time their server is up and running. This should never be less than 99.7%.

- **Scalability** - Can the account be upgraded with the growth of your business? Whether you need to add email accounts, more space or more traffic, it should be as easy as sending an email or making a phone call.

- **Helpful technical 24/7 support** - You want a technical support team that is always on hand to solve your problems and answer your web hosting questions quickly and in a friendly manner.

- **Technical support contact** - Is support available by phone or only by an email 'ticket system?' Trust me, there are times you will want to talk with your technician, rather than chew all your nails off while waiting for an email response.

- **Quick response to e-mails** - Technical support via 'ticket systems' can work very well when response time is lightning fast.

- **Online Community** - Is there a community forum set up for discussion among other users of the service? Some of these are well organized with great searchable databases. In other cases, they are simply a waste of time. I prefer to get my answers straight from the 'techies.'

- **Volume discount** - Do you get a discount if you sign up for a full year?

- **Upgrade charges** - Does the company charge setup fees for upgrades? If they do, I suggest that you continue your search for a hosting service that doesn't charge for upgrades. Any company that already has your business shouldn't penalize you for wanting to spend more money on their service!

- **Bonus Software and Webmaster Resource Center** - Do they offer free shopping cart software? Are additional tools such as guestbooks, form mail and other scripts provided free of charge? Note: You'll get a whack of bonus software with a cPanel host.

- **Satisfaction Guarantee -** Is there an unconditional money back guarantee? If so, how long is it good for?

Choosing the right service the first time is crucial, because switching hosts is costly, time-consuming and tedious work. I know because I've done it, and don't ever plan to do it again! ☺

6 REASONS NOT TO USE FREE HOSTING

Many new webmasters are tempted to use free hosting services on which to build their affiliate businesses. Here are 6 reasons why you should stay away from free hosting services.

1. **Loss of Credibility** – Would YOU buy from a business that can't afford $7.95 per month to host its own web site? I wouldn't. My impression of businesses on free servers is akin to street vending. I might buy an inexpensive little trinket, but never anything of value.

2. **Banner Advertising on Your Pages** – In exchange for space on their servers, the host places their own banner advertising on your pages. Their banners don't make you money and detract from your business.

3. **Long Domain Addresses** – Which address will your visitors remember? http://members.atsomefreeserver.com/~johnsbusiness/ or http://johnbusiness.com?

4. **Lack of Features** – Free hosts generally restrict the amount of space you can take up on their servers. The sites offer few, if any, of the most basic features necessary to run an ecommerce site, e.g. cgi-bins and shopping carts.

5. **Slow Loading Pages** – Most free server pages load very slowly. Slow loading pages are the primary reason people cite for failing to complete online order placement. Let's not chase our visitors away before they have a chance to become customers.

6. **No Customer Service** - Your site is down? Tough luck!

Other than using a web hosting service to practice your HTML skills, free hosts are worth precisely what you pay for them... nothing.

TRUE STORY: BAD MR. FREE WEB HOST

Too many webmasters, myself included, have learned the lesson about free web hosting services the hard way.

Several years ago, I placed a recently completed site on a free hosting service. While I disliked the banner ads that showed up above and below my pages, I understood that was how the company made their money and the price I paid for the space.

So, my new site was up and I submitted it to the search engines to bring in some traffic. My efforts started to pay off and **pretty soon the money was rolling in**. Cool! I start working on new projects. Sometime later however, I notice that the site **stopped generating revenue**, so I checked to see whether the site was offline or if perhaps the sales links were broken.

I typed in my URL and up came a different site in my browser window. Thinking I'd entered the address incorrectly, I typed it in again. The same strange page comes up instead of mine. So I try it again... and again. Nope, right URL, DIFFERENT site. **My site was gone**. In its place was a full page of advertising.

Why was this done? Well, of course I never found out, no one responded to my queries. Granted, this was a scam of the worst kind. Get suckers like me to build a site and bring in visitors, then steal their traffic.

Although this was an unusual circumstance, I learned a valuable lesson – being that you get what you pay for. So I pass the lesson on to you. Register your own domain name and pay for a good hosting service. Both are relatively inexpensive, and they put your business on the right track from the start.

---

3 Basic Site Building Options

From coding HTML with Notepad, Homesite and Dreamweaver, and using free Wordpress blogging software to full-blown content management systems (CMS) such as ArticleLive, to having sites built for me by designers, I have experimented with almost every type of web-site building process since 1997.

During that time, I discovered that building a web site can be a quick, cheap and simple process, or it can be time-consuming, expensive and frustrating if you go about it the wrong way.

To make sure *you* know all your options and go about building your site the right way, in this section you'll find the 3 Basic Site Building Options from which you should choose at least one.

OPTION #1: HIRE A DESIGNER

Unless you personally know a Web site designer and are totally confident in his or her work, this option can be a total crapshoot. Due to differences in artistic interpretation, there is no guarantee that you will be thrilled with the resulting design. Furthermore, a 5 to 10 page mini site can easily cost $1,000 or more, and

Cost isn't the only issue with using a designer to build your site, however.

On one project, my partners and I hired programmers to develop proprietary 'matchmaking' software – similar to that used by Match.com and Date.com. We loved the result, and the price was very reasonable.

However, the final product was more than a year overdue, and although all aspects of the program's functionality were carefully articulated point-by-point in a thick contract, it took many more months to 'tweak' the site to perfection.

The point here is that even 2 teams of articulate Web professionals can incur lengthy production delays. Delays generally result in cost over-runs and missed revenue opportunities.

As an affiliate marketer, the time it takes to make changes to your site is often the most pressing factor. For example, if your merchant tells you about an outstanding deal that is only available for the next 3 days, how frustrated would you be if your webmaster / web site designer was on vacation for the next 2 weeks?

That's why it is SO important for you NOT to rely solely on a designer and to learn how to add content and links to your own site.

Don't get me wrong. I DO post small projects for header graphic creation and script installations at Elance.com, Scriptlance.com and Rentacoder.com. I've used each of these services and have always been very satisfied with the work done.

Basically, the only way I would allow a web designer total control over my web site was if I hired that designer as an employee and I could count on him or her to work when I needed them.

Otherwise, using a web designer to build your site is the least favorable option.

OPTION #2: BUY A PACKAGE DEAL

One web site building option that has most of the features any Super Affiliate would ever need in a Web site, is Ken Evoy's 'Site Build It!'

Although the initial outlay may seem rather steep, Site Build It! is a great option for someone who wants to save time and money by buying all the website building necessities in a neatly packaged bundle.

Even if you could arrange domain registration, Web hosting, autoresponders, HTML editors, etc., to the tune of $25 or $30 per month, you still wouldn't enjoy the benefit of accessing all those utilities through a single interface. More importantly, you won't be getting all the site research and analysis features included.

Moreover, newbie webmasters who use SBI! report amazing search engine rankings achieved *without* having to pay for advertising.

Not only is it an excellent business-building system for newcomers to affiliate marketing, but the SBI ecommerce package will serve you well as you grow your business to include your own products.

Site Build iT! Web Site
http://webvista.sitesell.com/buildit/

BEST OPTION #3: DO-IT-YOURSELF

I've saved the best site-building option for last – do it yourself – and I will show you step-by-step how to build your site using blog technology and free software.

What is a blog? A blog (short for 'web log') is simply a type of website that lets you add (post) and edit content via a web-based interface. Posts are listed in chronological order with the latest shown at the top of the page and content can be easily categorized according to your needs. Blog technology has made site building so simple, quick and inexpensive that anyone – and I do mean *anyone* – can build their own web site.

Shown to the right is a screen capture of my *Net Profits Today* blog, located at:

http://www.netprofitstoday.com/blog/

That blog uses Wordpress software which is available free of charge through better hosting services.

Better yet, even the most novice webmaster can install a Wordpress blog in under 5 minutes, a process covered in the *7-Step Wordpress Blog Installation* section.

FIGURE 31 NPT BLOG

Almost no knowledge of HTML is required, as Wordpress provides a built-in WYSIWYG editor.

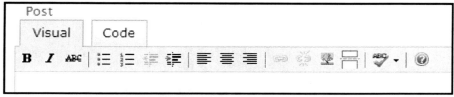

FIGURE 32 WORDPRESS WYSIWYG EDITOR

WYSIWYG stands for what-you-see-is-what-you-get.

The entire Wordpress interface is very clear and intuitive. For example, if you want to add a category, you simply click on 'Manage' then 'Categories' and at the top of the resulting page is an 'Add New' link. In addition to ease of installation and use, webmasters that blog regularly attain higher search engine rankings than webmasters who build static sites with individual HTML pages.

When you visit the blog, you will notice the 'Leave a Comment' and links to comments posted by NPT blog readers. The Comments facility is built right into Wordpress and helps build community and increase your readership.

Bloggers therefore enjoy increased revenue and lower advertising costs by attracting more free traffic to their sites. If blogging appeals to you, (and I certainly hope that it does!) be sure to read the *7-Step Wordpress Blog Installation tutorial* in the next section.

The Super Affiliate Handbook also covers essential points for those who build HTML pages using an HTML editor in the section called '*10 Design Rules-of-Thumb for HTML Pages.*'

Blogging Basics

By far, the easiest web site to start is a blog. More specifically, installing a Wordpress blog takes no more than 5 minutes and is push-button simple. To get started, you should have a domain name and a cPanel web host --- which you can do all in one step at BlueHost. Ready? Set? Let's go!

7-STEP WORDPRESS BLOG INSTALLATION

STEP 1: CPANEL LOGIN

Login to cPanel with the information provided by your host.

The URL will usually be something like:

http://yourdomain.com/cpanel

A screenshot of the cPanel interface is shown here on the right.

FIGURE 33 CPANEL LOGIN

STEP 2: FANTASTICO

Scroll down the page until you come to the **Fantastico** icon, as shown in the picture to the right.

Click on the icon.

FIGURE 34 FANTASTICO

STEP 3: WORDPRESS

Scroll down the left navigation bar until you see the word **Wordpress** (under the 'Blogs' header), as shown here to the right.

Click on the link.

FIGURE 35 WORDPRESS LINK

STEP 4: NEW INSTALLATION

On the resulting page, click the "**New Installation**" link as shown in the graphic to the right.

FIGURE 36 NEW INSTALLATION LINK

71

STEP 5: FILL IN THE BLANKS

The next page has **6 blanks** for you to fill in - the others are already done pre-filled by Wordpress.

Read the short instructions included about choosing a directory.

In this example, I chose to install my new blog to a directory called 'testblog.'

I filled in the site name as 'The Test Blog.'

I entered the description as 'This is only a test...'

'Admin access data' and 'Password' are the username that you will use to login to your blog's interface.

'Base configuration' requires a nickname, your email address, the Site Name and a description of your blog. The latter two will appear on the blog itself.

Once you have filled in the blanks, click the "**Install Wordpress**" link at the bottom of the page.

FIGURE 37 FILL IN THE BLANKS

STEP 6: FINISH INSTALLATION

The next page gives you information about the MySQL database that will be created, the installation directory and the URL of your new blog.

Take note of that information.

Next, click "**Finish Installation**".

FIGURE 38 FINISH BLOG INSTALLATION

STEP 7: CONFIRM INSTALLATION

The following page **confirms** the installation and provides a link to the Wordpress Administration Panel login along with the username and the password that you selected.

Note that the address for the Wordpress administration panel will always be:

*http://yourdomain/yourdirectory/**wp-admin***

Fill in your **email address** to send the details about the installation to yourself.

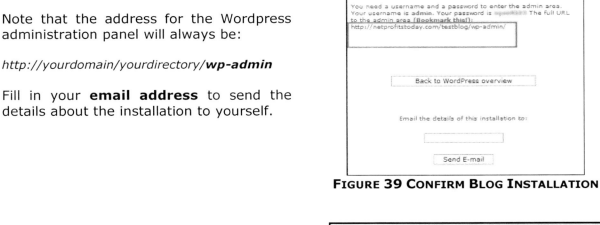

FIGURE 39 CONFIRM BLOG INSTALLATION

The next image is a partial screenshot of how the blog appeared after successfully installing Wordpress on a test blog at http://NetProfitsToday.com

FIGURE 40 SEE YOUR NEW BLOG ONLINE

TAKE A TOUR OF THE WORDPRESS ADMINISTRATION PANEL

To familiarize yourself with the functions of your new blog, login to your Wordpress Administration Panel. It will be located at http://your-domain.com/your-blog-directory/*wp-admin*

The login screen will appear as it does in the screenshot to the right.

Once you have logged in, you will see the 'Dashboard' or main Wordpress interface as it appears in the screenshot on the next page.

FIGURE 41 WORDPRESS LOGIN

FIGURE 42 WORDPRESS ADMINISTRATION PANEL

Click on the various tabs listed along the top of the page. For example, when you click on 'Manage,' another navigation bar appears below the first as shown in the next graphic. This navigation bar gives you access to managing your posts, pages, categories, comments (including those awaiting moderation) and your files.

Clicking on 'Manage' opened the 'Manage > Posts' page from where you can see the posts and comments that were installed with your blog. From this page, you also have the option to view, edit and delete the post; as well as edit, delete or unapprove the comment.

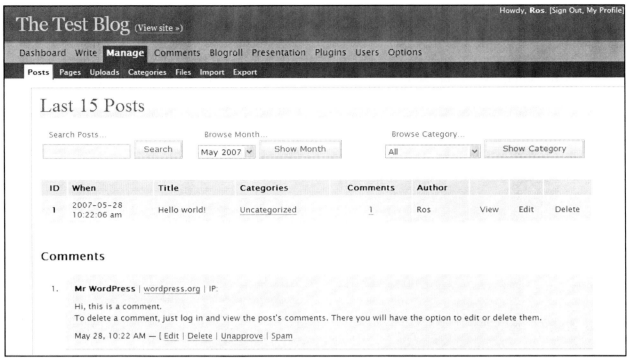

FIGURE 43 BLOG "MANAGE" PANEL

Browse around the administration panel for a while and see what else is offered. More information about individual functions of each tab in the administration panel are detailed on the official Wordpress site at http://codex.wordpress.org/Administration_Panels

Alternatively, you may want to check out 'WordPress for Beginners' at http://codex.wordpress.org/WordPress_Lessons

HOW TO ADD A PAGE TO YOUR WORDPRESS BLOG

Login to your Wordpress administration panel located at either *http://yourdomain.com/wp-admin* or *http://yourdomain.com/your-blog-directory/wp-admin* depending on whether you installed it in your domain's root directory or created a separate directory for your blog.

Click on the tab marked 'Write' (this is the Wordpress administration panel for my RosalindGardner.com blog). From within the Write Panel, click on the "Write Page" tab shown in the figure below.

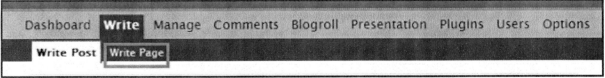

FIGURE 44 SELECT THE "WRITE PAGE" PANEL

Once you are in the "Write Page" panel (shown in the screenshot below) use content you've developed for that specific page to fill in the Page Title and Page Content.

Once you have finished entering your content, click "Publish" to make the page visible on your blog.

Otherwise you can either "Save and Continue Editing" to keep working on the page, or click "Save" to work on the page later.

FIGURE 45 ADD YOUR CONTENT

If you choose to "Save" a page without publishing it, you can find it again by clicking "Manage," then "Pages" from your main Wordpress administration panel.

The screenshot below is a sample of how the filled-in text looks in the Write Page panel.

FIGURE 46 "ABOUT US" PAGE EXAMPLE

The finished page can be seen at http://rosalindgardner.com/about/

Now it's your turn. Create content for your 'About Us' page and create that page in your blog. Let's start by adding those categories that you put together when you were researching your niche.

HOW TO ADD BLOG CATEGORIES

For this exercise, we will use the Sage-Hearts.com blog as an example.

The following screenshot shows how the category list appears for that site within the blog's Manage > Categories interface.

Notice how the main and sub-categories are shown with subs listed below their parents, i.e. 'Dating Tips for Men' is a sub-category of 'Dating Tips'.

ID	Name	Description	# Posts	Action	
14	Dating Site News		12	Edit	Delete
1	— Everything Else		46	Edit	Delete
15	Dating Tips		18	Edit	Delete
11	— Dating Tips for Men		16	Edit	Delete
12	— Dating Tips for Women		10	Edit	Delete
13	Just for Fun		9	Edit	Delete
17	Movies and Books		2	Edit	Delete
9	Romance 101		5	Edit	Delete
3	The Love Shoppe		11	Edit	Delete
4	Your Dating Stories		3	Edit	Delete

Categories (add new)

FIGURE 47 ADD CATEGORIES TO YOUR BLOG

The number of posts and the option to edit or delete each category is also provided.

To add a category to your blog:

- Login to your Wordpress Administration Panel.
- Click on 'Manage.'
- Click on 'Categories' in the sub-navigation panel.
- Scroll to the bottom of the page where you'll see the Add New Category form (see screenshot below).
- Enter the name and description (optional) of your category.
- Click the 'Add Category' button to finalize the operation.

The next graphic shows the 'Add New Category' interface.

Note: To create a sub-category, follow the points above and select a 'category parent' from the drop-down box labeled as such.

Now that you've established your blog categories, let's write a post.

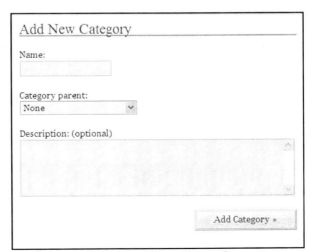

FIGURE 48 ADD A NEW BLOG CATEGORY

HOW TO POST TO YOUR BLOG

Writing a post in WordPress is easy.

1. Login to your WordPress Administration Panel.
2. Click the Write tab.
3. Enter a Title and content for your post.
4. Choose a Category for your post.
5. Select 'Allow Comments' and 'Allow Pings' under Discussion if you want to receive comments on your post. (Hint: You do!)

To see how your post looks before it is published, click the Preview link under the Title box. When you are finished, click Publish.

Wasn't that easy? Now let's see how it looks in practice. The screenshot below shows the "What Makes a Relationship Great?" post in the 'Write Post' panel on the Sage-Hearts.com blog.

FIGURE 49 WRITE A BLOG POST

Pretty simple, eh?

The screenshot to the right shows the post in the preview window (using the 3k2redux klein theme by Michael Heilemann & Chris J Davis).

USING QUICKTAGS

Look again at the screenshot above, and see how the 7th word in the first sentence 'those' is bracketed with <em> and </em>.

That code creates italicized text and is easy to do using the Quicktag codes in the Wordpress WYSIWYG editor.

FIGURE 50 PREVIEW YOUR POST

Simply highlight the word you want to italicize (or bold) with your cursor, then click the little italicized 'i'.

Most of the Quicktag codes are self-explanatory. For a detailed explanation of the WYSIWYG editor's 'quicktags' go to: http://codex.wordpress.org/Write_Post_SubPanel#Quicktags

If you need more information about all the different features of blog post writing, visit the Wordpress Write Post page at http://codex.wordpress.org/Write_Post_SubPanel

HOW TO ADD AN IMAGE TO A POST (OR PAGE)

The old proverb, "a picture worth a thousand words" is particularly applicable to website content, as surfers have incredibly short attention spans. Placing product pictures within your endorsements is therefore essential. For example, imagine a fashion site with endless descriptions of cut, color and fabric *without* pictures of the clothing described. How painful! Fortunately, your merchants will provide you with graphic images of their products.

The same theory holds true when a surfer is scanning an informational article or blog post, such as the "What Makes a Relationship Great?" post discussed in the *How to Post to Your Blog* section.

I therefore wanted to add an image of a happy smiling couple to the upper-most left hand corner of the post – as I do with almost all my blog posts.

I sourced the picture (shown right) through my membership at ClipArt.com, saved it to my computer and then uploaded and added it to my post easily.

CUSTOMIZE BLOG FILE UPLOAD SETTINGS

First we have to customize your blog's upload settings. To do that, login to your Wordpress Administration Panel (or "Dashboard") and click on the "Options" tab, followed by the "Miscellaneous" tab, where you will see the title 'Uploading' and the default folder is set as "wp-content/uploads."

You can select and enter a new directory, and choose whether you want to organize your folders uploads into month- and year-based folders by ticking the box as shown in the next screenshot.

FIGURE 51 CUSTOMIZE FILE UPLOAD SETTINGS

Next we want to make sure that the permissions for your upload folder are set correctly.

You can do this with either FTP software or via cPanel.

SETTING FILE PERMISSIONS WITH FTP

For FTP, login to your host using FTP software (FileZilla), right click the folder you chose for your images and the little window in Figure 52 will pop open. Select "File attributes" in that box.

Change your permissions to 'All Write' privileges, or "Numeric value: 777" as shown in Figure 53 below.

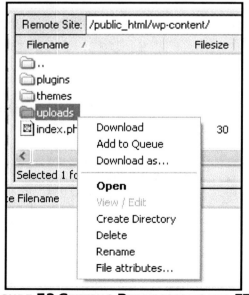

FIGURE 52 SETTING PERMISSIONS VIA FTP

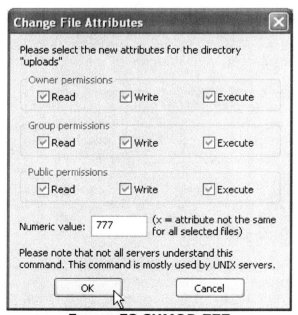

FIGURE 53 CHMOD 777

SETTING FILE PERMISSIONS WITH CPANEL

The other option is to login to your host account's cPanel, and use the File Manager to accomplish the same permission tasks as above.

Login to cPanel and click on 'File Manager.'

Navigate to the folder you chose for your uploads and double-click.
Click on 'Change Permissions' located in the upper right-hand corner of the page, and tick on each of the boxes under User, Group and World until 777 appears beside Permissions, as shown in the following screen shot.

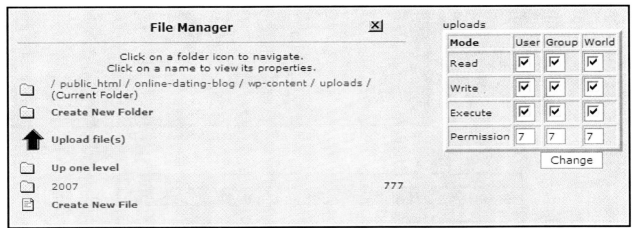

FIGURE 54 SET FILE PERMISSIONS IN CPANEL

UPLOAD THE IMAGE TO YOUR BLOG

Navigate to the Write > Write Post sub-panel within your Wordpress Administration Panel – or open your draft message.

Scroll down the page until the Upload form appears (see right) and click on 'Browse' beside the 'File' blank.

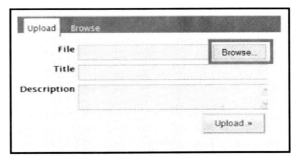

FIGURE 55 BROWSE FOR YOUR IMAGE

A new window labeled 'Choose file' will appear.

Browse to the directory to which you saved your image.

Click on the name of the image that you want to upload, which then appears next to 'File Name.'

Now click on 'Open.'

The location of the image on your computer will appear in the blank beside the word 'File' as shown in the graphic below.

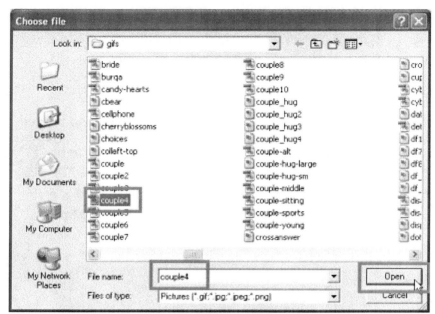

FIGURE 56 CHOOSE IMAGE FILE

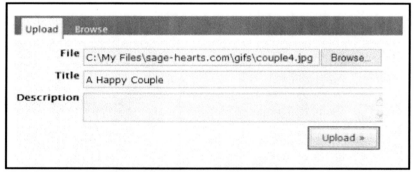

FIGURE 57 LABEL YOUR IMAGE

Now fill in the Title and Description blanks for the image, and click the 'Upload' button. The window under the 'Browse' tab will open as shown in the image to the right.

Select to show either a thumbnail, full size or title for the graphic.

Click 'Send to Editor' and the image link will appear within your post as shown highlighted in the screenshot below.

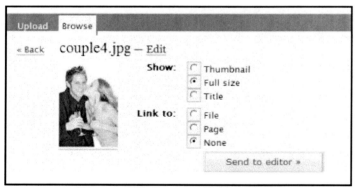

FIGURE 58 CHOOSE IMAGE SIZE

Notice how the Title that I entered during the uploading process shows up as *alt='A Happy Couple.'* When a visitor cursors over the picture, a little box will appear showing 'A Happy Couple' in text.

FIGURE 59 IMAGE IN A POST

Finally, when you click on Publish or Preview, you will see your image within the post.

HOW TO INSTALL LINKS IN YOUR POSTS AND PAGES

This is the best part. We're at the point where you will learn how to put those money-making links into your blog posts and pages.

So, without further ado, here are the steps:

1. Login to your blog and select Write Post sub-panel to start a new post.
2. Enter the text to which you want to add the link.
3. Cursor over that text.
4. Click the 'link' Quicktab in the WYSIWYG editor.
5. Enter the URL that you want to link to into the box that appears.
6. Click OK.
7. The link will appear fully coded within your post.
8. Don't forget to click Save! ☺

In the screenshot to the right you can see the highlighted text and the box where you'll enter your link.

The next screenshot below shows the link inserted and highlighted along with the text.

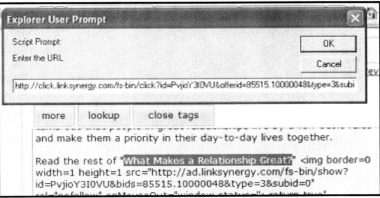

FIGURE 60 ADD A LINK TO YOUR POST

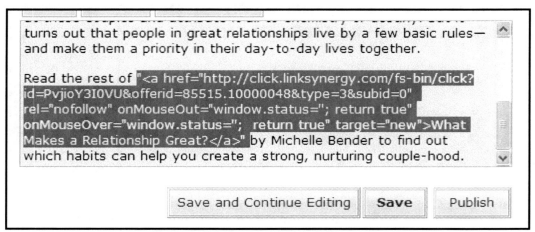

turns out that people in great relationships live by a few basic rules—
and make them a priority in their day-to-day lives together.

Read the rest of "<a href="http://click.linksynergy.com/fs-bin/click?
id=PvjioY3I0VU&offerid=85515.10000048&type=3&subid=0"
rel="nofollow" onMouseOut="window.status="; return true"
onMouseOver="window.status="; return true" target="new">What
Makes a Relationship Great?</a>" by Michelle Bender to find out
which habits can help you create a strong, nurturing couple-hood.

| Save and Continue Editing | **Save** | Publish |

FIGURE 61 INSERTED LINK EXAMPLE

HOW TO INSTALL A THEME: GIVE YOUR BLOG A NEW LOOK

You can easily change the look of your blog by installing a new theme. In this section, you'll learn how to download, upload and install a new Wordpress theme.

For the purposes of this exercise, we will install a theme called "Brajeshwar" which is a 3-column, white, fixed width, zero image theme with both left and right sidebars.

It is described as a 'minimal, simple, crisp, clear and light 3 column design. This plugin independent theme highlights the excerpt of the latest article on the home page. The font styles have been updated to be compatible with Microsoft Windows Vista.'

STEP 1: DOWNLOAD THE ZIPPED THEME FILES

To find the theme, go to http://themes.wordpress.net/ and enter "Brajeshwar v7.3.1" (without the quotes) into the search box.

Themes are packaged as zip files.

The number in brackets, i.e. Download (11540) outlined in the screenshot to the left, indicates the number of times that theme has been downloaded.

To download, click on the download link below the theme's graphic. This opens the 'File Download' window shown in the following screenshot.

FIGURE 62 INSTALL A THEME: BRAJESHWAR V7.3.1

STEP 2: SAVE THE THEME FILES

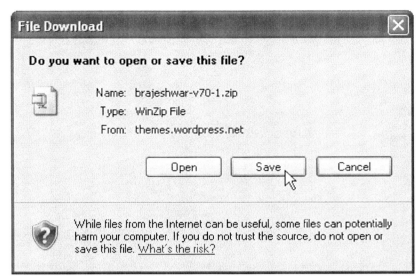

FIGURE 63 INSTALL A THEME: DOWNLOAD & SAVE

Click on "Save" and save 'brajeshwar-v70-1.zip' to your computer.

To make the theme files easier to find later, save the files to a directory on your computer named for the domain and your blog.

For this example, I installed this theme to the blog on RosalindGardner.com.

Update: I now use the Premium News Theme by Adii on the site.

Because the blog is installed in the root directory of that domain, I saved the zipped theme files to a directory on my computer named:

C:\My Documents\My Files\rosalindgardner.com\wp-content\themes as outlined in the next screenshot.

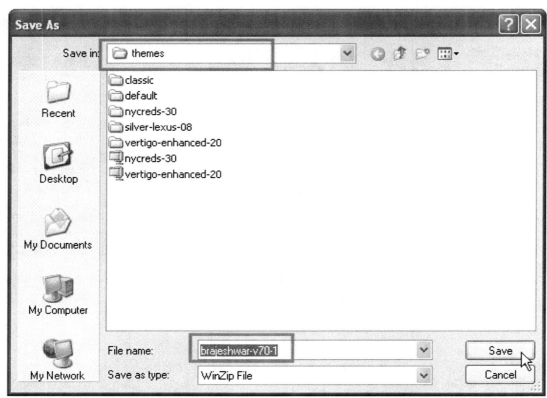

FIGURE 64 INSTALL A THEME: SAVE THE ZIPPED FILE

When your files have finished downloading, a 'Download complete' window will open.

Click on 'Open' as shown in the screenshot to the left.

This will open WinZip (your extraction utility) and show all of the files associated with the theme.

FIGURE 65 INSTALL A THEME: DOWNLOAD COMPLETE

STEP 3: UNZIP (EXTRACT) THE THEME FILES

When WinZip opens, click on 'Extract' as shown in the screenshot below.

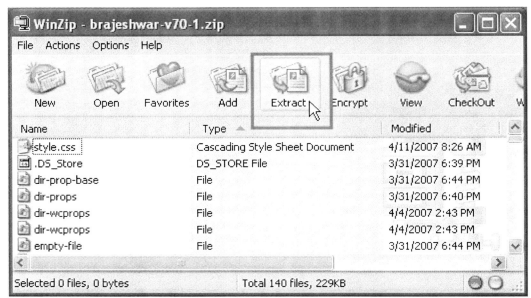

FIGURE 66 INSTALL A THEME: FILE EXTRACTION #1

This will open a new window (shown in the next screenshot). When the next window opens, be sure to check the 'Use folder names' box as outlined in the next screenshot. Then click on 'Extract'.

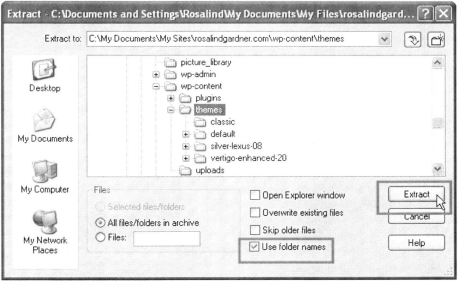

FIGURE 67 INSTALL A THEME: FILE EXTRACTION #2

STEP 4: UPLOAD THE THEME TO YOUR BLOG

Open your FTP software and connect to your site, as shown in the screenshot below.

This will be FileZilla if you are a Windows user, or CyberDuck if you are a Mac user. FTP software was discussed under 'File Transfer Protocol' of the Basic Software section.

Navigate to and open the 'themes' file folder on your blog. You will see two folders in that file, one named 'classic' and the other 'default.'

Those are the themes that were installed with the blog.

Now locate the file folder on your computer where you saved your new theme and transfer the theme's folder to your blog's wp-content/themes/ folder.

When your files have been transferred, the folder will appear as it does in the *Upload Theme Files to Your Blog* screenshot shown right.

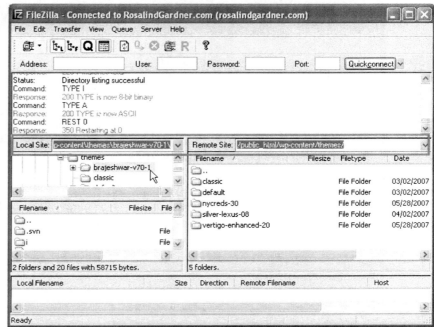

FIGURE 68 INSTALL A THEME: UPLOAD THEME FILES TO YOUR BLOG

STEP 5: ACTIVATE YOUR NEW THEME

Login to your Wordpress Administration panel and click on 'Presentation.'

In the window that opens, you will see the 'Current Theme' displayed at the top of the page and 'Available Themes' displayed below as shown in the next screenshot.

FIGURE 69 INSTALL A THEME: THE PRESENTATION PANEL

To activate the Brajeshwar v7.3.1 theme that you uploaded, click on the linked name of the theme or the graphic for that theme. The new theme will now show up under 'Current Theme.'

To see how your new theme appears, click on the "View Site" link located near the top of the Wordpress administration panel's page.

SEARCH FOR YOUR OWN THEME

Don't worry if you decide that you don't really like your new theme that much after all. You can easily search for, download, install and activate another theme.

Themes on the WordPress Theme Viewer may be searched for according to the number of columns, basic color, fixed or fluid width, left or right sidebar, square or rounded corners, with or without images, and whether the theme is 'widget-ready' or plugins are required.

Returns may be sorted according to date, title, downloads or tag.

Small thumbnails of the themes are returned by the results.

When you see one that you like, click on the thumbnail to see a larger image. You may also click on 'Test Run' to see the theme in action. Download and activate your new theme using the steps above.

When I found the Brajeshwar theme used in our installation example, I had searched for a theme that had 3 columns, was widget-ready and had a fluid width. I sorted the returns based on the theme's popularity, or the number of downloads.

To search for your own theme, go to http://themes.wordpress.net/.

For more information about Wordpress Themes, visit the "Using Themes" page on the Wordpress Codex at http://codex.wordpress.org/Using Themes.

Add Your Content

The average affiliate produces a visitor-to-sales conversion between half and one percent. In other words, they achieve an average 'conversion rate' if they make 1 sale for every hundred visitors sent to a merchant's site.

Quite frankly, I think that's dismal. You CAN do much better than that.

My conversion rates average *between 2.5 and 6 percent*, and many are much higher depending on the type of product sold.

To get those results, I consistently follow my own rules in the chapter on 'How to Choose Affiliate Programs.' I also often purchase and test products before promoting them on my site. I do this after I've joined the program, and when I can, I use my own affiliate link to buy the item. The price is then reduced by the amount of commission I receive from the sale. The cost is also a business write-off.

But the real 'secret' is great site content and LOTS of it.

NOTE: If you are *not* a writer, don't worry about how you'll put all this content on your site --- as you will also learn how to get content from other sources.

I always give the product or service 'added value' by creating content around it. I tell my customers exactly why I think it's a good product or service. If it has a few drawbacks, but I still think it's a good buy, I'll tell them that too. I give my customers enough information about the product to help them decide whether or not it is right for them, which gives me a big leg up on the competition. Then I offer 'extras' like informative articles, reports and newsletters that further increase my sales and conversion rates.

In the following sections we'll look at different ways in which you can develop content and different types of content to use on your site. I recommend that you plan to incorporate all or most of the following content elements in your own web site.

6 Ways to Build Content

I write almost all the content for my own sites - only because I'm such a control freak. If I were smarter, I would outsource most of my writing and take even more holidays! ☺ So, don't worry if you are not a writer. You have 5 options for content development – in addition to writing your own content. Each is discussed in greater detail in this section.

- Create Your Own Content
- Hire a Ghostwriter
- Buy Resale & Private Label Rights
- Source Copyright-Free (Public Domain) Work
- Use Other Authors' Content
- Repurpose Your Content

1. CREATE YOUR OWN CONTENT

I like to write. Actually, I *really* enjoy writing. When people ask me what I do for a living, I don't say that I'm an affiliate marketer. I tell them that I'm a writer, and *then* I explain how I make money from my writing as an affiliate marketer.

The best thing about writing your own site content is that you can inject your personality and create your own brand.

It's your site. You can choose to portray yourself as funny, curmudgeonly or sweet.

In time, your visitors start to recognize your 'voice.' If they like you, they look forward to hearing more of what you have to say.

Eventually you build rapport with your readers and develop friendships through your correspondence. That, more than commissions, is what makes this business so sweet.

2. HIRE A GHOSTWRITER

If you are allergic to writing, then you can have someone else do your writing for you.

Many webmasters build content for their sites quickly and cheaply using ghostwriters hired through Elance and Rentacoder.

The graphic to the right shows a *poor example* of a project posting at Elance for ghostwritten articles. The poster is looking for '20 reviews for dating sites.' That description is insufficient to explain exactly what is expected of the writer.

Despite the fact that the project poster mentions earlier in the project description that he has had "problem with copyrights," he is looking for 'small kudos, small darts,'

PROJECT DESCRIPTION
We need reviews for dating sites: description – 1-2 paragraph;   small kudos;   small darts.   List for the sites will be provided.

FIGURE 70 HIRE A GHOSTWRITER: ELANCE PROJECT SAMPLE #1

Hmmm... I wonder where he got that idea?

Hint. Take a look near the bottom of my eHarmony review at http://sage-hearts.com/dating_services/eharmony.html. Oh well, the ghostwriter probably won't know what the heck 'small kudos, small darts' means anyway.

Be original.

Come up with your own review structure and spell out exactly what you want.

The figure to the right is an example of a well-written project posting at Elance for ghostwritten articles.

This request for 'bingo articles' is much better, especially since he or she is looking for 'quality, fun articles' written by someone who is a 'fan of online bingo.'

Here is another tip about hiring ghostwriters - don't underpay them!

I've seen article packages sell for $2.00 per article, and the writing is absolutely terrible.

For example, in the section below is a portion of an article about *cell family plans* that appears to have been ghostwritten.

Project Description

I would like 100 bingo gaming articles written for my websites and also for distribution. I require quality, fun articles written by an enthusiastic fan of online bingo which will look good on my websites and people will want to republish on theirs.

I need somebody with English as their first language to write these articles as I want to spend as little time as possible editing them and do not want cheap "keyword stuffed" articles which hold no value for the reader.

If you are a fan of online bingo and can write 100 articles, each containing a minimum of 450 words on all aspects of online bingo such as:

Bingo origins / history
Bingo rules
Bingo "tactics"
Variations of bingo
Bingo in the UK and different countries
Bingo experiences
Online bingo room reviews
Bricks and mortar bingo experiences
Online bingo "scams"

Please attach examples of previous bingo articles when placing a bid and be prepared to complete the project within 30 days of accepting the project.

FIGURE 71 HIRE A GHOSTWRITER: ELANCE PROJECT SAMPLE #2

You are here looking for cell phone family plans, which ones offer the best wireless plans for the money and which have the best free cell phones.

Cell phone family plans that include free cell phones and great cheap wireless plans

Well try and give you as much information regarding cell phone plans for families as well as finding the best deals on free cell phones and cheap wireless plans.

Whether or not your looking to simply stay in touch with your family easily or your looking to save money on your current wireless plan, family cell phone plans can do that by placing all the cell phones in your family onto one wireless plan. Another great aspect of getting a cell phone family plan is that many wireless plans provide free mobile to mobile minutes so you can stay in touch with you family without running up the bills.

That article appears to have been written to a keyword density formula for the terms "cell phone" and "cell phone plans." Furthermore, the writing is boring, and both the spelling and the grammar are simply atrocious.

To get high quality ghostwritten articles you must pay a good writer a fair price for their work and be specific about the 'tone' of the article. Moreover, you will get quality material when you hire writers that are actually *interested* in the topic they are writing about.

3. BUY RESALE & PRIVATE LABEL RIGHTS

Private label rights (PLR) and packages with niche content are all the rage at the moment.

PLR are articles and ebooks for which you buy the right to use any way you want.

Typically they are supplied as unformatted text files or Word documents, to which you can add or modify content, including the title and authors name… meaning you can put your own name on the article.

PLR packages are quite inexpensive compared to ghostwritten articles. Private label rights articles average 10 to 20 cents, whereas a good ghostwriter will charge between 10 and 30 bucks for one well-written article.

You could take a PLR ebook and break it up into individual articles and then use those articles on your site, in your blog or your newsletter.

Conversely, you might want to combine a number of PLR articles into an ebook to give away as incentive to signup for your newsletter, or even to sell for a profit.

You could even sell your new book on eBay and generate affiliate sales or bring traffic to your site through links in the book.

Consider using the first paragraph or two of each article in your autoresponder series and include a link to the complete article on your site to bring your visitors back to your site.

Before you buy a private label rights package, read the terms carefully. You want to make sure that you have the right to change, modify, cut, delete the content in any way you want, and put your name on it.

A number of PLR distributors are listed at NetProfitsToday.com listed in the "Develop Site Content" category under "Private Label Rights" and "Buy Content for Your Site." Some deal in a number of different markets, whereas others target specific niches such as dogs, self-help and health.

4. OBTAIN WORKS IN THE PUBLIC DOMAIN

Public domain works are books, poems and articles for which the copyright has expired and that have *NO copyright protection*.

Anyone can copy, modify and use or sell them.

Once you modify a public domain work it becomes your property. The modified work receives an automatic copyright just like it would if it were an original work.

To learn how to source public domain works, please visit the "Recommended Resources" section.

5. USE OTHER AUTHORS' CONTENT

GoArticles.com, EzineArticles.com and a number of other article directories allow you to use the material that authors post to those sites, free of charge.

The stipulation is that you will respect authors' guidelines and those of the article directory managers. In almost all cases, authors require that you place their resource box at the bottom of the article, which invariably includes a link back to their site.

Therein lies the drawback, however. That link out of your site is not usually an affiliate link, and I don't recommend that you post any 'leaky' links on your site.

You're much better off using PLR articles which you can claim as your own and have no linking requirements.

6. REPURPOSE YOUR CONTENT

Repurposing content means taking content that you have created - or paid to have developed for you - and using it in a different way.

For example, you might use a portion of an article in your autoresponder series.

By repurposing your content and creating new formats for your material, you can extend your reach and increase the size of your audience. Those who read your newsletter but not the articles on your site will derive the benefit of the information in that article which before resided only on your site.

Here are 5 more ways you can reuse your content:

1. Articles can be recorded to audio files and uploaded to your site for those who would rather listen than read.

2. Articles can be combined into a report, booklet or full-scale ebook and offered as incentive to sign up for your newsletter. You could also turn them into paid content!

3. Turn your autoresponder series into a downloadable report.

4. Interview experts in your field and upload the audio to your site. Have the audio transcribed and turned into an ebook or a series of articles. Use quotes from the transcripts in a variety of different articles.

5. Modify your content to suit different audiences. For example, an article entitled "6 Strategies for Successful Online Dating" could easily be re-written as "6 Online Dating Mistakes to Avoid."

Use your imagination to find new and different ways to reuse your existing material.

Not only will you increase your reach and your profits, but you'll also save time in the process!

5 'Must-Have' Site Pages

The number of affiliate webmasters that don't include the following 5 basic pages on their sites is appalling. They are losing sales by result.

Do yourself and your business a big favor. Take a few hours to create the content for these 'must-have' pages. To make it even easier for you, I include examples for your use in a few cases.

1. CONTACT PAGE

A visitor who makes time to send a question demonstrates their interest in the site and the product offerings, and timely responses to their questions increase the likelihood of making the sale.

Instead of using clickable email links, I recommend you use contact forms for two reasons. First, forms eliminate a lot of the spam that you get from the idiots who use email address harvesters. Second, your visitors' email software won't be popping open when they least expect it.

2. PRIVACY STATEMENT

Every commercial web site needs a privacy/security statement. Privacy statements explain how information on your site is collected, safeguarded and used. It is an explicit statement made on behalf of the site owner to the site user, and is a legal, binding document. Including a privacy statement instills user confidence and trust, reduces liability, and increases your web site's conversion rate.

I've included the template below that I use for the privacy statements on my sites.

Feel free to use it on your site. Simply replace YourSite.com with your site's name or URL, fill in the blanks where appropriate, and replace the words '<u>by clicking here</u>' with the link to the contact page on your site.

```
Sample Privacy Statement

YourSite.com has created this privacy statement in order to demonstrate our
firm commitment to privacy. The following discloses our information gathering
and dissemination practices for this website: YourSite.com.

We use your IP address to help diagnose problems with our server, and to
administer our Web site.

This site contains links to other sites. YourSite.com is not responsible for
the privacy practices or the content of such Web sites.

YourSite.com employs the services of _____ for the YourSite.com
Newsletter. _____ and YourSite.com agree not to sell or rent the email
addresses of any YourSite.com Newsletter subscriber to any third party.

Public Forums
This site may make chat rooms, forums, message boards, and/or news groups
available to its users. Please remember that any information that is
disclosed in these areas becomes public information and you should exercise
caution when deciding to disclose your personal information.
```

Choice/Opt-Out
This site gives users the following options for removing their information from our mailing list database to not receive future communications or to no longer receive our service. You can contact YourSite.com by clicking here.

Correct/Update
This site gives users the following options for changing and modifying information previously provided. Change or modify information by clicking here.

Contacting the Web Site
If you have any questions about this privacy statement, the practices of this site, or your dealings with this Web site, feel free to contact us by clicking here.

3. DISCLAIMER

Do you plan to promote business opportunities, health-related items or any product that may make claims about extraordinary success achieved by its users? If so, you should include a disclaimer on your site to protect yourself from legal action by association.
Here is the disclaimer that I've placed on the NetProfitsToday.com site.

SITE DISCLAIMER

NetProfitsToday.com does not represent or endorse the accuracy or reliability of any of the information, content or advertisements contained on, distributed through, or linked, downloaded or accessed from any of the services contained on this website, nor the quality of any products, information or other materials displayed, purchased, or obtained by you as a result of an advertisement or any other information or offer in or in connection with the services herein. You hereby acknowledge that any reliance upon any Materials shall be at your sole risk. NetProfitsToday.com reserves the right, in its sole discretion and without any obligation, to make improvements to, or correct any error or omissions in any portion of the Service or the Materials.

THE SERVICE AND THE MATERIALS ARE PROVIDED BY NetProfitsToday.com ON AN "AS IS" BASIS, AND NetProfitsToday.com EXPRESSLY DISCLAIMS ANY AND ALL WARRANTIES, EXPRESS OR IMPLIED, INCLUDING WITHOUT LIMITATION WARRANTIES OF MERCHANTABILITY AND FITNESS FOR A PARTICULAR PURPOSE, WITH RESPECT TO THE SERVICE OR ANY MATERIALS AND PRODUCTS. IN NO EVENT SHALL NetProfitsToday.com BE LIABLE FOR ANY DIRECT, INDIRECT, INCIDENTAL, PUNITIVE, OR CONSEQUENTIAL DAMAGES OF ANY KIND WHATSOEVER WITH RESPECT TO THE SERVICE, THE MATERIALS AND THE PRODUCTS.

NetProfitsToday.com respects the rights (including the intellectual property rights) of others, and we ask our users to do the same. NetProfitsToday.com may, in appropriate circumstances and in its sole discretion, terminate the accounts of users that infringe or otherwise violate such rights of others.

4. DISCLOSURE STATEMENT

On December 11, 2006, the Federal Trade Commission said that companies that engage in word-of-mouth marketing must disclose those relationships. Word-of-mouth marketing is peer-to-peer communication for the purpose of earning a profit.

Affiliate product endorsements placed on blogs and web pages is considered word-of-mouth marketing and therefore requires disclosure.

Rather than identify each and every affiliate link on my site, I opted to place a disclosure statement alongside my disclaimer at NetProfitsToday.com.

The text of the disclosure reads as follows:

DISCLOSURE STATEMENT

The contents of this web site and blog is written and edited by me, Rosalind Gardner.

The compensation I receive as an affiliate marketer to provide opinion on products, services, websites and various other topics does NOT affect the topics or posts I make in this blog.

I abide by word of mouth marketing standards and believe in honesty of relationship, opinion and identity.

Unlike so many who promote Internet marketing products, I am NOT a product launch monger who promotes ever product - good or bad - that hits the market.

The views and opinions expressed on this blog are purely my own. I always provide my honest opinions, findings, beliefs, or experiences on those topics or products.

In rare cases, I will mention products that I have not personally reviewed. However, this only occurs when I am familiar with the manufacturer's previous products and am satisfied that he or she produces only high-quality goods. Regardless, I will mention if and when I do not have personal experience with the product.

Any product claim, statistic, quote or other representation about a product or service should be verified with the manufacturer, provider or party in question.

To create your own disclosure statement, DisclosurePolicy.org has a neat disclosure policy generator available at http://www.disclosurepolicy.org/generator/generate_policy

5. 'ABOUT US' PAGE

It's natural to want to know with whom you're doing business – both online and off.

When you get the impression that someone is hiding behind the typical anonymity of the Web, you're less likely to trust the products recommended on the site and therefore unlikely to buy from that site.

Having an 'About Us' page on your site instills that trust in your visitors and will increase your sales numbers.

The screenshot to the right is taken from my 'About Us' page at Sage-Hearts.com.

Notice how I've included a picture of myself and the reasons I had for creating my Web site.

That makes me a 'real' person to my visitors and is one of the reasons that site has been so successful.

FIGURE 72 "ABOUT US" EXAMPLE

Because they help improve your credibility, increase visitor trust and sales, the 5 pages discussed in this section are the FIRST pages you should place on your site / blog. Don't do business without them!

Essential Content for Affiliate Sites

In this section, you'll learn about the two types of content that are absolutely essential for every affiliate site – product endorsements/reviews and informational articles.

PRODUCT ENDORSEMENTS AND REVIEWS

The best conversion to sales rates are achieved when you write product endorsements and reviews for your merchants' products.

Below is a portion of the Match.com endorsement at Sage-Hearts.com.

Dating Site Reviews

Match.com

Match.com first appeared in April 1995 as an online classifieds tool. With limited features and usability, Match.com soon attracted a community of over 60,000 singles in less than a year, quickly becoming a leading online matchmaking site.

FIGURE 73 SAMPLE PRODUCT ENDORSEMENT

By early 1996, nearly 500,000 members were finding each other at Match.com, and engagement and marriage announcements started to pour in. On March 30, 1996, the *first baby of a Match.com-inspired marriage* was born, and to date they have confirmed at least 50 more babies, almost 1200 marriages, and hundreds of thousands of relationships.

Today, Match.com is the leading (and largest) subscription-based online dating site, offering adults worldwide a fun, private and secure environment for meeting other singles. Match.com claims more than **15 million members with profiles** posted who are active users.

Try Match.com Free for 3 days

In January 2006, Match.com launched MindFindBind™, a new program it created with the help of Dr. Phil McGraw. Created specifically for Match.com, MindFindBind™ is a Web-based program designed to educate singles about the ins and outs of dating and relationships. It includes more than 50 new Internet-only video segments with Dr. Phil that aim to inspire and enlighten, workshops that are a lot more fun than work, an occasional audio blog, and provocative dating tips and techniques. Participants can move through the program at their own pace, in the privacy of their own homes.

To help my visitors decide whether a visit to the merchant's site is worth their while, I also include a list of product features on the product review page, as shown in the screenshot on the right.

The benefit to affiliates for providing more information is that if they decide that the service doesn't offer what they want, they will stay on your site and look for another service that does.

You can see the full Match.com review at:

http://tinyurl.com/2en5z3

Match.com	
Last Reviewed	May 2007
Category(ies)	Dating Service
Free Basic Membership	Yes
Regions Served	All
Relationships	Heterosexual Gay Lesbian Exotic, Risque Single Parents PenPals
Site Highlights	Photos
	Email Read Notification - Find out when someone reads your email
	Happen Magazine - Includes regular articles such as Leave the "Baggage" at Home and 6 sure tips to score a sweetie
Database Search	Who's Online sex, age and sexual Orientation City, Zip Code and distance from your location

FIGURE 74 PRODUCT FEATURE LIST

The trick is to give your visitors just enough information to pique their interest without overwhelming them with text. In other words, make your review 'compelling.'

HOW TO WRITE A COMPELLING PRODUCT ENDORSEMENT

Don't you hate being on the receiving end of a sales pitch? That's why the best way to promote your affiliate program products is to **endorse** them, honestly and sincerely.

In order for your endorsement to be persuasive, you should have personal experience with the product and be enthusiastic about it. Given those two factors, writing the endorsement then becomes easy.

That's why super affiliates frequently buy the products they sell. They study the product or service inside and out, backwards and forwards. They note all the features, both good and bad.

Writing the recommendation takes time and care. You need to carefully consider all you want to say and anticipate your readers' reactions. When you anticipate your visitors' concerns, you are able to address them *before* they become unanswered questions that cause them to click away.

The primary ingredient in a compelling personal testimonial is an explanation of how you benefited from use of the product or service. The product feature list is secondary.

People want to know how the product will improve their lives.

For example, if you are promoting the latest health regime, emphasizing the point that it contains coral calcium is unlikely to convince anyone of its worth. What the heck is coral calcium?

Tell your visitors sincerely how using the product made you feel more fit and energetic and that will get them interested.

If you want to see examples of product endorsements in action, watch TV infomercials. Infomercial writers are the kings and queens of 'compelling.'

AN ALTERNATIVE TO PRODUCT REVIEWS: COMPARISON CHARTS

An alternative to individual product reviews is a side-by-side comparison review chart. A very basic structure for the chart is laid out in the table below.

[Product Type] Compared			
Name	Product 1	Product 2	Product 3
Rank	#1	#2	#3
Product Image			
Feature 1			
Feature 2			

Feature 3			
Price			
Affiliate Link	Buy Now	Buy Now	Buy Now
Review Link	More Info	More Info	More Info
[Product Type] Reviews			
Product 1	Summary review – 200 – 400 words in length.		
Product 2	Summary review – 200 – 400 words in length.		
Product 3	Summary review – 200 – 400 words in length.		
Summary Conclusion			
Relatively short summary of findings above. Include rating and selection criteria.			

These comparisons convert to sales especially well when the affiliate has experience with the product and can express their findings using first-person terms, such as "I found the XYZ Heart Rate monitor the most comfortable to wear."

INFORMATIVE ARTICLES

Well-written highly relevant articles also help to attract free search engine traffic to your site. You can also place some of your articles on other webmasters' sites or article directories to bring in more free traffic via the link in your author's resource box.

But first and foremost, your visitors are searching the Internet for information. If you give them the information they want *before* sending them to your product review pages, your sales conversions will soar.

For example, I know that single people who may be considering online dating have a number of questions about internet dating safety, background checks and how to improve their chances of success when using a dating service. I therefore provide informative articles on my dating site such as:

- How to Write a Personal Ad
- Internet Dating Safety Precautions
- Should I Get a Background Check?

Each of these articles links to a product that is relevant to the topic. The personal ad article links to a page with recommended dating services, and the latter 2 articles link to investigative services such as Records Registry, which provides background services.

THE 'SECRET' INGREDIENT EVERY ARTICLE NEEDS

Whether you write your own articles or use a ghostwriter, there is one secret ingredient that is more important to your article than anything else. Any guesses?

It's your HEADLINE! If your headline doesn't compel your visitors to read the article, then it won't matter if you have written the best article in the world. As headlines can be a challenge for new marketers, I've included 21 fill-in-the-blank ideas to help get you started.

7. Top 10 _____ Do's and Don'ts
8. What's HOT and NOT in _____
9. When Not to _____
10. Your Must-Know Guide to _____
11. _____ with Pizzazz!
12. _____ and Grow Rich
13. _____ on the Cheap
14. 5 Ways to Get More from Your _____
15. 5 No-Fail Strategies for _____
16. 6 Secrets to Successful _____
17. 7 Ways to Avoid the Most Deadly _____ Mistakes
18. 8 Ways to Avoid the Worst _____ Mistakes
19. 9 Formulas for Fantastic _____
20. 10 User-Friendly Facts for _____
21. 10 Tips to Jump-Start Your _____
22. 11 Questions You Must Ask When You're _____
23. 12 Tactics to Open Up _____
24. 13 Tips That Will Make a _____ Smile
25. 10 Time-Tested Tips for Becoming a _____
26. 25 Quick _____ Tips to Use Now
27. 26 Holiday Gifts for _____

Now that you are set with all the ways to develop content and the type of content to place on your site, it's time to add some revenue-generating programs to your site.

Monetize Your Site

The time has come to start making money from your site. You will do this by joining and placing links from advertising networks and affiliate programs on your site.

Join Contextual Advertising Networks

In an April 20th, 2006 press release, the Interactive Advertising Bureau (www.iab.net) reported that "overall internet advertising revenues (U.S.) for 2005 totaled $12.5 billion, a new annual record exceeding 2004 by 30%. Q4 2005 internet advertising revenues totaled a record $3.6 billion, representing a 34% increase over same period in 2004."

Do you want a piece of that pie? Then consider placing ads from contextual advertising networks on your site. In the following section we will look at the most popular ad network, however, there is a *larger list of contextual advertising networks* in Appendix A.

GOOGLE ADSENSE

Google Adsense is perhaps the best-known provider of contextual ad units for affiliates. AdSense is an advertising program run by Google and is a quick and easy way to generate revenue from a content-rich website.

Webmasters enroll in this program to allow text and image advertisements served by Google to be placed on their sites. Google's search technology ensures that the ads are based on the content of the page and/or the user's geographic location. The ads generate revenue on a per-click basis.

The figure to the right shows a screenshot of how 2 of the 4 Adsense units appear on the 'Interracial Dating' page at Sage-Hearts.com.

Notice how the ads relate to the topic of interracial dating?

Meet Interracial Singles
Hot, Sexy & Single - Lets Mingle! Free Sign Up & 7 Day Trial
www.True.com

Interracial Singles Photo
Free membership, photo gallery, and more. Meet other diverse singles.
www.InterracialSingles.net

Ads by Google

FIGURE 75 GOOGLE ADSENSE EXAMPLE

Therein lies the art behind making Adsense work for you.

Provided your page content is focused on a specific theme and targets just one or two keywords or keyword phrases, Adsense will 'reward' you with ads related to the content of that page. Because your visitors are already interested in that topic, they're more likely to click on the ad… and bingo! You earn a commission for the click.

How much commission?

Well, Google is not telling. However, their reasons may have something to do with the legal contracts between Google and its premium distribution partners. However, estimates put the rates between 40 and 60% of Adwords rates and Adsense earnings.

Although Google's terms of agreement prohibit Adsense publishers from reporting their earnings, tales of riches abound. The following table includes just 3 examples of those who have had great success with Adsense.

ADSENSE SUCCESS STORIES

Chris Pirillo, best-selling author and creator of the Lockergnome series of online publications, reports clearing more than $10,000 a month.

Jason Calacanis says his sites made $45,000 within the first four months of launch.

GOOGLE ADSENSE DO'S AND DON'TS

I've played with Adsense positioning over and over and over again and here are the points that I've learned.

1. Do NOT place Adsense on your homepage, especially if you use PPC to advertise your site. Give your visitors a chance to look around before giving them the opportunity to click away.

2. Do NOT place Adsense on your product endorsement pages. You should make more money selling the product than you will with Adsense. If your visitor decides not to buy the product, it is better that they use your navigation to find another product on your site, than click away for just a penny or two.

3. Do NOT over-crowd your content pages with Adsense advertising. Google allows you to place up to 3 instances of Adsense per page on your site. I've seen all manner of ludicrous placement that screams "Get me outta here!". Those sites may earn money from Adsense, but they aren't earning money from affiliate commissions.

4. DO put Adsense on your non-monetized pages such as your forum and general content pages that do not link to product endorsement pages.

5. DO NOT underestimate your site's viability as an 'affiliate site' and turn it into an full-blown Adsense site without testing and tracking your income results. Before you add MORE Adsense to your pages, try *improving* your product endorsements. Your aim should be newsletter signups and conversions to product sales through affiliate programs... not clicks.

With those do's and don'ts in mind, visit Google Adsense to set up an account right now at: http://www.google.com/adsense

Join Affiliate Programs

The first step to earning revenue from affiliate programs is knowing where to find them, so in this section you will learn about affiliate networks, directories and how to find merchants with stand-alone or 'in-house' programs.

AFFILIATE NETWORKS

Affiliate networks may also be referred to as 'pay-for-performance network,' 'cost-per-action (CPA) network' or 'marketing solution provider.'

Affiliate networks act as third-party "honest brokers" and function as middlemen between merchants and affiliates. Merchants use affiliate networks to list their products and the details of their affiliate programs, and affiliates can apply to those they are interested in and qualify for.

For merchants, joining an affiliate network places thousands of eager affiliates right on their doorstep. The marketing value and simplicity of having another company administer their affiliate program is worth the (sometimes) hefty prices charged by the networks.

Joining an affiliate network is free for affiliates, and the process of finding and selecting programs is simplified through categorical search facilities. Because merchants pay top-dollar for a good network's management services, affiliate networks in general tend to offer higher-quality programs. Being able to access your statistics in a centralized interface is another big benefit to joining a network.

Each affiliate network is set-up and operates differently.

Networks generally handle sales tracking statistics, provision of marketing tools, and most networks consolidate affiliates' earnings into a single monthly paycheck.

To join most networks, you enter all your contact and payment details (name, address, phone number, etc.) just once. After your application is accepted, you can apply to each merchant's program separately. In some instances, approval is immediate, and in others you may have to wait a day (or seven) for the merchant to get back to you.

Some networks allow you to see a list of all the merchants in the network before you join, while others require that you signup with their network first.

Marketing material for each merchant is readily available, and HMTL code for links is usually generated with a single mouse click. You simply cut and paste the code into your Web site pages. Banners are usually hosted on the network's servers, saving you bandwidth charges.

Commission Junction, Linkshare and Performics are the major affiliate networks. Clickbank specializes in digital products and has a built-in affiliate network.

In *Appendix A*, you will find a long list of affiliate networks and more information about a few individual affiliate networks including network URLs, signup restrictions, program types, minimum payouts and payment processes, tracking, the availability of multi-tier programs and more.

SIGN UP FOR COMMISSION JUNCTION NOW

You will be unable to see advertisers (merchants) listed at Commission Junction unless you have an account with them. So, let's join Commission Junction now.

During the signup process, you will be asked for your Web site or newsletter name, URL and description as shown in the graphic below.

I suggest that you simply put in a newsletter name and a brief description for now. You will be able to change and add sites to your profile later.

FIGURE 76 COMMISSION JUNCTION ACCOUNT SIGNUP

Once you have established an account, click on 'Get Links' from the homepage.

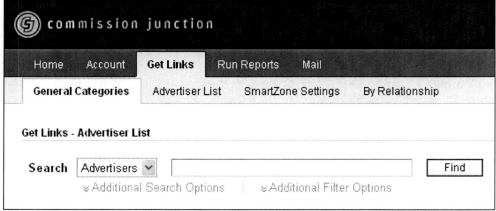

FIGURE 77 FIND PRODUCTS AT COMMISSION JUNCTION

You can search for Advertisers or Products either by name, or drill down through the main category list as shown in the screenshot below.

Financial Services
Banking/Trading - Credit Cards - Credit Reporting - Investment - Loans - Real Estate Services

Food & Drinks
Gourmet - Groceries - Restaurants - Tobacco - Wine & Spirits

Phonecard Services
Online/Wireless

Recreation & Leisure
Astrology - Betting/Gaming - Communities - Events - Matchmaking - New Age - Outdoors - Party Goods

FIGURE 78 COMMISSION JUNCTION'S CATEGORY LIST

I clicked on 'Matchmaking' and found 32 different advertisers at Commission Junction alone!

Advertisers in Recreation & Leisure > Matchmaking   Display By ALL COUNTRIES

Results 1 - 25 of 32

☑ Apply to Program   Select All

Advertiser	3 Month EPC (USD)	7 Day EPC (USD)	Network Earnings	Sale	Lead	Click
Top 9% in EPC of all CJ affiliate programs. Great Expectations - Dating Service » View Links	$75.42	$63.01		Sale: 25.00% USD, $50.00 USD Lead: $15.00 USD Performance Incentive		
Earn More Than $140 Per Membership! PerfectMatch.com » View Links	$58.88	$44.67		Sale: $27.50 - $115.00 USD Lead: $1.50 USD Performance Incentive		
You can earn over $100 per membership eharmony.com » View Links	$57.65	$54.06		Sale: 20.00% - 40.00% USD, $20.00 - $75.00 USD Lead: $0.50 USD		
YAHOO! Yahoo! Affiliate Program » View Links » View Products	$40.77	$31.09		Sale: $1.50 - $22.00 USD Lead: $4.50 - $8.00 USD Performance Incentive		

FIGURE 79 COMMISSION JUNCTION PRODUCT SEARCH RESULTS

While you are in the Commission Junction (CJ) interface, take a look at commissions paid by each of the merchants. Based on what I see in the graphic above, I would note that PerfectMatch.com pays between $27.50 - $115.00 USD per sale, $1.50 USD per lead, and has a 'performance incentive.'

Performance Incentives allow advertisers to increase commissions based on performance during a given month and that goal must be reached within the month.

For example, PerfectMatch.com will increase commission rates by 18.00% when the number of 1-month membership sales is equal to or greater than 20. Sell more than 30 memberships in a month and the commission goes up by 36%.

We'll investigate all the particulars of individual affiliate programs in *20 Questions to Ask Before You Join an Affiliate Program*.

'IN-HOUSE' PROGRAMS

What happens if you can't find a merchant that sells Barbie doll supplies and accessories through an affiliate program? Suppose you've searched the affiliate networks and directories and still had no luck?

Here's a search technique that will help you locate exactly what you are looking for.

In this case, go to Google and type "+Barbie +doll +affiliate" into the search box. Don't include the quotes, but do include the plus signs. The plus signs ensure that each word entered appears on the pages returned in the search results.

However, the pages returned aren't guaranteed to have a Barbie doll accessories affiliate program. Some of the sites may be affiliates themselves, but looking around their site should give you clues as to the identity of the merchant.

Other sites that are returned by your search will in fact be merchant sites.

While reviewing individual sites and pages, look for links on the site that say, "Webmasters," "Make Money," "Affiliate (or Associate) Program," "Partners," "Earn $" and other phrases that indicate that the company has an affiliate program.

AFFILIATE PROGRAM DIRECTORIES

Affiliate Program Directories are web sites that contain lists of links to affiliate programs that have been compiled and organized by various webmasters.

Programs are typically categorized by product type (e.g. educational, business, etc.) and include brief summaries of each program with sufficient information to allow directory users to choose which programs they would like to join. Some also provide program ratings as supplied by program users.

When searching through the directories, you'll discover that many of the merchants listed *are* also affiliated with networks. Research the networks first, because in all likelihood, you'll be redirected back to them anyway to sign up for many of the programs.

Affiliate Program Directory Caution
Affiliate program directories should be your last resource for finding affiliate programs, as listings on these sites are often outdated and no longer relevant.

Affiliate program directories are therefore best used to find merchants that have stand-alone or 'in house' programs that are not associated with the big affiliate networks.

Although there are hundreds of affiliate program directories, I've listed only one below.

AssociatePrograms.com - Approaching 6,000 program listings, AssociatePrograms.com offers the most comprehensive list of affiliate programs anywhere on the Net. The site is easy to use, and listings appear alphabetically in the search results, making it easy to locate programs again later. Listings are kept brief, with only salient points like commission structure and product descriptions. If you have first-hand experience with any of the programs listed, you are invited to share your opinion and rate the program.

In summary, look for products and services to promote at affiliate networks, directories and merchants' 'in-house' programs. However, resist the temptation to sign up for every good-looking program and product until your basic Web site is in place!

More importantly, don't join a program until you've finished reading the next section.

20 Questions to Ask Before You Join an Affiliate Program

Before you join any affiliate program, there are a number of questions that need to get answered. Below is a list of 20 questions you should consider before affiliating with most merchants.

If you can't find an answer on the merchant's site, phone or email them. If contact information isn't readily apparent on their Web site, don't waste more of your time on that merchant - find another program.

If you don't get a response within a reasonable time frame, say 24 to 48 hours, then pass on the program. They may be more responsive to their customers and current affiliates, but will you know? Discovering that they are LESS responsive when you have a real problem is a bigger problem still.

On the flip side, be sure that the answer to your question is NOT included in the affiliate package before contacting the program manager. They're busy people, and answering questions that have been covered elsewhere, wastes their time. That makes for a lousy first impression.

OK, let's review those questions.

1. IS THE COMPANY REPUTABLE?

Most merchants are reputable operators but just because someone has a Web site does not mean that they're legitimate and/or trustworthy.

Obviously, you don't have to ask Dell or eBay™ how long they've been in business. The concern here is about promoting an **unknown merchant** that may turn out to be a **fly-by-night or dishonest** operator.

A few years ago, I was robbed by just such an operator to the tune of more than $700! Despite sending many emails and leaving a number of telephone messages, I heard and received nothing in return.

I could have avoided that problem by doing just a little research.

Commission Junction posts the date that merchants join their affiliate network. When I see that the company has been associated with Commission Junction for a year or more, I feel confident that they are in business to do business. Furthermore, some networks require merchants to have funds on deposit to ensure that affiliates are paid what they are due.

You can also search Yahoo! Search Marketing to see how many 'sponsored listings' are returned for a specific product and company. If more than one listing is returned, the rest of the sites are probably affiliate sites. However, if only one listing is returned, the company may not permit affiliates to advertise their trademarked name.

Search Google for the site name. For example, if you want to promote the web host 'HostRocket,' do a search at Google for "HostRocket."

Are thousands of results returned?

Good!

Now visit a number of sites that came up in the regular listings. Read the reviews and check for affiliate links on the site. Are the reviews positive and enthusiastic? You can also contact the webmaster of one of those sites and ask about their experience with the program.

2. IS THERE AN AFFILIATE AGREEMENT?

Most affiliate programs have agreements in place, primarily to cover their butts. However, these agreements should also cover yours.

If the program you are considering doesn't have an agreement published on the site, move on. Without an agreement, it's much too easy for them to shaft you for money you've earned.

3. WHAT ARE THE TERMS OF AGREEMENT?

Affiliate agreements are usually lengthy and peppered with long-winded legalese. Read it. Read it completely and carefully or you could be in for a nasty surprise.

For example, let's say you invest several hundred dollars in PPC advertising to promote a particular product. In return, you earn a thousand or two from that program during the first month of promotion. It would be very unpleasant to discover that the company only pays quarterly. Who wants to invest several hundred or thousands of dollars to promote a company that won't invest five or ten bucks to write you a check every month?

If you end up in a dispute with a company, agreements are usually interpreted under the laws of the state, province or country in which the company is located. Disputes are usually resolved by binding arbitration in that same state, province or country. Is it worth traveling from Rhode Island to California to argue over a couple hundred bucks?

Probably not. Protect yourself against nasty surprises by reading affiliate agreements from top to bottom.

4. MAY I TERMINATE THE AGREEMENT? IF SO, HOW?

Most agreements contain a 'termination clause' that outlines the terms under which you or the company can end the affiliation. In most cases either the affiliate or the company may choose to cancel an agreement at any time without written notice of cancellation to the other. As an affiliate, you'd simply take down your links and that would be that. Do make sure that is the case, however.

Way back when affiliate programs were new, I was required to sign and return a paper agreement that bound me to a 2-year contract with a merchant. I felt uncomfortable agreeing to such a stipulation without proof that their product would convert well to sales, or that they would pay on time.

I should have trusted my intuition. The company was excruciatingly slow to pay. I got sick of hearing 'the check is in the mail.' Furthermore, the checks never jibed with their own statistics reporting.

Frustrated with the situation, I removed all their links from my site and effectively ended our association, about a year before the agreement expired.

Fortunately, the company did not take me to task on this point, and it all came out in the wash eventually. After an inexcusable delay, they finally paid all that was owed to me.

Learn from that. Don't sign an agreement that binds you to a company for a specified period of time. Your luck in terminating the contract may not be as good as mine.

Avoid companies that require signed agreements. There are plenty of other programs that will be happy to have you join their program without strings.

5. IS MY SITE ELIGIBLE FOR THIS PROGRAM?

Pay particular attention to criteria that have been set for acceptance into an affiliate program.

For example, the following excerpt is from the advertiser detail section at Commission Junction for its own recruiter program:

Publishers will be accepted into the program based on the following criteria:

- Quality and appropriateness of site(s)
- Volume of traffic
- At least a one-dollar sign ranking in the Commission Junction network
- Own domain name
- Compliant with the Commission Junction publisher service agreement
- Directly related to performance marketing

My site met all the criteria, but my application was rejected. I wrote to question their decision and asked for reconsideration.

Here is a portion of their response:

> In addition, **publishers must be based in either the U.S. or U.K.** and have at least a one-dollar sign CJ ranking, their own domain name, and a Web site that is compliant with the Commission Junction publisher service agreement and directly related to pay-for-performance advertising. Preferred publishers will have at least a one-star or higher Alexa rating.

My site met all of the other 'additional' criteria, except that I am located in Canada. As I know of many sites promoting the CJ publisher program that aren't based in the U.S. or the U.K., this geographic restriction made no sense to me. I wrote again to question this point. CJ's subsequent responses were simply verbatim repeats of the previous paragraph.

Therefore, read and understand ALL the criteria thoroughly. If you don't understand a clause, ask about it. The merchant's response may not be fair or make sense, but at least you'll have done your homework thoroughly.

6. IS THERE A FEE TO JOIN THE PROGRAM?

Ninety-nine point nine percent (99.9%) of merchants don't charge a fee to join their affiliate programs. If they do, it's an MLM, or Multi-level marketing scheme or a reseller program.

Six Figure Income (SFI) is an example of an MLM scheme that refers to itself as an affiliate program. In order to earn income with SFI, you must purchase some of the company's products each and every month to 'qualify' for sales earnings that you've generated within a month.

I believe MLM (network marketing) and reseller programs should refer to themselves as such, and leave the term 'affiliate program' for programs that are free to join.

To highlight the differences between MLM, reseller and affiliate programs, I compare and contrast each of those marketing methods below.

- **Cost to Join** - Affiliate programs are FREE to join, whereas resellers must BUY the products they sell. Multi-level marketers usually must buy sufficient quantities of the products they market to qualify for earnings at a certain 'tier' or level.

- **Payment Scheme** – Affiliates typically earn a percentage of the purchase price, while resellers retain 100% of the proceeds from product sales.

- **Tiered Programs** – Some affiliate programs offer webmasters the opportunity to earn a percentage in the '2nd tier' by paying a fee for each new affiliate that joins the program, while some others pay a percentage of their 2nd tier affiliates' earnings. Others pay in both situations. Although this structure is akin to MLM schemes, unlike multi-level marketers, affiliates are not required to purchase products in order to be eligible to build their affiliate 'downline.'

- **Product Fulfillment** – Resellers and many multi-level marketers must handle their own product fulfillment, including carrying inventory, order processing and shipping. In the case of affiliate marketing, the merchant handles all of the above.

- **Product Pricing** - Each affiliate sells the product for the same price. Resellers can often set their own prices, although competitors may undermine their efforts by offering the same product for a lower price.

- **Lead Generation** - Although affiliates can collect names and email addresses from visitors to their sites, the affiliate rarely knows exactly who buys their affiliated merchants' products. Because resellers handle product fulfillment themselves, they collect names and email addresses from those who buy their products, in addition to those who sign up for their opt-in lists on their sites. This benefits the reseller in that they can do follow-up or 'back-end' sales to existing customers.

As with any opportunity, there are advantages and disadvantages to each type of marketing and each method can yield decent profits.

Although the Super Affiliate Handbook deals only with affiliate marketing, you may wish to consider adding relevant products for which you have resale rights to your site when you've gained experience as an affiliate and are ready to expand your online marketing horizons.

7. DOES THE PROGRAM REQUIRE EXCLUSIVITY?

An exclusivity clause is one that stipulates that if you promote that merchant's products you may not partner with merchants selling similar products.

When Barnes and Noble started its affiliate program, it had an exclusivity clause. If you sign up with them now, you'll notice that is no longer the case. Hmmmm... Was that clause detracting from their share of the affiliate market? Even if that company was the only provider of its type of service on the 'Net, I wouldn't agree to exclusivity.

You can be sure that the moment you agree to be exclusive, a better product or service will come along, and you'll be stuck with a bad agreement.

This is your business, not your marriage. Keep your options open.

8. WHAT IS THE PROGRAM TYPE?

There are essentially three types of affiliate programs: pay-per-sale, pay-per-lead, and pay-per-click.

- **Pay-Per-Sale** programs are also known as **Partnership** and **Percentage Partners** programs. These programs pay either a fixed dollar amount or a percentage of sales generated by your links.

- **Pay-Per-Lead** programs pay a set amount whenever your customer fills out a survey or requests a quote or some information.

- **Pay-Per-Click** affiliate programs are similar to Pay-Per-Lead. Essentially you are paid each time one of your visitors clicks on the link through to that program's site.

As Pay-Per-Lead and Pay-Per-Click programs require huge volumes of traffic to generate serious revenue, I prefer Pay-Per-Sale programs because they are performance based.

Doing business as an affiliate is about giving your visitors valuable information so they can make good product choices. Sending huge quantities of traffic to a merchant site so they can collect email addresses and spam large groups of people is valuable only to the merchant.

Target a market effectively, give them what they want, and you'll be rewarded handsomely with a percentage of the sale!

9. WHAT IS THE COMMISSION RATE?

This is a VERY important question! It's not the MOST important, but it *is* close! ☺

It's absolutely essential that you understand commission structures and compare payout rates between affiliate programs. This will affect to what extent you promote individual products.

Let's look at some real examples. Let's say you want to build a site around credit cards, in which you get paid a commission each time someone fills in an application.

First you'd search advertisers and products at Commission Junction, by inputting the word 'credit cards' into their search box.

You then sort the results according to **payout per lead**, from highest to lowest amounts, by selecting 'Lead' at the top of the column. When you click on 'Sale,' advertisers are sorted according to **payout per sale**, from highest to lowest.

Here are a few examples of what I found during a quick search.

Citibank Business Cards – Pays $5.00 for a complete Rewards or Platinum Select card application.

Discover Card - Commissions start at:
$25 per approved Platinum Card Account
$25 per approved Affinity Card Account
$25 per approved Titanium Card Account
$15 per approved Student Card Account

First USA/Bank One - Offers a wide variety of credit card products including airline and travel rewards to exclusive co-brand card products. Commissions start at $30.00 and go all the way up to $50 per approved credit card.

What a variety of commission structures and payout amounts amongst these merchants!

It would be a real disappointment to heavily promote the First USA/Bank One program, thinking that you are paid $50.00 per application, when in fact the applicant has to be approved before you are credited with the lead.

Compare that to the Citibank structure that only requires the visitor to complete the application.

As a rough guideline, **look first** for companies that pay the highest per sale and per lead commissions in your category of interest. Once you've established a short list, then you can start weeding out those that don't make the grade.

10. HOW LONG DO COOKIES LAST?

You may have heard that it takes 7 exposures to a product before people feel comfortable to buy that product. So what happens if a visitor from your site clicks through to your affiliated merchant site today but doesn't buy anything until a week later? Will you still get credit for the sale?

Whether or not you earn a commission depends on the duration of the 'cookie'.

A cookie is coded piece of information, stored on a computer that identifies that computer during the current and subsequent visits to a web site.

Some people worry that cookies put viruses on their computer, but there is no need to worry! Cookies are simply text files that cannot be used in any way to harm a computer.

Each cookie is coded to identify that computer during the current and subsequent visits to the merchant's web site.

For example, if you visit http://iwantu.com from my dating service review site at http://sage-hearts.com, the cookie stored on your computer will be called *yourname*@dating.iwantu.txt and look something like this:

BIGipServerhttp_pool#855746752.20480.0000#dating.iwantu.com/#1024#17018579 2029540480#1283039984#29540196#*

FIGURE 80: COOKIE EXAMPLE

More important to affiliates, is that cookies are coded to expire after a set amount of time. So, if the merchant gives cookies that last for 90 days, you get credit if a visitor from your site returns to the merchant and makes the purchase within 90 days.

If your visitor purchases the product after the 90 days, and the cookie has expired, you won't get credit for the sale.

So it literally **pays you to look for long-lasting cookies** when choosing affiliate programs.

11. WILL I GET CREDIT FOR RECURRING SALES?

What happens when you stop promoting your merchant partners' sites? In most cases, you'd simply stop earning. Your income would stop and the checks would stop coming. Because your income is limited by the number of customers you send to the merchant in a given month, you have to keep marketing your site to bring in new customers. Over, and over, and over again.

Make a sale, get paid and that's it. Your customer may buy more of the same product from your merchant partner, but you only get credit for the first sale. The merchant benefits indefinitely from your introduction of the customer to the product, and you get only one credit?

Does that sound fair? You bet it's not!

However, there ARE affiliate programs that **pay commissions on all recurring charges**, such as monthly newsletter subscriptions and web hosting packages. As long as your customer keeps ordering the product, you get **residual commissions** that keep coming in month after month, after you made the initial sale.

So, here's the bottom line. If the affiliate program doesn't pay residual commissions on recurring charges, **you're losing money**.

12. DOES THE PROGRAM PAY LIFETIME COMMISSIONS?

There is a difference between 'recurring' or 'residual' commissions, and 'lifetime' commissions.

A program that pays **residual commissions** pays you every time the customer renews their subscription to a specific product.

A program paying **lifetime commissions** pays the affiliate a commission for each and every product that the customer buys from that merchant, including residual commissions, if applicable.

For example, let's say that you are earning recurring commissions on Mr. Samson's web hosting subscription at *Best Host Company*.

If the company doesn't offer 'lifetime commissions' and Mr. Samson upgrades to his own dedicated server at *Best Host Company*; you won't get paid commissions on his monthly server fees because it's a different product.

If XYZ Company offers 'lifetime' commissions however, the customer you refer to them is "yours" for life, regardless of which *Best Host Company*'s products they buy. In the scenario above, you would be paid a monthly commission on the dedicated server fees for as long as Mr. Brown remains a subscriber.

Joining programs that offer residual or lifetime commissions is an excellent way to build a steadily increasing income. Once you make a referral, the checks keep coming in. So even when you take a vacation from your affiliate business, the checks for your residuals, will also keep coming in.

How many other businesses pay you to take a vacation?

13. IS IT A 2-TIER OR MULTIPLE-TIER PROGRAM?

A "two-tier" program is one that offers two sources of income, the first for bringing in business, and the second for recommending new affiliates. Some programs pay a fee for each new affiliate that joins the program, while some others pay a percentage of the 2nd tier affiliate's earnings. Other programs pay in both situations.

When the subject of 2-tier programs comes up, the question often arises as to whether two-tier affiliate programs are MLM (multi-level marketing) schemes.

Well, let's take a look at a definition of 'MLM,'

"Also known as network marketing, MLM is essentially any business where payouts occur at two or more levels. For example, any company that compensates you for the sales you make, and also pays you a small percentage of the sales made by those you've recruited as sellers, is an MLM company."

According to that definition, 2-tier affiliate programs are MLM programs.
Does it matter? Should it matter?

Don't let the MLM association scare you or put you off. There are many reputable MLM organizations including Avon, Mary Kay Cosmetics and PartyLite Gifts, Inc.

MLM gets its bad reputation from companies that focus only on recruiting new members and downline-building. Essentially the only 'products' these companies sell are memberships, which you must purchase in order to be eligible to build your own downline of members.

Your primary concern is whether the company you sign up with is selling real goods and/or services that benefit its customers.

Focus first on marketing the product, and **secondly** on recruiting affiliates. That's why it's called **2-tier**.

14. ARE SALES STATISTICS REPORTED IN REAL TIME?

Can you imagine waiting a month to find out if you made a sale for a particular program?

Suppose you were spending money to advertise a program and it took a month to assess the success of your promotional efforts. Would you join that program?

No?

Good!

When signing up for an affiliate program, be sure that it offers real-time sales tracking, or something fairly close to 'real-time.' Real-time actually means immediate, within seconds. Some sites have statistics that are delayed by 20 minutes or an hour. That's acceptable. We can live with that.

Real-time sales reporting is another good reason to affiliate with merchants in affiliate networks like Commission Junction.

To be competitive, most of the affiliate networks provide real-time reporting to their merchants and affiliates. Being part of the network means you don't have to hunt around to find out whether real-time reporting is a feature of the program that you want to join.

15. ARE MERCHANT COPY & SALES TOOLS OFFERED?

Most merchants offer their affiliates advertising copy and banner ads for placement on their sites. In many cases, you'll be able to generate the code with a click of your mouse, which you then paste into your page or in your newsletter. Some merchants also offer product datafeeds for their entire range of products. Using datafeeds, you can build a 1,000 item site in mere seconds!

Many merchants also host the banners from their own sites, which saves you the trouble of downloading and saving the graphic to your computer, then uploading it to your server. Banners that are kept on the merchant's server also reduce your bandwidth.

Sales tools make an affiliate's job easier. In the "10 Types of Merchant Copy and Sales Tools" later in this section we'll look more closely at how to put these tools to use.

16. HOW OFTEN DO I GET PAID?

Compensation plans vary from merchant to merchant and program to program. Be sure you know what the payment plan is, or you could be in for a nasty surprise!

Payment schedules vary depending on the program. I'm affiliated with programs that pay **weekly**, **biweekly**, **monthly** and **quarterly**.

17. HOW DO I GET PAID? CASH? PAYPAL? FOOD STAMPS?

Payments are usually by check or direct deposit, although some companies pay in merchandise or service credits.

PayPal has become a very popular payment method for many merchants. It is an account-based system that lets anyone with an email address securely send and receive online payments using their credit card or bank account.

When given the option of taking a check or payment by PayPal, I always take the check, as PayPal's fees eat into my commissions. That said, some merchants won't give you the option, you'll probably have to sign up for a PayPal account anyway.

Most Internet companies do business and pay in **US Dollars**. Be sure to confirm the currency that the company deals in however.

For example, Ken Evoy's company, and his 5 Pillar Affiliate program are based in Canada. You will automatically be paid in Canadian dollars if you live in Canada, and American dollars if you live anywhere else in the world. His program allows you to change that option if you are a Canadian who prefers to be paid in US Dollars.

18. DOES THE MERCHANT USE THIRD PARTY BILLING?

One nice thing about associating with merchants that are part of a bigger affiliate network is that you can count on the affiliate network to make sure the merchant has put enough money into their account to pay your commissions.

Some networks go so far as to indicate how well each merchant's account is funded, allowing you to choose whether or not you should promote their products. Other networks will suspend the merchant's account until they've deposited sufficient funds.

You don't get that kind of security when you sign up for a program that is administered by the company itself. While you don't need to worry about Amazon or Match.com, it's sometimes hard to be sure about smaller unknown companies.

One way to gain some security in that regard is to find out whether the company uses third-party billing to process their payments and handle affiliate commissions. A third-party processor takes in money from the customers, and makes sure that the affiliate receives what is due to them.

Depending on the affiliate agreement, you may end up splitting the payment processing costs with the merchant. For example, one dating site I promote offers a 50/50 commission split and uses CCBill for payment processing. That fifty percent is reduced to 42.5 percent after CCBill's 15% fee is also split.

19. Is There a Minimum Payout Amount?

Many programs require that you earn a minimum amount before they will issue you a check. For example, some merchants set their minimum payouts at $50 or $100. This makes sense (cents?) if your earnings for the month are $2.00 and it costs the merchant five dollars to cut you a check.

20. Is Co-Branding Available?

Co-branding is a form of customization, whereby the affiliate program permits you to "brand" a copy of the landing page on their site, with your logo and/or your site's "look and feel."

Visiting a co-branded site gives your visitors the impression that they are still on your Web site and may improve visitor trust in 'your' products resulting in increased sales.

Many merchants offered co-branding when affiliate marketing first began on the 'Net.

However, few merchants offer co-branding nowadays. It's simply too much work for them to approve each and every affiliate's logo graphic. For sites that allowed affiliates to automatically upload logos, there was always the potential that the logo was inappropriate and/or not in keeping with the image the company wanted to maintain.

In summary, don't get cheated out of your hard-earned commissions.

Ask all the right questions and make sure the affiliate programs are solid prospects before you join.

Other Program and Product Considerations

You'd think that asking 20 questions would be enough to consider, but OH Noooo!

In this section we'll find out how to choose between similar programs, what to do if you find a great product without a program and how to assess a product.

How to Choose Between Similar Programs

If you are having a hard time choosing between two similar products, the commission scheme and/or the brand name may be the deciding factor.

If all else is equal – the product, site, program, etc. – you should pick the program that pays the higher commission.

For example, if you promote a review site that compares several similar products and services, you should carefully evaluate commissions on each different product to determine which product or service should be most actively promoted.

Sometimes it becomes somewhat tricky to compare potential income between two or more programs when the commission structures differ only slightly. Here are examples from two dating services that I promote. First I compare product pricing.

Dating Direct	**Yahoo Personals**
▪ 1 Month costs just $19.95 ▪ 3 Months costs just $34.95 ▪ 12 Months costs just $84.95	▪ 1 month for only $19.95 ▪ 3 months for only $44.95 ▪ 12 months for $99.95

Dating Direct is slightly less expensive than Yahoo! Personals and therefore might be more acceptable to my customers.

But I don't stop there. Next, I check the commission rates.

Dating Direct pays *75% per sale*. ▪ $15.00 per 1 Month subscription ▪ $26.21 per 3 Month subscription ▪ $63.71 per12 Month subscription	**Yahoo! Personals** pays a *flat fee per subscription*: ▪ $10.00 per 1 Month subscription ▪ $20.00 per 3 Month subscription ▪ $40.00 per12 Month subscription

That works out to between 40 and 50% per sale, and considerably less than Dating Direct. So far, Dating Direct is emerging the clear winner, right?

Not exactly. You need to read the fine print.

When you read the fine print at Yahoo!, you see that you can earn a 75% bonus over the base commission for each subscription when you generate more than 30 subscriptions during a calendar month. That raises their commission rates to between 70 and 88%.

Here are the new commission totals for **Yahoo! Personals**: ▪ $17.50 per 1 Month subscription ▪ $35.00 per 3 Month subscription ▪ $70.00 per12 Month subscription

With that kind of incentive, I'll have no problem generating at least 30 subscriptions a month at Yahoo!

Brand name is a big factor to consider.

By now you've probably heard that it takes 7 exposures before people are willing to buy a certain product.

By offering brand name products, the exposure and trust in a product has been accomplished for you, so that you don't have to bring the visitor back to your site up to seven times, before they are ready to buy.

All else being equal, if you are given the choice between a totally unknown product, and a nationally-known brand name, it's usually prudent to choose the brand name.
So, using the example above - even if Dating Direct's commissions had been higher than Yahoo! Personals commissions, I would probably promote the latter more heavily to take advantage of their brand recognition.

Yahoo!

HOW TO CHOOSE BETWEEN MULTIPLE COMMISSION OPTIONS

Some merchants offer only one commission scheme depending on the product they sell, while others let their affiliates choose amongst a variety of schemes for the same product.

For example, Cashring gives its affiliates 4 different commission scheme options including; their 'RevShare' (percentage) program, 'Pay-Per-Signup' (pay per sale), Pay-Per-Profile (lead), and Pay-Per-Click commission schemes.

While this allows flexibility to channel your traffic and optimize your revenue, the options can be confusing. Here are the descriptions for each of the schemes Cashring offers.

1. **Rev Share** - Earn recurring commission for life! Each time a visitor you sent us joins any of our sites, you get up to 70% of the income generated by the membership fees, as long as that person is a member on our site!

2. **Pay-per-Signup** - Looking for immediate payment? Our pay-per-signup program pays up to $100 for every membership regardless of its duration. We are so confident of our member retention that we are willing to pay you up to 140% of the membership initial cost.

3. **Pay-per-Profile** - Earn up to $10.00 for every confirmed profile registered on our sites. We accept worldwide traffic and don't require email confirmation for you to get paid, so what are you waiting for?

4. **Pay-per-Click** - For every unique visitor you send us, we will pay you up to $1. Unique visitors are based on unique IP addresses sent during a 24-hour period.

Choosing a program can get even more confusing when you read the 'More Info' sections that accompany each of the commission schemes.

For example, this is the 'fine print' attached to the pay-per-profile option:

> *For every surfer you send us who registers a FREE profile, you can earn upto $10.00!*
>
> *Everyday, you will receive $0.05 per profile by default. The payout for the day will automatically be adjusted at midnight (Eastern time) based on the overall ratio of all your pay per profile campaigns for the same day. e.g: If by midnight, you referred a total of 4 paid signups out of 40 free profiles, then your payout will automatically be adjusted to $5.00 per profile for all campaigns.*
>
> *The ratio is based on: number of paid signups/number of free profiles.*
>
> *1:5 $10.00*
> *1:6 $8.30*
> *1:7 $7.10*
> *1:8 $6.25*
> *1:9 $5.50*

```
1:10 $5.00
1:12 $4.10
1:15 $3.30
1:17 $2.90
1:20 $2.50
1:25 $2.00
1:30 $1.60
1:40 $1.25
1:50 $1.00
1:75 $0.65
1:100 $0.50
1:200 $0.25
1:500 $0.10

Worse than 1:500 $0.05
The average conversion rate is 1:12, giving you an average of $4.10
per free profile.

Pay Per Profile Advantages

Registration is FREE and requires no credit card
No email confirmation necessary
We accept profiles from all the countries of the world
Approved profile: Is when a Profile is posted and approved by the
Admin.
```

... and that's just the pay-per-profile fine print!

Deciding which option to choose depends primarily on the quantity and quality of traffic that you get to your site.

If you get lots of *un-targeted traffic*, i.e. visitors who are not interested in a specific offer, then the pay-per-click option may be best.

If on the other hand your promotional efforts attracts less traffic, but the visitors you do receive are highly qualified, i.e. they were searching specifically for the information they found on your page, then the RevShare option is perhaps your best choice.

Lastly, if the people who visit your site tend to be freebie-seekers, then the pay-per-profile option may be the most lucrative.

As a content publisher who focuses on increasing conversion rates, I almost always choose to run percentage programs, which usually tend to offer the highest payouts. However, in order to determine which is truly the most lucrative program for you and your traffic, you will have to know your conversion ratios.

Here is an example based on my experience with the Cashring RevShare program.

Clicks	Free Signups	Sales	Commissions
10635	1836	306	$19,745.46

According to the table, approximately 1 in 6 visitors signed up for a free profile, and 1 in 6 of those people bought a paid membership. Earnings amounted to $1.86 per click, $10.75 per free signup (profile) or $64.52 per sale.

Had I been running the pay-per-profile scheme instead of the RevShare program, (see the 'fine print' section above) my total earnings would have been $15,238.80 as it pays $8.30 per free profile when the conversion ratio is 1:6.

Even if my conversion to sales had been 1:5, which pays $10.00 per free profile, I'd have earned less than I did from the Revshare program.

The point is that you will need to test your traffic when you are starting out to determine your site's conversion ratios.

GREAT PRODUCT, NO PROGRAM - NOW WHAT?

If you find a great product that doesn't appear to be supported by an affiliate program, it's time to put your knowledge of affiliate marketing to work.

Phone or email the merchant, tell them how much you love their product and ask if they have an affiliate program. If they say that they don't, or don't know what affiliate programs are, you'll have to explain the concept and process to them. Here are some sample emails. Feel free to adjust the wording to your needs.

```
Dear [Merchant Name],

I just visited [Merchant's Domain] and think that your [product name] are
absolutely fabulous! I would love the opportunity to sell them at [your
domain address].

I wasn't able to find affiliate program information at [Merchant's Domain],
however. Is there one in place?

If not, would you be interested in an affiliate partnership with [your store
name]? Our site receives 5,000 unique visitors a day who are interested in
[site theme]-related goods. I know they'd also love [Merchant Store Name]
[merchant product].

If you are interested, please feel free to contact me if you have any
questions about how to start an affiliate program for [Merchant Store Name].
I have personal experience in with affiliate programs and can help save you
time and money in the set-up.

Thanks kindly for your consideration, and I look forward to hearing from
you.

Sincerely,

[Your name]
*************************************************
[Your full name, site address and telephone number]
```

If the merchant responds that they are interested in a partnership, you might consider sending them another email similar to the one below.

```
Dear [Merchant Name],

I am SO pleased that you're interested in an affiliate alliance with [Your
Store Name] to promote [Merchant Store Name] products.

There are 3 different ways to set up an affiliate program.

Join an affiliate network that handles almost all of the work associated with
the program, including processing orders and affiliate payments. This is
perhaps the most costly solution, but requires the least effort and will put
'[Merchant Store Name]' in front of thousands of affiliates eager to sell
your product.

Sign up with a shopping cart service that includes affiliate-tracking
software. Although less expensive, this option is slightly more work in that
you'll need to advertise the program to gain more affiliates.

Buy and install affiliate program software on your own server. This option is
the least expensive with a one-time purchase of software, but the most time-
consuming to administer in terms of keeping track of affiliate sales and
payment handling.

If you have questions, please feel free to contact me.

I look forward to working with you!

Sincerely,

[Your name]
********************************************
[Your full name, site address and telephone number]
```

With a bit of effort and extraordinary luck, you may convince the merchant to start an affiliate program for which you become the only affiliate! That would be like having worldwide exclusive rights to market a product.

While that would be nice, it's unlikely that a merchant would go to the trouble of setting up a program for just one affiliate.

But you *should* take advantage of the situation until they actively start to market their new affiliate program. ☺

PROGRAM EXAMPLES

Here are two examples of affiliate programs that I have joined. One was very well run and managed, while the other – well, was definitely NOT.

A WELL-RUN PROGRAM

I once joined an affiliate program that sent me a welcome letter that did not include information on how to access the affiliate interface. Their email address bounced when I wrote to ask them for the information, and their contact form was also broken!

Needless to say, I don't promote that product. The trouble is, I can't cancel the account either. Dumb. Dumb. Dumb.

Below is an example of an affiliate program welcome letter from the InfoGoRound.com affiliate program that contains all the necessary ingredients to make working with that program easy.

Subject: Welcome to the InfoGoRound.com Affiliate Program!

IMMEDIATELY READ AND SAVE THIS EMAIL!

Hi Rosalind Gardner,

Welcome to the InfoGoRound.com (IGR) affiliate program!

You are now ready to earn money simply by referring new IGR members through your IGR affiliate link as follows:

http://www.infogoround.com/cgi-bin/click.cgi?id=rosgardner

To view IGR's *current* compensation details, visit this page:

http://www.infogoround.com/affiliate.html

(We'll email you whenever our compensation details are updated - which of course includes news on special affiliate promotions and competitions!)

You can check your referral stats on a daily basis by logging in here:

[Affiliate name and password embedded in link, therefore, no need to login.]

And here's a copy of your IGR *affiliate* account login info:

[Username]
[Password]

We recommend you spend at least 15 minutes actively promoting IGR per day - starting today...You could earn and win as much as $5,000 or more this month alone!

It's great to have you on our team Rosalind Gardner.

Bryan Winters - CEO, InfoGoRound.com

The affiliate welcome letter above first thanks me for becoming an affiliate then gives the information I need to assess my affiliate statistics, a link to the product, and contact information for the company should I require further help or information...a truly promising start to our affiliate relationship.

That letter provides ALL the information that an affiliate needs to start promoting their product.

Merchants should *all* be so thorough in their affiliate welcome letters. Building rapport early in the game increases everyone's chances for success.

AN EXAMPLE OF THE TYPE OF PROGRAM TO AVOID

As an affiliate marketer of Internet dating services, I'm always on the lookout for good quality dating sites and products to offer my single visitors. Merchants help me out when they let me know about their new products and affiliate programs.

I was therefore thrilled when one of my friendly affiliate competitors got in touch to tell me that he'd started his own Internet dating service and affiliate program.

Having launched a community membership site myself, I could fully appreciate the huge amount of time and money my friend invested to develop this new site. He was justifiably proud of his accomplishment and I was excited by the prospect of having a product to promote that would benefit everyone - my customers, my friend and me.

Unfortunately, it didn't quite work out that way.

The first stumbling block was the low commission rate.

His top rate was 30%, with no commissions on recurring sales. This puzzled me. As an affiliate marketer of dating programs, he would have been aware that new sites offer at least 50% on new and recurring sales to entice good affiliates to sign up. If commissions on recurring sales are not offered, then the rates on new sales should be increased to between 70 and 100 percent.

In most cases, his affiliate program would have struck out for me at that point.

However, as this was my friend's site, it occurred to me that perhaps his product was so unique that the potential for high volume sales might offset the lower commission.

Hoping for the best, I continued my review.

When I arrived at the site, the first thing I noticed was *'6 registered members'* prominently displayed at the top of the homepage. That normally wouldn't be a problem, except for the fact that my customers are looking for friends and soul mates. If I send them to a site where there are only six people to meet, they'll likely be disappointed. Worse, by wasting their time, they lose trust in my judgment and then I lose them as customers.

That's not good.

My customers are literally my bread and butter.

Giving them what they want is how I stay in business. Paying for traffic that I send to a merchant site where there is nothing to buy, will put me out of business.

(This is how a membership site should be structured. When starting a dating service, the merchant pays for advertising to bring people to their site. To entice visitors to sign up as members, he will initially offer his services for free. When the database is large enough to attract paying customers, the affiliate program manager then invites potential affiliates to join their program.)

Although my friend's program had already struck out for my customers and me, I was still curious, so I kept on looking.

I clicked next on a link labeled 'Dating Resources.' Expecting to find Internet dating tips and advice, I found links and banners pointing to Lavalife, FriendFinder and other affiliated dating sites instead. When I asked him about placing affiliate programs on his site, my friend said he simply wanted to supplement his income until the dating service got *rolling.*

I can understand his motivation. However, what he doesn't understand is the concept of customer 'hijacking.'

As an affiliate, you pay good money to get visitors to your site. You pre-sell your merchants' products and the merchant honors their end of the bargain by completing the sale and sending your commission check.

You don't want to pay the merchant to send YOUR customers to THEIR affiliated merchants.

I didn't need to look any further. I told my friend that I'd wait to sign up for his program and my reasons for holding off. Fortunately, he understood my concerns and quickly alleviated some of the problems I mentioned.

Knowing when NOT to sign up for an affiliate program is sometimes a tough call.

However, the process is very simple. Put yourself inside your customer's head. If the product doesn't benefit them, the program strikes out. It's as simple as that.

5 Ways to Assess a Merchant's Product or Service

Promoting quality products is absolutely crucial to your success. Therefore keep the following 5 questions in mind as you find products and services to promote.

1. **Is the product or service relevant to your customers and your site?** Banners for credit card applications look out of place on a dating service review site. I've tried to 'extend' the range of services on my niche sites a few times, and it has been a mistake each and every time. Those 'added features' serve only to detract from your site's main focus.

2. **Is the company's site attractive and functional?** Would *you* buy from a site that looked unprofessional, had broken links or was a hassle to navigate? Don't send your visitors to tacky sites. Your reputation is at stake.

3. **Is it a quality product at a reasonable price?** Would YOU buy the product you plan to sell? To sell effectively, you must believe in the products and services you carry. Listing products you aren't enthusiastic about shows in what you say about them.

4. **Do you have experience with the product?** I've purchased most of the products I promote. Having first-hand knowledge about an item gives me an edge over other affiliates selling the same product. If the commission is 50%, you will only need to make 2 sales to get your money back.

5. **Does the company provide excellent customer service?** This is essential. I occasionally get email complaints from people who bought services through my site because the company didn't respond to their request for service or information. Unfortunately, there is usually very little I can do, except use the contact number or email address given only to affiliates, and pass the request along. If you are successful in getting their concerns resolved, Bravo! That reflects well on you.

Now that you know where and how to find programs and how to assess products, it is time to revisit *Commission Junction*. Make a list of those programs that you want to join once your site is ready.

10 Types of Merchant Copy and Sales Tools

Most merchants provide promotional tools and ad copy that you can place on your site. All you have to do is visit their affiliate interface, then cut and paste their text and banners into your pages. In most cases the links will be automatically coded with your affiliate ID.

Below are 10 different sales tools that merchants may offer their affiliates. I've included examples where possible.

1. TEXT LINKS

Text links are usually formatted in HTML with your affiliate ID attached. For example, this is a snippet of code that I got from Commission Junction when looking for links for Yahoo! personals.

STANDARD TEXT LINKS

```
<a     href="    http://www.tkqlhce.com/click-1316974-10303900"     target="_top">Find romance at Yahoo! Personals</a><img  src=http://www.qksrv.net/image-168978-10278403"  width="1" height="1" border="0">
```

All I do is cut and paste HTML code into my Web page, and my visitors see the text:
'Find romance at Yahoo! Personals'

'ALL-IN' TEXT LINKS

The Friendfinder dating service affiliate program codes a link that sends traffic to a page titled 'Top Dating Sites' so your visitor can pick the site or sites that appeal to them most. The page has a list of each one of their dating sites, and each one is coded with your affiliate ID. Here is that link:

http://seniorfriendfinder.com/go/page/site_directory_dating.html?pid=g9517

I would code the link to read "Top Dating Sites"

2. BANNERS AND GRAPHIC ADS

Banners are graphic images that come in a variety of different sizes.

The most popular sizes are 468 x 60 pixels, 125 x 125, 234 x 60, 120 x 60, 120 x 90, and 88 x 31. 'Skyscrapers' are generally 120 x 600, which is the average window height of a computer display.

Some companies have half page banners that are about 480 x 480 pixels in size. Others offer full-page ads with numerous graphics and text and come in a zipped file that you extract to a file on your computer.

This screenshot shows a **typical 468 x 60** pixel banner ad.

FIGURE 81 468 X 60 BANNER EXAMPLE

The figure below shows a 468 x 60 banner ad that promotes the *Internet Marketing Center's* (IMC) 'Secrets to Their Success' monthly online publication.

Note how the banner appears to be a paragraph with a text link, rather than a graphic ad.

NEWS FLASH — Private Tours of Successful Web Sites Now Available! Take a personal tour of hugely profitable web sites owned by real people just like you and me that are *making real money ($100,000+) on the Internet...* click here now to book your tour and discover the "*No BS*" strategies they are using!

FIGURE 82 BANNER GRAPHIC WITH TEXT

The merchant (*Internet Marketing Center*) has created this banner because graphic banner ads are not clicked as frequently as text links.

The figure to the right is an example of a 120 x 240 pixel banner ad supplied by Yahoo! Personals. Note the caption "Summer Love."

Use care when choosing banner ads that refer to specific seasons, holidays or events.

They become stale quickly and if not removed in a timely manner will make your site appear out of date, which in turn will lower your conversion to sales.

What you want to avoid are '**banner farm**' pages. Banner clusters provide no useful content, amount to nothing more than ugly 'clutter' and simply confuse your visitors.

FIGURE 83 120 X 240 BANNER EXAMPLE

I recommend that in most cases you should use only one banner per product page.

3. INTERSTITIAL (POPUP) BANNERS

An interstitial banner ad is advertisement that appears in a separate pop-up browser window while the main page is still loading, forcing exposure to the advertisement before visitors can see the main content.

Be careful if you choose to use this type of advertising.

While the response rates may be higher, many Internet users have installed 'popup killers' on their computers, so they will never see your ad. They also may not be able to move forward within your site if they use 'popup-stopping' software.

Because popups interrupt the surfing flow, they also breed resentment.

I stopped visiting About.com for a long time due to their use of interstitials. Although it appears that they've ceased their use of *interstitial inessentials*, About.com still uses popups far too frequently for my liking.

4. CUSTOM LANDING PAGES

Friendfinder provides a number of different custom landing pages to which their affiliates can send traffic. Examples include location, gender, race and specific pages on the site. Here is an example of FriendFinder's custom landing page for 'Women Seeking Men near Palo Alto.'

FIGURE 84 CUSTOM LANDING PAGE EXAMPLE

The link I use that helps my customers find "Women Seeking Men near Palo Alto, California between the ages of 18 and 25" is shown below.

Note how the link is constructed to return the desired results. For example "show=F" returns female members of the site. If we replaced the F with an M, then the page would return men between the ages of 18 and 25 near Palo Alto.

http://friendfinder.com/search/g9517-pct?show=F-M&age=18-25&geo=Palo Alto,CA

5. PRODUCT REVIEWS

Not many merchants provide their affiliates with full-scale product reviews, which is wise. Overuse of the same articles and product reviews detracts from both the merchant's and the affiliate's reputation.

I recommend that affiliates use the merchant's review as a 'guideline' for writing their own product reviews and articles.

However, if you can confirm that a specific product review or article is not used too frequently, then you can save yourself a lot of work by grabbing it and using it on your site.

You can see an example of a product review for Endless Summer Patio Heaters, sold by Yardiac, a Commission Junction merchant, on my Roamsters.com travel blog at:
http://roamsters.com/break-out-the-patio-heaters

6. EMAIL COPY

Smart merchants write their own "advertorials" and format them both in HTML and in plain text for affiliates to distribute via email.

Smart affiliates customize merchants' email promotions to give it their own 'voice.' They recognize that hundreds of other affiliates will be using the same material, so their efforts look cheesy when they're caught trying to pass off someone else's material as their own.

The table to the right shows an example of a text/HTML promotional email for *GotoMyPc*, accessed through the Commission Junction interface.

As the email includes HTML code, affiliates who prefer to send text-only mailings will replace the 'Click here' and *setup in only 2 minutes'* link with direct links to GotoMYPC. They would also change the copy to remove 'click here' as that no longer applies.

The would also change 'PC Users: Download the Free Trial Now - Click the following link and setup in only 2 minutes' to something like 'PC Users: Download the Free Trial Now - 2 minute setup.'

> **Access Your PC from Anywhere - Free 30-day Trial**
>
> GoToMyPC allows you to securely access and use your office computer from any Web browser anytime, anywhere. Free Trial. Click here.
>
> * TELEWORKERS: Work on your office computer from home, easily and securely, with just an Internet connection.
>
> * TRAVELERS: Access and use your computer and files from hotels, airports, Internet cafes - anywhere with Web access.
>
> * AFTER-HOURS ACCESS: Access and use your office desktop, email and other corporate resources after hours from any location connected to the Internet.
>
> Never be without a forgotten file again and see why GoToMyPC is changing the way people work remotely. Try it Free!
>
> PC Users: Download the Free Trial Now - Click the following link and setup in only 2 minutes.

7. INTERVIEWS

Very few merchants use this technique, but I think it's absolutely brilliant.

Affiliates are allowed to publish interviews that the merchant marketers have given. The interviews tend to have great conversion rates because it appears that more information is being shared with the reader than through typical product advertising.

Think of the 'infomercials' that you've seen in which the creator of some miracle gel extols its benefits in response to an interviewer's questions. It uses the same principle and sells products like crazy!

8. PERIODIC ARTICLES

Unlike interviews and email advertorials that get stale from overuse, periodic articles are always new and fresh. Jim Edwards is very good at offering his affiliates up-to-date topical articles to help promote his line of Internet marketing products. These are especially helpful if you don't have an idea for this week's feature article in your newsletter.

9. MERCHANT DATAFEEDS

Building an affiliate web site that sells between 5 and 20 products is relatively quick and easy to accomplish.

An experienced webmaster could build a site like my Internet dating service review site, http://101Date.com, on which 11 services are promoted in as little as a day. Someone with less experience might spend a week signing up for the programs, designing a template, and inputting the product information and affiliate links.

Spending a week or even a month on a site that delivers big rewards over the years is a relatively minor investment. Moreover, those products and their prices change infrequently, so the site requires very little ongoing maintenance.

But how much time and effort is invested by affiliates who promote thousands of items like magazines, garden products, posters, t-shirts or lingerie? How difficult would it be to place tens of thousands of links to music CD's, or movie DVD's on your site?

A MoJoSounds.com affiliate might want to promote only adventure movies, but his state of mind might be a 'horror' by the time he's input more than 500 descriptions, links and graphics!

If the same affiliate planned to let his visitors know about the latest and greatest discounts by listing prices, would he ever get any sleep?

Sure he would!

By using the MoJoSounds.com product datafeed, that affiliate could build a 500+ item site in less than an hour. He could even build a 10,000 item site in less than an hour!

So what is a product datafeed? A product datafeed is a spreadsheet or text file which typically lists product names along with their categories and subcategories, descriptions, coded affiliate links, product graphic image URL's, prices and even applicable keywords.

Affiliates can manipulate datafeeds in various ways to display content on their sites. Those with programming knowledge may insert the feed into databases on their servers.

Other affiliates prefer to use *dynamic website templates* that some merchants offer. These templates are completely customizable and the resulting site automatically updates itself.

Shawn at Nature Hills Nursery sent me a zipped package containing all the necessary files. Using my HTML editor, Homesite 5.0, I then added my affiliate I.D. to the config.pl file, as shown in the *Figure to the right.*

```
// setup
$affiliate_id = '84626';
$header_color = '#E0EEDF';
$left_menu_color = '#E0EEDF';
$product_nav_color = '#EEEEEE';
$main_border_color = '#E0EEDF';
$product_row_limit = '10';
$nopic_row_limit = '50';
```

FIGURE 85 MERCHANT DATAFEEDS: DYNAMIC FEED CODE

I uploaded all the files to the /garden/Nature-Hills/ directory that I created on my server at Rosalinds.com and Voila! it looked exactly as it does at:
http://www.naturehillsaffiliates.com/templatesite/

You can see how the Nature Hills Nursery datafeed appears on my demo site at http://rosalinds.com/Nature-Hills/

Although I've added my own header and changed a few of the colors around, the product display is exactly as you see on the Nature Hills site.

GOLDENCAN AFFILIATE DATAFEEDS

GoldenCAN.com (http://goldencan.com) offers a service to affiliate marketers that lets them combine millions of products in hundreds of thousands of categories, thousands of coupons and recent price drop products, multiple merchant searching and price comparisons, from different merchants - all in one line of code.

Options include store, coupon and search integration.

With *store integration*, your visitors can search a merchant's entire inventory without leaving your site.

Using coupon integration, you can display thousands of coupons, promotions and 'recent price drop' information from one or more merchants.

Lastly, search integration gives you a way to display search results from multiple merchants.

Shown below is a working example of a Golden store integration datafeed from eBags that I've placed on our travel blog at Roamsters.com.

Notice how visitors may browse by type of luggage, brand, or scroll down the page and see images of the various products offered. Everything within the content portion of that page is dynamically generated, which means that once you place the Goldencan code within the page, you won't have to muck about inserting affiliate links and product pictures.

The actual page is located at http://roamsters.com/travel-gear/find-luggage-at-ebags/

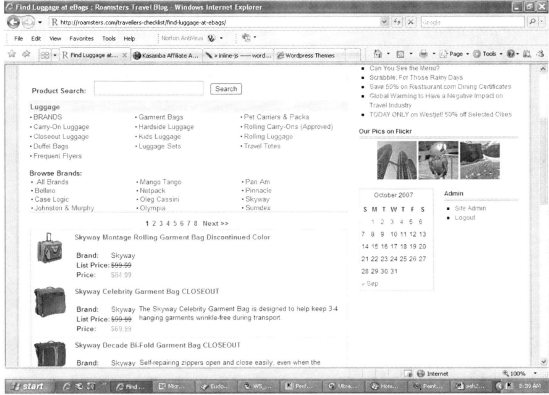

FIGURE 86: GOLDENCAN FEED

The next screenshot is an example of how Goldencan's coupon integration and price drops feed for eBags displays in practice. The actual page is located at:

http://roamsters.com/travel-gear/ebags-coupons/

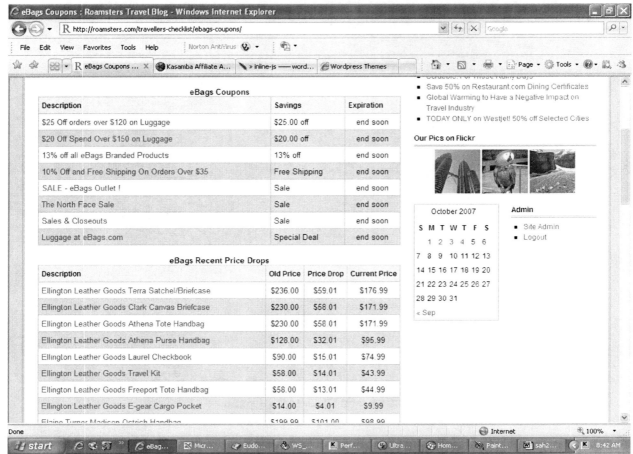

FIGURE 87 MERCHANT DATAFEEDS: COUPON INTEGRATION

When you signup for GoldenCan you will see FREE and 4th Click under the heading Fee-Structure. Your account is credited with 100% of your traffic to Free merchants.

For 4th click merchants GoldenCan replaces your affiliate ID with their own on every fourth click and will receive the affiliate commission should that click result in a sale.

Dynamic templates only work on servers running PHP and MYSQL.

However, affiliates whose hosts do not run PHP and MYSQL can still create product datafeeds by building static pages on their computer using software such as *WebMerge*, written by Richard Gaskin of FourthWorld.

The Webmerge Interface screenshot shown right shows how the Webmerge software interface appears.

http://Rosalinds.com/CandyCrate is a demo site that I built using Webmerge and a datafeed from Candy Crate.

FIGURE 88 WEBMERGE INTERFACE

138

Not all merchants offer product datafeeds - yet. They're shooting themselves in the foot. Many super affiliates no longer join programs that don't make datafeeds freely available.

I've signed up for countless affiliate programs that I later decided not to promote because I just couldn't fathom working that hard for a 15% commission.

Would I promote their products if it took me an hour to design a template and build a 10,000 item content site? You bet I would!

Smart merchants enthusiastically provide datafeeds without charge. They know that richer, more specific content on affiliate sites increases conversion rates and sales. Making it easier for customers to get all the information they need about a product without endless clicking is a smart thing to do.

To save time and make more sales, look for merchants that offer product datafeeds. My daddy always said, 'Work smarter, not harder,' and affiliate marketing doesn't get much smarter or easier than using a datafeed.

In summary, use merchant ad copy and tools to kick-start your site and sales campaigns.

Use copy sparingly, however. Visitors click 'Back' buttons quickly when they've seen the same copy a hundred times on other affiliate sites. Plan to replace the merchant copy on your site with your own articles, newsletters and product endorsements over time.

Market Your Site

'Build it and They Will Come' is a pipe dream. Webmasters must actively market their sites to attract visitors.

4 Primary Marketing Methods

The section below covers the 4 primary methods that I use to market my affiliate sites --- listed in order of preference --- including pay-per-click advertising, email marketing, article distribution and search engine marketing.

1. PAY-PER-CLICK ADVERTISING

The fastest way to gain exposure on the Internet is to buy keyword listings on Pay-per-click Search Engines.

It always surprises me when I hear a newbie Internet marketer tell me that they haven't yet opened up a pay-per-click account, but are waiting for their site to get listed by the free search engines.

That approach worked several years ago, but it doesn't work nearly as well now.

When I started my first online business, advertising online was free, easy and accomplished through the search engines. You submitted your site to AltaVista, HotBot and Excite, and 2 days later you saw your homepage on their first page of results. Traffic started flowing in, and so did the sales. It was wonderful!

But those days are gone. You can now wait months for an HTML site to get spidered by the free search engines, and end up 425th or 2,307th in the search listings. Even showing up 50th, won't bring you enough traffic in a week to buy lunch.

Although blogs are better at attracting search engine traffic, nothing beats sending highly targeted traffic to your site via the PPC's.

Pay-per-click advertising should *top* your list of marketing strategies. Only after you start getting copious amounts of traffic to your site, and making similar amounts of money, should you even think about spending time 'tweaking' your meta tags for better search engine placement.

There are now well over 500 pay-per-click search engines. I recommend that you start with accounts at the following PPC's (and in the following order) at:

- Google Adwords
- Microsoft Ad Center
- Yahoo! Search Marketing

More information about pay-per-click advertising is available in the Bonus Tips chapter, in the article *Will PPC Advertising Be Profitable in Your Niche?*

2. EMAIL MARKETING

Permission-based email marketing works! Studies have shown that permission email yields response rates that are ten times better than banners.

Because your subscriber has voluntarily signed-up or "opted-in" to receive your information, it allows you to:

- Offer products and services for sale to that subscriber
- Survey subscribers to gather information for new products
- Build a rapport with the subscribers

Many Internet marketers invite visitors to join their mailing lists by offering a free 'ecourse.'

An ecourse is a series of informative shorter articles delivered automatically through an autoresponder service (e.g. Aweber.com) to those who subscribe. Each message is designed to bring visitors back to your site or introduce them to your merchants' products through your affiliate links.

Studies suggest that the ecourse (or autoresponder series) should contain no fewer than 7 messages, however I know webmasters that have a year's worth of messages programmed into their autoresponders.

Visitors can also be encouraged to sign up for your ecourse when you offer them something for free. The 'freebie' can either be a report or a free sample from one of your merchants.

For example, I used to offer Michael Webb's "101 Romantic Ideas" ebook as a free download when visitors signed up to receive my "Singles eScene" newsletter at Sage-Hearts.com.

The EMAIL MARKETING: NEWSLETTER SIGNUP FORM EXAMPLE shown to the right shows a screen capture of the newsletter (ecourse) signup form.

Obtaining permission to use Michael's book was simple.

I emailed and asked him if I could use it, and he said yes. Furthermore, he also rebranded the ebook so that links inside the book are my affiliate links.

FIGURE 89 EMAIL MARKETING: NEWSLETTER SIGNUP FORM EXAMPLE

Sweet!

When visitors sign up to receive your ecourse or the free download that you offer, they are also subscribed to receive 'broadcast messages' - so you don't have to do anything extra to make sure they receive your newsletter.

You might broadcast a weekly or bi-weekly newsletter containing news and information relevant to your site. Regular ongoing contact builds rapport and trust with your subscribers, and encourages them to revisit your site time and again.

Use your newsletter to notify your subscribers about special promotions and sales held by your merchant partners.

It's best to link from your newsletter to a special 'sales' page on your site, as opposed to sending them directly to the merchant's site. That way you can test the effectiveness of your offers by keeping track of the number of visitors who visit that page via your newsletter.

With 150,000+ subscribers on my 'singles' list, the effect is fairly immediate and always positive. People rush off to the site to take advantage of the offer, and I just got a nice little bonus for doing a little bit of work.
NOT building a mailing list, or allowing it to languish is allowing money to slip out of your hands.

Think about this...

Suppose you have 5,000 unique visitors arrive at your Web site in an average week. Even though they had an initial interest in your site's subject, the vast majority of these people will never return to your site, because they will forget about it or won't remember how to get there.

Now imagine if you had a free newsletter or course to offer them in exchange for their opt-in name and email address. At a sign-up rate of 10% you'd be getting 500 new opt-in subscribers per week, or 6,000 per year!

STAY CAN-SPAM COMPLIANT

I recommend that you use a professional mailing list or autoresponder service to keep track of your subscribers and broadcast your messages. These services automatically handle all your signups, unsubscriptions, and bounces.

The biggest advantage to having a professional service maintain your mailing list is that it protects you from spam complaints. Most affiliate networks that permit email marketing of their merchants' offerings insist that you be able to produce evidence of subscriber opt-in.

Under the **CAN-SPAM Act**, which became effective Jan. 1, 2004, companies are liable for illegal spam sent by their affiliates. As such, most affiliate networks that permit email marketing of their merchants' offerings insist that you be able to produce evidence of subscriber opt-in.

Shown right is a sample clause relating to the subject of customer spam complaints and affiliate responsibilities in that regard.

If Publisher conducts e-mail campaigns to its users, Publisher must, if requested, be able to supply the name, date, time and IP address where the consumer signed-up and/or gave permission to the Publisher to conduct such e-mail campaign. Publisher is solely responsible for all consumer complaints relating to e-mail campaigns conducted by Publisher. Publisher will respond to all consumer complaints in a timely fashion and shall immediately remove any person from its database who makes such request for removal. In addition, all e-mail must contain a functioning unsubscribe link which, when activated by a user, actually and permanently removes the user's e-mail address from the publisher's database.

Thank goodness that type of clause is standard practice throughout the industry!

I detest receiving offers for Viagra, 'incredible' business opportunities and other topics in which I have no interest. It's garbage pure and simple and wastes time and energy to click into the trash. The 'do unto others' rule is a good one to follow when contemplating the use of unsolicited email. The clauses above make it possible to lose your source of income, which should be a good incentive to play by the rules.

Using a mailing list service will also prevent having your ISP close your account down because you sucked up too much of their bandwidth by sending 30,000 emails to your subscribers.

Although there are a many different autoresponder services available to Internet Marketers – and I've tried and used most of them since 1998 - I now only use and highly recommend Aweber's autoresponder service.

3. ARTICLE DISTRIBUTION

Placing an ad in an ezine can cost anywhere from a few dollars to thousands of dollars. However, submitting your articles to ezine editors and article directories costs nothing more than your time.

When your articles are published in those venues, people interested in your subject matter will read them and visit your site. Depending on the ezine's subscriber base or traffic to the article directory, the potential for bringing new visitors to your site can be enormous.

To start distributing your article, simply write a short "how-to" article on a topic relevant to your Web site topic. At the end of each article, add your 'byline,' or 'author's resource box,' with your personal bio and your site's URL.

A typical byline is 3 to 4 lines long. One of the bylines that I use when I publish my own articles looks like this:

> Article by Rosalind Gardner, author of the best-selling "Super Affiliate Handbook: How I Made $436,797 in One Year Selling Other People's Stuff Online." To learn how you too can succeed in Internet and Affiliate marketing, please visit http://NetProfitsToday.com

To get your article published in ezines, look for sites with topics that are complimentary to your own, not direct competitors.

For example, after the Super Affiliate Handbook was released, I contacted Allan Gardyne whom I knew had visitors who were interested in affiliate marketing and that he didn't sell his own affiliate marketing tutorial. I asked if he would like to publish my article '10 Ways to Gain Visitor Trust and Increase Your Conversion Rates' in his Associate Programs Newsletter.

Allan published the article and traffic to my site doubled for the next week, and because Allan archives the newsletters on his site, that article STILL sends traffic to my site!

Onsite archiving has an additional benefit. Your site's popularity increases as links to your site appear on more and more pages. With increased exposure, your name becomes better known and your credibility as an expert grows. This effect becomes cumulative, as 'experts' are frequently interviewed for other publications, which again increases their popularity.

Placing your articles on article directories is even easier to do because you don't need to contact the site's webmaster directly to solicit their interest in your material.

Article directories generally have submission pages on which you simply fill out a form that includes fields for your name, email address, URL, title of the article, the article body and your byline.

Different directories have different formatting requirements. Some require straight text insertions, while others want the article in HTML format. A few directory webmasters will ask you to provide an autoresponder address through which their visitors can have the article sent to them via email.

Although some article submission sites will ask for your specific terms of use or author's guidelines, articles placed on most directories are freely available to other webmasters for use on their sites according to the rules of that particular directory.

For example, Rozey Gean of Marketing-Seek.com attaches this note to the end of every article:

> **Please Note**: The author of this article has authorized its distribution with the requirement that it be published in its entirety, without changes, including the author's resource box. Please respect the authors' wishes by getting their permission to reprint their articles if they so request.

Here is a **short list** of article submission sites to get you started:

- Article Announce   http://groups.yahoo.com/group/article_announce
- Free Content   http://groups.yahoo.com/group/free-content
- Idea Marketers   http://www.ideamarketers.com
- Marketing Seek   http://www.marketing-seek.com

There is a **BIG list** of 860 article directories at http://www.articler.com/9746/big-list-of-article-directories.html

TAKE THE PAIN OUT OF ARTICLE SUBMISSIONS

Submitting your articles to individual directories can be time consuming.

To speed up the process considerably and gain even more exposure, I use Jason Potash's "Article Announcer" software. When I first bought Article Announcer, I used an already popular article to see if the program could effectively increase circulation.

Here is what happened.

On September 19th, 2005, I searched for my article "Broke, Desperate and at the End of Your Tether?" and discovered that there were **149 instances** published around the 'Net. The ARTICLE SUBMISSION TEST 1 screenshot to the right is a graphic image of that result.

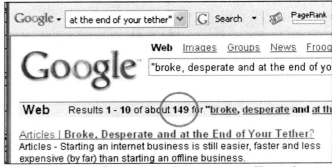

FIGURE 90 ARTICLE SUBMISSION TEST 1

After taking 45 minutes to learn how to use the "Article Announcer" software, I chose to submit the article only to article directories, and not to announcement lists or ezine editors. The 'Article Submission Test 2' screenshot shows what I discovered just **4 days later**, on September 23rd.

An additional 101 occurrences of the article had appeared in only 4 days! That's HUGE!

Just imagine the phenomenal traffic you'll drive to your site if you did that once a week or even twice a month.

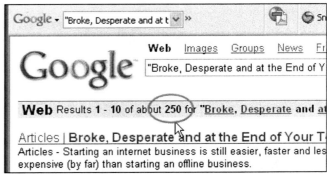

FIGURE 91 ARTICLE SUBMISSION TEST 2

In addition to a huge selection of editors, directories and lists to which you can submit, you can add your own resources to the Article Announcer software as you find them.

4. SEARCH ENGINE MARKETING

I'm going to start this section with a CAUTION about trying to rely *only* on free traffic.

There is an approach to affiliate marketing that focuses almost exclusively on search engine marketing as its primary method of driving traffic. The approach involves building tens and hundreds of little sites around topics that are chosen not out of interest, but for pure profit potential. Each site may make a paltry $20 to $100 per month.

The content on these sites is typically written according to a **keyword density formula** that involves repetitive use of chosen keywords and keyword phrases throughout the article.

Besides the fact that this method of writing usually results in dull, uninformative drivel that adds useless "web clutter," and does little or nothing to actually inform the site's visitors... this method has repeatedly proven to be **unsustainable.**

Many affiliates who use this technique have had their sites de-ranked and/or de-listed by search engines such as Google, which do their best to keep 'formulaic' web sites out of search engine results.

Because these affiliates relied primarily on search engine traffic, their $40,000.00+ per month incomes plummeted to less than $1,000.00 overnight, when their traffic 'dried up' completely.

Many have since given up on affiliate marketing and returned to day jobs.

Don't let that happen to you!

By all means, do your best to bring free traffic to your sites, but hedge your bets and combine those efforts with paid advertising.

OK, forewarned is forearmed.

Now let's look at how to bring free traffic to your sites.

Despite my caution above about relying only on search engine traffic, getting your site found and listed by the major engines is important. In order to do this, make sure your pages are properly optimized. Page optimization and submissions are dealt with in more detail in the 'Build Your Web Site' section.

Search engine crawlers visit sites and automatically build listings, generally *without the need to submit your site*. One of the quickest ways to get a visit from Google's spider, is to have a paid listing in the Yahoo! directory.

Here is a list of the best 3 places to submit your sites and pages.

- Google.com
- MSN.com
- Yahoo!

To learn more about how search engines work, visit SearchEngineWatch.com.

Fresh content is the other 'secret' to getting listed and staying listed. Regular blogging has proven the best way to get individual pages on my site listed in Google. Blog entries are typically shorter than newsletters and can be used to quickly post new merchant offers or deliver the latest industry news. Blogging is covered in detail in the *Blogging Basics* section of the book.

Using Aweber's RSS to Email technology, your blog posts can be delivered automatically to your newsletter subscribers, giving them still more reason to revisit your site, and thus increasing your search engine visibility even more.

Are you considering site submission services & software? A keyword search on 'website submission' or 'submission services' at Google or Yahoo yields hundreds of companies offering to submit your site to the search engines for a fee. Many of these services say they'll hand-submit your site to hundreds of engines all for the unbelievably low price of $9 - or for an incredibly good value at $999.

You should know that there are only a handful of important search engines, and that you can submit to these yourself for free. You will however need to submit regularly as search engines drop your site after a period of time unless re-submitted.

For more information about search engine optimization, please read *8 Ways to Make Your Site "Google' Friendly* in the Bonus Tips chapter.

10 Secondary Marketing Methods

1. GET LISTED IN THE YAHOO! DIRECTORY

As the time of writing, Yahoo! charges $299 (non-refundable) for their 'Yahoo! Express' expedited listing service, and $600 for adult-oriented sites. I think you'll find that it's a small price to pay for the amount of traffic that Yahoo! will send to your site.

Payment does not guarantee inclusion in the directory. Payment guarantees that a member of Yahoo!'s editorial staff will look at your site, consider your suggestion to include the site in the directory, and respond to you within seven business days from the date that you submit your site for consideration. Payment also guarantees that Yahoo! will respond to your suggestion within seven business days, by either adding or denying the site.

If your listing is denied, you have the right to appeal and/or make changes to your site within a certain amount of time and re-submit without making an additional payment.

If your site is accepted, you'll be charged $299 the following year to maintain the listing.

The expensive downside covered, it is well worth the money to list your site with Yahoo! because Yahoo! still has the Number 1 Alexa ranking. It's Top Dog.

That means it gets more traffic than any other site on the Web. THAT's the biggest reason 'why.'

Being listed in Yahoo's handpicked, human-compiled directory is one of the best ways to make sure that Google's (Alexa rating = 5) crawls and picks up your home page quickly. A link from Yahoo! will also improve your Google page rank. Even without the Yahoo! link, Google will find your page eventually, but if you are looking for lots of traffic fast, a Yahoo! listing (http://yahoo.com) is where it's at.

2. GET FREE DIRECTORY LISTINGS

Look for directories that include categories relevant to your site's topic. Some may require a reciprocal link in exchange for your listing, while those that are still building their databases may list it for free.

The **Open Directory Project** (ODP) bills itself as the largest 'human-edited directory' on the Web. Although the chances aren't good that your site will be accepted, submit the site anyway. You have nothing to lose, and you might get lucky.

Why is it unlikely that your site will be listed by the ODP? Unfortunately, most of those human editors are affiliate marketers who don't look favorably on competition from other affiliates, good content aside.

The Yahoo! directory does not accept free listings in their commercial categories, so affiliate sites, which are commercial sites, are not be eligible for free listings.

Other affiliate marketing coaches will suggest that you should apply for a Yahoo! directory listing once you have content on your site but *before* your affiliate links are in place. That is nothing more than a scam tactic and a dangerous one at that.

The Yahoo! directory is constantly being reviewed for relevancy. What would happen if you use this tactic, start earning decent commissions and then suddenly have your listing removed when the reviewer discovers that it is in fact an affiliate site?

First, your earnings will decrease. Secondly, I wouldn't count on having the site approved for a commercial listing after trying to scam Yahoo!

3. SYNDICATE YOUR CONTENT WITH RSS

RSS stands for **'Real Simple Syndication'** and is another way for you to **publish information**. For example, the Roamsters feed URL is http://roamsters.com/wp-rss2.php

Those using **RSS feed readers**, who have subscribed to the feed, are notified when a new post is made.

A single 'news' item will typically include a headline, a snippet of content and a link to your site.

The *Feedreader Interface* screenshot, shown to the right, shows how an item appears in *FeedReader*, an RSS feedreader.

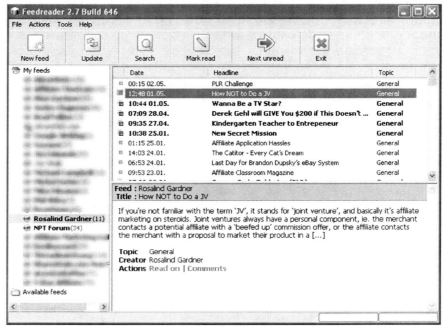

FIGURE 92 FEEDREADER INTERFACE

There are many RSS feed readers, also known as **'aggregators'**. A **list of readers** can be found at http://www.2rss.com/readers.php

FIGURE 93 FEEDBURNER

As many people now use web-based news readers provided by Google and Yahoo!, another option is to 'burn' your feed using FeedBurner, a service that provides custom RSS feeds and management tools to bloggers, podcasters and other web-based content publishers.

FeedBurner gives webmasters a new URL for their feed.

If you visit Roamsters.com, you will see a smaller version of the orange FeedBurner 'chiclet' (shown in the graphic to the left) at the top of the right-hand navigation on each page. That leads to Feedburner via the link, http://feeds.feedburner.com/RoamstersTravelBlog; a page where visitors can select from a good selection of web-based news readers and feed delivery via email. Feedburner's other services include traffic analysis and an optional advertising system.

Making your content available in this way is particularly useful as more people move away from accepting information by email.

4. USE AN EMAIL SIGNATURE

You send email every day, don't you? Well, make it work even harder for you!

Cheap but effective, an email signature line gets your message out every time you send an email.

My Sage-Hearts.com signature is shown to the right.

> Rosalind Gardner
> Online Dating for Savvy Singles
> http://sage-hearts.com

HOW TO CREATE A SIGNATURE FILE IN MICROSOFT OUTLOOK

- Open Outlook.
- Under the "Tools" menu, click on "Options."
- Click the "Mail Format" tab.
- Click "Signature Picker" at the bottom of the screen.
- Choose "New" and follow the prompts to name your signature file.

Once you make the new signature file the default, it will be inserted automatically at the end of every email you send, thus generating referral fees without any further work on your part.

HOW TO CREATE A SIGNATURE FILE IN EUDORA

- Open Eudora.
- Under "Tools," click on "Signatures." This will open the Signatures box on the left side of your screen.
- Right-click in the box, and select "New."
- A box pops open titled 'Create New Signature' and prompts you to "Enter Signature Name" in the form. Choose a name for your new signature, and then click 'OK.'
- A blank page opens. Type your promotional message and URL in this space. You have the option to be creative with font colors, sizes and types. When finished, click "File," and then "Save" to save your new signature.
- To set your new signature as the default signature, choose "Options" under the "Tools" menu, then "Composing Mail." In the drop down box beside "Signature:" pick the name you chose for your new signature.

That's it! Now every time you send out an email, your URL and promotional message will be included.

5. ADVERTISE IN RELEVANT EZINES

There are tens of thousands of ezines published online, and chances are excellent that there are many ezines published on a topic relevant to your site. Advertising in ezines is a low-cost and extremely effective way to bring qualified traffic to your site.

The Directory of Ezines is an excellent resource for quickly finding ezines targeted to your audience.

For a wealth of information about email advertising and to access targeted opt-in email lists where you can place your ads, check out http://www.bestezines.com

6. ISSUE PRESS RELEASES

Do you have an event scheduled or breaking news related to your site's topic? Send out a press release and announce it to the world!

For example, as a dating site webmaster you could survey your site visitors on their use of the 'Net to meet other singles. Ask them if they've met anyone from a dating site offline. Ask if they've bought gifts online to send to their 'online' friends.

Report your results in a press release.

A well-written release can dramatically increase your sales, expose your company to the masses, and greatly enhance the image of your business or products.

7. PARTICIPATE IN GROUPS AND FORUMS

Forums are like 'message boards' where members post messages for the entire group to read. Most forums are focused around a central theme.

Yahoo, Google, MSN and other major portal sites have discussion groups and clubs to which you can post messages.

Many newbies 'lurk' in forums, afraid to post their thoughts and questions.

That's SO sad and totally unnecessary. No one will bite you, provided the forum rules are followed. Even if you accidentally break one of the rules, chances are that you'll be politely reminded of the rules, asked to follow them in future, and given another chance to participate.

Responding to another group member's question with valuable information is the best way to gain respect and credibility in the groups.

To profit from forums, find and participate in forums related to your industry. Place your site's URL in your signature line. When you follow the rules listed in '*Forum Etiquette*' section in the *Bonus Tips* chapter and provide stellar information, people will want to hear more of what you have to say and will click on that link. Using the rules of forum etiquette posted below; get out there and learn, participate and prosper from forums.

RECOMMENDED WEBMASTER FORUMS

While there are thousands of forums related to affiliate and Internet marketing on the Web, relatively few receive daily postings. I've listed those that I find most useful below in alphabetical order.

Don't restrict yourself to just the forums listed below. If and when you find a new forum that looks interesting, be sure to check the dates of the latest postings, the number of responses to each posting and for the general absence of advertising material within the posts themselves.

Recent posting dates and numerous responses indicate an active community, and good forums use moderators to prevent blatant advertising by forum members.

- **Anthony Blake Online**
  Variety of entrepreneurial topics in a continuous thread presentation from the homepage. Search options available and preferences can be set.
  http://www.ablake.net/forum

- **Associate Programs Forum**
  Allan Gardyne's forum is a great source of information about affiliate programs from those who use them. Allan frequently shares sound advice in his own inimitable, levelheaded style.
  http://associateprograms.com/discus

- **GeekTalk**
  A friendly Community where "newbies" and "experts" share tips, ask questions, and network.
  http://www.geekvillage.com/forums/

- **How to Forum**
  Michael Green's forum is touted as the world's largest Internet marketing forum, where Internet marketers can exchange ideas, ask questions and get the answers they are looking for.
  http://www.howtocorp.com/forum/

- **NetProfitsToday Forum**
  This is my own forum and the NPT "Forumites" are generous with their time and helpful advice!
  http://www.netprofitstoday.com/forum

Learn about affiliate and Internet marketing from others and to share your own knowledge. So, find a forum, get in there, ask questions and speak up!

8. USE AUCTIONS TO SELL AFFILIATE PRODUCTS

Would you like to expose your products to 22 million people in over 100 countries? Yes? Then think 'eBay'!

In 1998, eBay's gross merchandise sales were $700,000 and by 2000, they hit $5.4 billion. This year the number should pass $30 billion.

The site has more than 168 million registered buyers and sellers and MORE than **724,000** Americans report that eBay is their primary or secondary source of income.

But here's a word of warning before you rush off to start listing your affiliate products on eBay. Affiliate products may NOT be sold directly on eBay's site. Be sure you understand the auction site's rules and regulations completely before you start to place listings. The following is taken directly from eBay's Links Policy.

EBAY'S 'ABOUT ME' PAGE LINKING POLICY

The About Me page may not promote outside-of-eBay sales or prohibited items, nor may it contain links to commercial Web sites where goods from multiple sellers are aggregated by a common search engine.

Violations of this policy may result in a range of actions, including:

- ❑ AboutMe page removal
- ❑ Listing cancellation
- ❑ Limits on account privileges
- ❑ Account suspension
- ❑ Forfeit of eBay fees on cancelled listings
- ❑ Loss of PowerSeller status

Despite the caution above, there ARE ways to use eBay's incredible market reach to promote your affiliate business.

For example, let's say that you sell health and fitness products as an affiliate. Obviously, you know a great deal about this subject, because you are a high-caliber, 'expert' affiliate who knows how to add significant value to all of your merchants' products.

So, you use some of your expert knowledge about fitness to write a report called '3 Steps to the Perfect Tush.' Within that report you've included your affiliate links and links to your main site.

Let's say that your digitally downloadable report sells hundreds of times at a dollar or two per copy. After paying the insertion, final sale and/or eBay store subscription fees, you still enjoy a profit.

With each sale you capture the buyer's email address and add them to your opt-in list or newsletter.

Within your well written report, your endorsements and affiliate product links continue to generate even more revenue for a long time to come. Do just a little bit of work to write that report and you too can use auctions to increase your affiliate income.

Register to become a seller at any or all of the online auction sites listed below:

- ▪ http://eBay.com.au (Australia)
- ▪ http://eBay.ca (Canada)
- ▪ http://ebay.co.uk(U.K.)
- ▪ http://eBay.com (U.S.)
- ▪ http://uBid.com

9. SOCIAL BOOKMARKING SITES

Adding social bookmark links to your blog or web site allows your readers to save and share your content.

Using a social bookmarking service, users click the bookmarking service of their choice, and save links to web pages that they want to remember and/or share. Because the bookmarks are usually public, and listed in order of popularity on the bookmarking service's site, many webmasters use social bookmarking as a marketing tool.

Unfortunately, the system is 'gamed' by webmasters who use bots to automatically bookmark their sites --- or get all their friends to click their links --- to achieve higher placement on the service.

This problem is pervasive amongst webmasters that promote products to other webmasters.

It may, however, be more effective if you work in a market in which consumers are less tech savvy such as pet lovers or photographers.

Here is a list of some of the most popular social bookmarking services.

- digg.com
- Netscape.com
- Technorati.com
- del.icio.us
- StumbleUpon.com
- reddit.com
- Fark.com
- MyBlogLog.com
- Slashdot.org
- kaboodle.com

10. SOCIAL NETWORKING SITES

Just as social bookmarking sites are 'gamed' by Internet marketers, so are social networking sites such as MySpace.com and Facebook.com abused, despite very clear policies against using those sites for spamming / marketing purposes.

Here is a portion of the MySpace terms of use agreement:

Non-commercial Use by Members. The MySpace Services are for the personal use of Members only and may not be used in connection with any commercial endeavors except those that are specifically endorsed or approved by MySpace.com. Illegal and/or unauthorized use of the MySpace Services, including collecting usernames and/or email addresses of Members by electronic or other means for the purpose of sending unsolicited email or unauthorized framing of or linking to the MySpace Website is prohibited. Commercial advertisements, affiliate links, and other forms of solicitation may be removed from Member profiles without notice and may result in termination of Membership privileges. Appropriate legal action will be taken for any illegal or unauthorized use of the MySpace Services.

To bring the point home that these sites are NOT to be used to spam members with marketing messages, in January 2007, MySpace announced its intention to sue 20 to 25 ad networks (including CPA Empire), seeking punitive damages from $20 million to $75 million per network. Individual affiliate marketers were also named in the case.

In mid-August, CPA Empire managed to get the judge to deny the MySpace motion for a preliminary injunction. Two of the affiliates involved each settled for $10,000.

With those warnings in mind, MySpace and other social networking sites may be worth investigating as a source of traffic provided you plan to post *informational content* that then links to your sites.

Look beyond MySpace for social networking sites that are highly specific to your niche. For example, if you work in the pet market, the following sites may be of value.

- Dogster.com
- Catster.com
- Hamsterster.com
- Petster.com

10 Ways to Market Your Site Offline

Offline marketing methods for affiliate sites are mostly a waste of time, and time IS money. However, if you have lots of both to spare, you may want to consider the following ways to go 'al fresco' with your site.

1. CAR DECALS

No doubt you've seen many cars plastered with Dot Com decals, and made a mental note to yourself to check out the web site when you got home or to your office. How many times did you actually look up the URL? If you're like me, the answer is 'never,' which speaks to the effectiveness of ruining your Mercedes' paint job with a Dot Com decal.

2. BUSINESS CARDS

These are highly effective marketing tools when you remember to put them in your wallet.

3. PERSONALIZED STATIONERY

Although it's unlikely that you will need to have business stationery printed as an affiliate marketer, I do recommend that you include your URL on any and all letters that you write. For example, your return address might look like this:

My Company Name
68 Someplace Avenue
Anywhere, State
USA 12345
(555) 444-2222
http://myURL.com

4. SPEAKING ENGAGEMENTS

The *last* thing I ever imagined myself doing was speaking at conferences.

But lo and behold, that *is* a picture of me speaking on the *"What Super Affiliates Want"* panel at the Affiliate Summit East conference held in Miami in July 2007. Seated beside me is my friend, Jeremy Palmer, another Super Affiliate.

Despite my overwhelming fear of public speaking, I've now spoken at numerous conferences and am well past the initial fear.

Not only has speaking boosted my business, it has helped connect me with others in the industry with whom I trade useful information from which I learn and pass along to my readers.

To boost your own business, consider speaking about your area of specialization at seminars and clubs.

5. CLASSIFIED ADS

Advertise your site in the classifieds section of local and regional newspapers. Do a small test first to see whether the return on investment (ROI) will be worthwhile.

6. TRADE PUBLICATIONS

The cost to advertise in a trade publication or journal can be prohibitive if you are starting a home-based affiliate marketing business on a budget. But it might still be worth your consideration.

TradePub.com offers free magazine trials in the following subject areas:

- Biopharmaceutical
- Business/Finance
- Computers
- Construction
- Education
- Engineering Design
- Farming & Agriculture
- Food & Beverage
- Government & Military
- Graphic Arts
- Healthcare
- Human Resources
- Industrial & Manufacturing
- Information Technology
- Insurance
- Internet
- Mechanical / Machine
- Meetings & Travel
- Multimedia Design
- Network / Communications
- Purchasing & Procurement
- Retail Sales & Marketing
- Telecom & Wireless
- Trade/Professional Services
- Transportation & Logistics
- Utility & Energy

Browse their extensive list of trade publications by industry, title, key word or geographic eligibility to find the titles that best match your interests. Simply complete the application form and submit it.

7. WEAR YOUR URL

Print some hats or t-shirts with your URL and logo and wear them proudly. Give them away so others may do the same. There is a slight chance someone will see and remember your site's URL until they get home to their computer.

If not, don't despair. Wearing your domain name proudly on your chest may have the beneficial side effect of helping to improve your posture.

8. GIVE AWAY PROMOTIONAL ITEMS

Become a sponsor at a conference related to your industry. Hundreds, if not thousands, of targeted consumers will be looking at your URL every time they pick up your pen or look at your mouse pad.

9. TELL YOUR FRIENDS AND FAMILY

This method works really well...not.

I spent 2 years working on a major joint venture project. The day the site opened, I emailed homepage links to some of my friends and invited them to check out our wonderful new site.

Some visited immediately and we were soon the proud recipients of several rave reviews. Months later however, many still hadn't even seen the homepage.

While this method rates a 1 out of 10 in marketing terms, more often than not it ranks 1st in the 'ego boosting' department. By all means, share your accomplishments with your friends and family. With luck, they'll 'pass it on.'

10. HAPPY CUSTOMERS

This is one way to market offline that is worth its weight in gold. Happy customers spreading the word about your site is always a good thing – online, offline or via ESP.

5 Marketing Strategies that Kill Time

I include the following list of marketing strategies simply as a caution for you. They are primarily a waste of time that took time away from the more relevant and effective marketing methods.

1. TRADE LINKS WITH RELEVANT NON-COMPETING SITES

Link trading, link exchange, or reciprocal linking is a web promotion strategy used by webmasters and site owners to increase "link popularity" as well as qualified traffic to their sites.

Page ranking in search engines is influenced by the link "popularity" of your site. The numbers of sites that link to yours, as well as the popularity of those sites determine link popularity. This is a relatively important factor as far as search engine placement is concerned.

You've probably seen sites with pages labeled 'Links.' These webmasters have listed links to their link trade partners, and the other webmasters have done likewise on their sites.

Links 'in' to your page from another site should include your site's name or primary keyword in the link, for better popularity.

Link popularity is improved when sites with a high page rank link to your site. A link from a site with a topic related to yours is more valuable than a link from an unrelated site. Your link popularity can actually be diminished if you trade links with sites that don't complement yours, or that have low page ranks or poor traffic numbers.

Having extolled the virtues of link trading, I'm now going to tell you about the disadvantages, which I see as being greater than the advantages.

A 'Links' page is an invitation for your visitors to leave your site without buying anything. Basically you are asking your visitors to go and buy at your competitors' sites.

Do you really want to do that?

I've rarely participated in a link exchange that actually brought worthwhile traffic to my site. Here are a few link exchange programs of which you should be aware.

Before pay-per-click came on the scene, link trading and links directories were all the rage. I used to spend hours writing and sending emails to complementary sites asking for link trades. I got my site listed in numerous dating link directories in exchange for placing their graphic on my site. Some insisted that I place their graphic on my homepage. You will still see many sites on which the bottom half of the page is a blinking mass (mess) of reciprocal links graphics to links directories. Tacky!

Note: Please don't mistake link directories for *real* directories like the Online Directory Project (DMOZ.org). The ODP doesn't require a reciprocal link to get your site listed, whereas these 'links' sites are in the business of trading links. Who benefits from these trades?

It's not the individual site owner, to be sure. Their site can't be located amidst the thousands of other affiliate sites listed in the directory.

Generally, the directory owner is also an affiliate of all the same programs that you are, and you can be sure that their affiliate links are encoded in the banners at the top, middle and bottom of their pages. Let's not forget the buttons on the side, or the 'Superior' listings on their site.

Some of these 'link exchange' directories have proven to be complete scams, the worst of which in the Internet dating realm was a site called Cupidnet.com.

They built a directory and got thousands of webmasters to link to their site in exchange for directory listings. At some point, and without informing any of their link trade partners, the site became an affiliate of American Singles, and the directory disappeared. Goodness only knows how many webmasters are *still* sending free traffic to Cupidnet.com, and receiving nothing in exchange.

Every link that leaves your site should generate revenue.

There are only a few circumstances when adding an unprofitable link to your site is warranted. Here is one example.

When I started Sage-Hearts.com, Internet dating was in its infancy. People were afraid to try online dating, and horror stories about dates gone bad offline were widely published. To counter the bad press, I directed my visitors to one of the first online sites specializing in background checks - Whoishe.com. They didn't have an affiliate program, (and still don't!) so I didn't earn a commission for the referral if my visitors bought their product.

However, my rationale for putting up the 'leaky' link was that if my visitors invested in a background check after coming to my site, they'd probably met someone through one of the dating services that I promote.

Basically, the only time you should put up a non-affiliate link, is if you consider the other site's information absolutely integral to your own. But keep looking for affiliate program products to replace that 'leaky' link as soon as possible!

In a nutshell - Links 'in' are good. Unpaid links 'out' are bad.

2. FFA's (Free For All Link Pages)

In your quest for traffic, you'll probably come across FFA, or Free For All, sites as well.

The promise looks so good! "Submit your URL to have your site appear on THOUSANDS of pages across our Network."

Webmasters list their URL's on the FFA page in hopes of generating traffic to their site. However, when you post to an FFA site, you get one line or a couple hundred characters to describe your site. Chances are good that your link will never be seen.

FFA's are nothing more than rotating lists of links.

Each and every time a site is submitted, the FFA site owner sends a confirmation email to the contact address provided by the listing webmaster.

THAT is the real purpose of the FFA site.

The FFA owner collects email addresses so he can send out his advertising message. He already knows that you, the listing webmaster, are interested in getting traffic to your web site, so he targets his message in that direction.

In most cases, he'll offer to sell you a service that promises to submit your site to THOUSANDS of FFA posting sites and search engines... and all for the low, low price of $59. Wow! In return, you'll receive THOUSANDS more confirmation emails from all those other FFA site owners.

Go ahead - give it a try, if you still want to. Just be sure you don't use your best email address. In the next table is a warning that I found posted on an FFA site, which should tell you something.

> Warning! Do NOT use your primary email address for this posting - you will receive many confirmation emails, and be added to many email lists (you will be posting to the entire network!).

For an example of an FFA site, visit the link below. If you can decipher any of the listing titles despite that horrible font, my hat is off to you.

http://www.free-for-all-links.com/

3. BANNER EXCHANGES

As the name implies a banner exchange allows you to display your advertising banners on member Web sites in exchange for allowing them to display their banner on your Web site.

But there's a catch. You must display two banners on your site so just one of your banners will be displayed on another member's Web site. Hmm... what happens to the other fifty percent? Those would be used by the banner exchange service to display their own advertising.

There are 5 big drawbacks to the banner exchange scheme for traffic generation.

- Banner exchanges don't generate significant traffic.
- You have no control over the appearance of the other members' banners.
- You end up with unrelated material appearing on your site.
- Banners suck up good bandwidth and slow your pages down.
- Banners rarely get clicked on and their conversion rates are terrible.

My advice - don't waste your valuable time and effort using banner exchanges.

4. START OR HOMEPAGE TRAFFIC NETWORKS

If every hit counts, then you might want to consider start page networks as a way to get free traffic to your site. Here's a quick run down of how these products work.
Sign-up and enter some basic information about the page that you want to promote. Set the Traffic Swarm code as your home page. Earn hits when you open your browser. Earn more hits when your friends sign up and open their browsers.

The more hits you have, the more times your site will show up on other members' browsers. Your links are then displayed all over the network - consisting of 1000s of other webmasters and 1000s of other sites like yours - and with Traffic Swarm, your site is also automatically included in the TrafficSwarm Search Engine.

Specifically, your links are displayed when other network users open their web browser, and when visitors leave THEIR website(s) via an exit "pop-under" window.

Sign up for an account at Traffic Swarm http://www.trafficswarm.com/

5. REFER-A-FRIEND SCRIPTS

You've probably seen these. You enter your name and email address, as well as those of a number of your friends. Push the 'SUBMIT' button and a message gets sent to all of those friends telling them what a great site you just found.

How effective are these scripts? All in all, probably not worth the time it takes to put up on your site.

I had one on one of my sites, and over a period of 4 months, only 2 folks used the form. I like to believe it's because they were too busy enjoying the site otherwise.

Here's my marketing strategy recommendation in a nutshell.

Bite the bullet and put some money into pay-per-click advertising to get the ball rolling.

Then start writing. Write articles, and more articles. Put them in your ezine, and send them to other ezine publishers.

Think 'income' and 'profit,' and then use the tools above to help you achieve both.

Manage Your Business

To keep your business on track, there are a number of tasks that need to be performed on a daily, weekly, monthly or quarterly basis.

Daily, Weekly, Monthly and Yearly Tasks

Use the following suggestions as a guideline for creating your own maintenance schedule.

DAILY TASKS

These are tasks that you should try to accomplish once a day. That said, as your business grows and you gain more experience as an affiliate, you will discover that it is no longer necessary to check your statistics or links every day.

Post to Your Blog - OK, you don't have to blog EVERY day. But to get more visitors and more sales --- post MORE often.

Check Your Email - Merchant partners send out new offers and the occasional affiliate newsletter, but in my experience most don't communicate with affiliates other than to advise of new offers. Likewise is true of the affiliate networks, which will notify you of new merchants and those that have left the network. Keep your eyes open for emails with the subject line: 'Check Your Merchant Status.'

You won't receive much email from customers, as most of those will be directed to the merchant.

However, if you DO receive email queries about products or services offered on your site, respond promptly with either the answer, or an offer to redirect their question as appropriate. Both the customer and the merchant will recognize and appreciate your effort. Because the customer asked YOU the question, it means that she trusts your site, and is probably planning to buy the product.

If you have an opt-in email list (as you should), you'll likely receive 'remove' requests from subscribers via email, despite the opt-out link within your newsletters. Remove their email address from the list immediately. Justified or not, spam complaints are something you don't ever want to get.

Monitor Your Site - Is your site online? Type your URL into your browser's address bar, refresh the page and find out at least once a day!

Pay-per-click advertising costs add up whether your site is functional or not. If your site is down, you are paying for advertising, but no one is buying.

Broken sales links are the bane of an affiliate marketer's existence. In many cases your HTML editor will have a built-in link checker.

If you don't have a link checker, NetMechanic is a service that will check to see whether your site is online, every fifteen minutes, 24 hours a day. If your site is down, they'll notify you by numeric pager, alphanumeric pager, or email, so you can resolve your downtime problems immediately.

Check out their free trial at http://netmechanic.com. The service will check your site every fifteen minutes for 8 hours so you can see how it works.

Check Your Stats - When I started out, I checked my stats hourly, and sometimes more often.

Now that I'm familiar with the income 'trends,' I check my 'key partner sites' daily to see how my business is performing. I recommend that you check your statistics daily until you know what to expect day-by-day and week-by-week.

Simply visit the statistics interface for each network and independent merchants and input your total revenues into Quicken or a spreadsheet. Using Quicken will also keep you informed as to whether certain checks are overdue.

Make Time for Yourself - A business that involves sitting at your computer for lengthy periods of time can lead to weight gain and repetitive strain injury if you don't take proper care of yourself. I personally try to exercise before I turn on my computer in the morning. That is the best way to not get 'side-tracked' by business interests.

WEEKLY TASKS

Add New Pages / Articles to Your Site - Try to add at least one new article page to your site/blog every week to keep it fresh. This will encourage your visitors to keep coming back.

Publish Your Newsletter - I publish the 'Net Profits Today' newsletter weekly and recommend that you publish your newsletter not less than once a week. Many other Internet marketers however, recommend publishing more frequently, and some report that their best results come from publishing once per day.

Add & Submit Keywords - Always be on the lookout for new keywords and keyword phrases to add to your pay-per-click advertising campaigns. Jot down your ideas and then add them to your Yahoo! Search Marketing, Miva and other campaigns on a weekly basis.

Research - Spend some time every week reviewing and researching the news in your industry as well as Internet marketing news. Learning about new methods and tools for doing business can save you time and money down the road.

MONTHLY TASKS

End of Month Statistics - Tally your income and expenses once a month to stay on top of your overall business picture. Enter data into your spreadsheets to see which direction your traffic and sales conversions are taking.

YEARLY TASKS

Year-end and Taxes - Whether you operate as a sole proprietor or incorporate your business, you'll need to prepare your taxes.

Set Goals for the Coming Year - Although I set daily, weekly and monthly goals, I find it very helpful to set annual financial goals and then create a master plan to execute those goals on a yearly basis.

Make up a 'cheat sheet' that lists your tasks and use it!

Evaluate Your Site's Performance

It's a great feeling to pick up commission checks from your mailbox and deposit them in the bank on a regular basis. Unfortunately, alongside those checks you'll find credit card statements and other bills for your business expenses. Make sure that the amount of those checks always exceeds the bills, or no one will be happy - not you, or your creditors.

To stay on top of your balance sheet and make sure your affiliate marketing business stays in the black; you must pay attention to a number of different statistics.

To learn exactly how well your business is doing and track its trends, you will need your Web site statistics and affiliate sales figures.

Once you've collected and recorded all the relevant data, the numbers then get crunched and analyzed. In the final analysis you will learn exactly where your site is, and where it tends to be headed.

STATS TO TRACK & NUMBERS TO CRUNCH

Before you start recording and analyzing data, you need to answer the following questions.

- What percentage of visitors to my site become customers?

- What is the conversion rate for each Affiliate Program?

- How much is each visitor worth?

- How much does it cost to bring a new visitor to your site?

Let's go through them one at a time.

1. WHAT PERCENTAGE OF MY VISITORS BECAME CUSTOMERS?

This percentage is known as the visitor-to-customer conversion rate, or simply, your conversion rate. When you hear other webmasters speak of their 'conversions' or say something like, "That program converts at 1.5 percent," they are talking about their visitor-to-customer conversion rate.

Average conversion ratios for affiliates range between .5 and 1.5 percent. Super affiliates often convert their traffic by much higher percentages. Some of my sites convert visitors to customers at rates between 6 and 20 percent.

In the following example, let's say your site receives 30,000 visitors in a month, and 375 of those visitors became new customers. The formula is shown in the table to the right.

> **Conversion Rate** = Number of new sales divided by the number of unique visitors.
>
> E.g. 375 new sales / 30,000 unique visitors is a conversion rate of 1.25%.

This is probably the most important number you will ever deal with in your affiliate business. It tells you exactly how well you convince your visitors to buy your affiliate merchants' products.

2. WHAT IS THE CONVERSION RATE FOR EACH AFFILIATE PROGRAM?

This calculation is similar to the one above. The only difference is that we use the commission and traffic statistics gathered from the individual affiliate programs, instead of totals for the site.

Knowing how conversion rates compare between programs is useful when deciding how to direct your promotional efforts.

For example, if you discover that Program 'A' converts at 1.25% and Program 'B' converts at 2.5%, it might be time to spend more time and effort to promote Program 'A.'

The formula for the equation is shown in the table to the right.

> **Program Conversion Rate** = Number of New Sales divided by Number of Unique Visitors Sent to Affiliate Site X 100.
>
> E.g. 22 (new sales) / 600 (unique visitors) X 100 = **3.66%**

3. HOW MUCH DOES EACH VISITOR COST?

This calculation determines your 'cost per visitor'. To get your 'net revenue per visitor' simply subtract the results of this calculation from your 'revenue per visitor'.

For example, if you spent $2500.00 in advertising, and sent 30,000 unique visitors to the merchant's site, your cost per visitor is $.083 per visitor.

The formula is shown in the table to the right.

> **Visitor Cost** = Advertising cost divided by number of unique visitors.
>
> E.g. $2,500.00 advertising / 30,000 uniques - $0.083 per visitor.

4. HOW MUCH IS EACH VISITOR WORTH?

Understanding how much your site earns per visitor will help you determine how much you can spend on advertising to acquire new customers.

To learn how much revenue you earn per visitor, you need to know your affiliate commission amounts.

Collect this data from each one of your affiliate merchant partners at the end of the month.

Recording the amount of commission you expect from each merchant also makes it easier to see if amounts are correct when your checks arrive.

The formula is shown in the table to the right.

To calculate net revenue per visitor, simply subtract visitor cost from revenue per visitor.

Revenue per visitor
Commission earned divided by number of unique visitors. For example, $7,000.00 commission / 30,000 uniques - $0.23 gross revenues per visitor.

In the examples above, each visitor would generate a net revenue of 14.7 cents.

Of course, a much easier calculation would be to subtract your expenses from your income!

Assuming however that you want to know all the nitty-gritty details, let's look at how you will collect all the necessary data to make your calculations.

COLLECTING DATA

Each time a surfer requests one of your Web pages, all the details and files associated with that page are recorded in what is called the **server log**, which is stored on your host's server.

To access this information, your host may provide full web site statistics reporting, or just the raw logs. If all you get is raw server logs, then you'll probably want to use log analyzer software, as raw logs are very difficult to make sense of otherwise.

Here is some of the information you can derive from analyzing your Web site's server logs:

- Traffic data including unique visitors, number of visits, pages viewed, hits, bytes. These numbers will be broken down on a monthly, daily and hourly basis.
- Number of visitors by country of origin.
- Numbers of spider/robot visits.
- Traffic source IP addresses.
- The number of times each page on your site was viewed.
- Which pages are used as entry and exit pages.
- The number and percentage of hits by file type.
- The number and percentage of hits by browser type.
- The number and percentage of hits by operating system type.
- Whether visits originated from bookmarks, search engine, newsgroup, links from external sites (other than search engines).

Most good Web hosts give you access to your server logs. If you don't know how to find your server logs, consult your host's help files or contact them and ask.

Affiliate Program Sales Data - In addition to information about your site's traffic, you'll need to collect information about each of the affiliate program products that you sell on your site.

You should already be checking your sales and commission information on a regular basis. In addition to number of sales and commission earned, now you'll also need to determine the number of unique visitors you send to the merchant's site.

If the statistics about the product that you sell is found through an affiliate network, like Commission Junction, be sure you gather information about the individual product, and not your collective Commission Junction statistics.

RECORDING DATA

I use Excel to compile and record my site's financial performance data.

I use it because once I've input formulae to calculate monthly totals, increases and declines, and conversion rates, I never have to do that math again. After that, I simply enter the raw data, and the spreadsheet does the calculations.

You may use any spreadsheet you are comfortable with, or you might prefer to use a calculator to do the math instead. That's up to you.

To help you understand and visualize the statistics recording and analyzing tasks, I've included tables below with statistical data from 3 products that I sell on one of my affiliate sites.

WEB SITE TRAFFIC

The first step is to record your web site statistics. In the following table, I've input the total number of unique visitors to the site, and calculated the average unique visitors per day and per month, as well as the increase or decrease from the previous month. **Note**: Changes from the previous month are not indicated for the month of January, as I haven't entered data for December.

To make these calculations more accurate and fair, I've divided the number of unique visitors by the number of days in the month to arrive at the averages. If I didn't do this, February might always appear to be a dismal month for sales, being between 8 and 10% shorter than the other months of the year.

To calculate percentage of change from one month to another, simply divide the second month's uniques by the preceding month's uniques.

For example: Feb **27626** / Jan **23839** = 1.16%

When calculating affiliate product performance (detailed on the next page), do NOT average out the traffic figures. In that case, February's lower traffic will usually be reflected in a similar decrease in the number of sales. Averaging the traffic out in that case would make February look VERY dismal indeed!

WebServer Stats	Jan	Feb	Mar
Unique Visitors	24634	25784	27907
Days in Month	31	28	31
Avg. Uniques/Day	795	921	900
Avg. Uniques/ Avg. Month (Avg./Day x 30)	23839	27626	27007
Increase/Decrease from Previous Month		3786	-619
% Change from Previous Month		1.16%	0.98%

ASSESS INDIVIDUAL PRODUCT PERFORMANCE

First we collect and record data from individual products to see how they perform from month to month. Once your Excel spreadsheet is set up with the correct formulae, this becomes as easy as inputting 3 numbers only:

- Clickthroughs
- Number of Sales
- Commission Amounts

All the other figures are then calculated based on the numbers we enter in the form.

In the next 3 tables are examples of 3 different products for which I've collected and recorded clickthrough and sales figures.

Product #1	Jan	Feb	Mar	Totals
ClickThroughs	8768	7548	7209	23525
Change from previous month		(1220)	(339)	
Sales	147	121	112	380
Change from previous month		(26)	(9)	
Commission	2,698.22	2,187.49	1,993.89	$6,879.60
Change from previous month		(510.73)	(193.60)	
Conversion Rate	1.68%	1.60%	1.55%	1.62%
Change from previous month		-0.07%	-0.05%	
Avg. Revenue/Sale	18.36	18.08	17.80	18.10
Change from previous month		-0.28	-0.28	
Avg. Revenue/Unique	0.31	0.29	0.28	0.29
Change from previous month		($0.02)	($0.01)	

Product #2	Jan	Feb	Mar	Totals
ClickThroughs	4647	7197	7328	19172
Change from previous month		2550	131	
Sales	34	42	45	121
Change from previous month		8	3	
Commission	988.17	1,712.60	2,302.02	$5,002.79
Change from previous month		724.43	589.42	
Conversion Rate	0.73%	0.58%	0.61%	0.63%
Change from previous month		-0.15%	0.03%	
Avg. Revenue/Sale	29.06	40.78	51.16	41.35
Change from previous month		11.71	10.38	
Avg. Revenue/Unique	0.21	0.24	0.31	0.26
Change from previous month		0.03	0.08	

Product #3	Jan	Feb	Mar	Totals
ClickThroughs	6690	6791	7827	21308
Change from previous month		101	1036	
Sales	40	48	50	138
Change from previous month		8	2	
Commission	1,018.89	1,049.70	1,248.87	$3,317.46
Change from previous month		30.81	199.17	
Conversion Rate	0.60%	0.71%	0.64%	0.65%
Change from previous month		0.11%	-0.07%	
Avg. Revenue/Sale	25.47	21.87	24.98	24.04
Change from previous month		-$3.60	$3.11	
Avg. Revenue/Unique	0.15	0.15	0.16	0.16
Change from previous month		$0.00	$0.00	

Next we'll look at how to compare the performance of individual products.

SIDE-BY-SIDE PRODUCT PERFORMANCE COMPARISONS

After evaluating how individual products perform from month to month, the products are placed side-by-side and their performance is compared.

This makes it easy to see that Product #1 is the best producer, not only in terms of commission earned, but also by its conversion rate and average revenue per visitor.

January	Prod. #1	Prod. #2	Prod. #3	Totals
ClickThroughs	8768	4647	6690	20105
Sales	147	34	40	221
Commission	2,698.22	988.17	1,018.89	$4,705.28
Conversion Rate	1.68%	0.73%	0.60%	1.10%
Avg. Revenue/Sale	18.36	29.06	25.47	$21.29
Avg. Revenue/Unique	0.31	0.21	0.15	$0.23
February	**Prod. #1**	**Prod. #2**	**Prod. #3**	**Totals**
ClickThroughs	7458	7197	6791	21446
Sales	121	42	48	211
Commission	2,187.49	1,712.60	1,049.70	$4,949.79
Conversion Rate	1.62%	0.58%	0.71%	0.98%
Avg. Revenue/Sale	18.08	40.78	21.87	23.46
Avg. Revenue/Unique	0.29	0.24	0.15	0.23
March	**Prod. #1**	**Prod. #2**	**Prod. #3**	**Totals**
ClickThroughs	7209	7328	7827	22364
Sales	112	45	50	207
Commission	1,993.89	2,302.02	1,248.87	$5,544.78
Conversion Rate	1.55%	0.61%	0.64%	0.93%
Avg. Revenue/Sale	17.80	51.16	24.98	26.79
Avg. Revenue/Unique	0.28	0.31	0.16	0.25

EVALUATE MONTH-TO-MONTH TRENDS

In the following table, the total commission and traffic amounts of all products are added together, and the site's performance is compared from month-to-month.

Total commissions and traffic for the year-to-date are added up, and average revenues per sale and per visitor is calculated.

Given this information, we can see that although the actual number of sales decreased between February and March, as did the conversion rate, the site's overall performance is improving with increased traffic, commission and earnings per visitors.

We're definitely heading in the right direction!

Totals	Jan	Feb	Mar	YTD
Unique Visitors	24634	25784	27907	78325
Change from previous month		1150	2123	
ClickThroughs	20105	21446	22364	63915
Change from previous month		1341	918	
ClickThroughs/Unique (%)	81.61%	83.18%	80.14%	81.60%
Sales	221	226	207	654
Change from previous month		5	(19)	
Commission	$4,705.28	$4,949.79	$5,544.78	$15,199.85
Change from previous month		244.51	594.99	
Conversion Rate	1.10%	1.05%	0.93%	1.02%
Change from previous month		-0.05%	-0.13%	
Avg. Revenue/Sale	$21.29	$21.90	$26.79	$23.24
Change from previous month		$0.61	$4.88	
Avg. Revenue/Visitor	$0.23	$0.23	$0.25	$0.24
Change from previous month		($0.00)	$0.02	

CALCULATE EXPENSES

In the table below, the site's expenses are added up.

Advertising costs are added and totaled separately, then added to other costs such as our hosting and Internet connection, to give totals for the month.

Advertising/PPC Costs	Jan	Feb	Mar	Totals
MSN	235.55	217.34	198.36	$651.35
Yahoo! Search Marketing	114.62	97.22	158.43	$370.27
Google Adwords	932.81	1018.33	1037.24	$2,988.38
Total PPC Costs	1282.98	1332.89	1394.13	$4,010.00
Expenses	**Jan**	**Feb**	**Mar**	**Totals**
Advertising/PPC	1282.98	1332.89	1394.13	$4,010.00
Hosting	9.95	9.95	9.95	$29.85
Autoresponder Service	10.50	10.50	10.50	$31.50
Cable Modem	29.95	29.95	29.95	$89.85
Total Expenses	1,333.38	1,383.29	1,444.53	$4,161.20

CALCULATE NET INCOME

Once both income and expenses are calculated, net income, or actual earnings from the site can be determined.

This is the amount leftover that you can use to spend on that new Mercedes, um, AFTER you pay your taxes!

Net Income	Jan	Feb	Mar	Year to Date
Total Revenues	$4,705.28	$4,949.79	$5,544.78	$15,199.85
Total Expenses	$1,333.38	$1,383.29	$1,444.53	$4,161.20
Net Income	$3,371.90	$3,566.50	$4,100.25	$11,038.65
% Return on Investment	352.88%	357.83%	383.85%	365.28%
Unique Visitors	24634	25784	27907	78325
Net Income/Visitor	$0.14	$0.14	$0.15	$0.14
ClickThroughs	20105	21446	22364	63915
Net Income/Clickthrough	$0.17	$0.17	$0.18	$0.17

Pay close attention to make sure the programs you promote are turning a profit.

Don't hesitate to drop a program if you find that the conversion rates are low or have suddenly dropped. The company may have made changes to their site, or the affiliate program. Go and check.

While this may seem like a lot of work to go through to track your site's performance, it really is a worthwhile endeavor.

Once all your formulae are set up on your spreadsheets, and you've done the inputs a few times, you'll be surprised at how simple it becomes. In fact, you may find that eventually you look forward to 'adding things up' at the end of the month to get a clear picture of where your site stands.

It's the only way to really know in which direction you've gone, and in which direction you should turn to pursue a correct and worthwhile course.

Grow Your Business

If you aren't working to grow your business, your business will decline.

From negotiating commission increases, using 404 pages and foreign currency rates to your advantage and adding components to your site that are designed specifically for affiliates, there are a number of ways to make sure your business continues to grow.

3 Ways to Negotiate a Commission Increase

How much is your effort worth?

It's a sad fact that as advertising costs and other Internet business expenses increase, net profits decrease. That is, unless you do something about it.

Simply because a commission rate for a particular affiliate program is posted at 15 or 20%, doesn't mean that rate is written in stone.

This is where it literally *pays* to have a personal relationship with the affiliate manager.

Most program management software allows merchants to set different rates for individual affiliates. Here are a few ways to entice managers to get in there and tweak your rates up a notch or five.

1. PROVE YOURSELF

If you find an excellent product that you know you can sell, it sometimes makes good sense to sign up for the affiliate program despite low commission rates in the hope that your performance will lead to a higher rate.

You would promote the product for a few months, and during that time establish a friendly working relationship with the affiliate manager.

After proving yourself as a webmaster who knows how to drive high traffic volume and convert visitors to sales, ask the affiliate program manager to raise your commission rates. Be specific, and ask for a set dollar amount or percentage of the sale.

The worst that can happen is that the manager denies your request, in which case you may choose to drop the program, or seriously restrict traffic to their site.

In many cases, when valued affiliates drop programs or restrict traffic, affiliate managers quickly respond by negotiating better deals for those affiliates.

The key here is to prove your value as an affiliate first, then ask the company to acknowledge that value in monetary terms. It's called building leverage.

The good companies always will compensate properly, and well, there are enough good companies that you don't need to deal with those that don't value your true worth.

2. ASK AND YE SHALL RECEIVE

If you've proven yourself as a valuable affiliate who sends LOTS of traffic and generates LOTS of revenue, with whom the merchant partner likes to do business, most often they will be willing to negotiate a higher commission structure for you.

Dating service affiliate managers often email and ask me to review and list their services on my dating service review sites.

When I receive these requests, I immediately visit the site and quickly look it over to make sure that it appears professional, attractive, and suitable for my audience.

My next step is to visit their affiliate home page to check their commission rates and program specifications. I often find the commission rates are too low to proceed with the affiliation.

However, I don't just click away and forget their request.

Regardless of whether or not I liked the program, I will respond, provided that their email was personalized.

If I liked both the site and the product, I tell the owner or affiliate manager that I think they've got an excellent service that might be eligible for inclusion on my site, if they are willing to raise their commission rates. I then specify the minimum terms that I am willing to accept and leave the ball in their court.

Half the time, I don't hear back from them.

That's OK, because it's the other half that counts. Merchants who understand that earning fifty percent of my sale is preferable to 90 percent of nothing are usually happy to accept my terms.

At that point, we're on our way to building a happy, profitable relationship.

3. CLAIM YOUR DUE

I recently had a call from a merchant partner asking me to send more traffic to one of their niche dating sites.

She cited that my conversions for that site were in the 40 percent range - which is very high - and that we would both benefit from the increased traffic.

The program in question pays per free member signup, rather than a percentage of actual sales, and although I don't usually sign up for 'pay per lead' programs, the company didn't offer a 'percentage of sale' option. I signed up for it only because it was one of very few in that specific niche. I used the program as inducement to get folks to my site, but once there, directed my visitors' attention to more profitable options.

The commission per lead was very small, so I didn't want to make any more effort in that direction.

During our conversation, the affiliate manager pointed out that at 20 percent, my free-to-paid member conversions were also very high, and that I should consider joining their percentage program.

I was shocked. That was the first time I'd heard that they even offered a percentage of sales option for that program. I asked when they made that change, and was told that it had been in place for a few months. I asked why affiliates hadn't been informed of this program improvement. She told me that no notice had been sent because they were busy and under-staffed.

I did a quick scan of my sales statistics while we were still on the phone, and saw that my commissions were around $600 less than I would have earned through the percentage program.

I felt cheated.

I may be blonde, but I'm not (that) dumb. I bluntly told the manager that it wasn't fair to use their staffing situation as an excuse to shortchange affiliates on their commissions, and that I would stop sending traffic to the program altogether, unless amends were made.

Sure enough, she switched me over to the percentage program immediately, and sent me a check for more than $600 to rectify the deficit.

I took a risk by stating exactly how their actions affected me, but it was a risk worth taking. I'm now happy to send that program all the traffic I can deliver.

Strive for excellence in all your affiliate endeavors, and demand that you be compensated appropriately for your efforts.

(It also pays to have your facts and figures handy so that you can do the math quickly when having important discussions with affiliate program managers.) ☺

More Ways to Profit

Yes, there are always more ways to profit!

PROFIT FROM *404 ERROR PAGES*

You've probably seen "*404 - Page Not Found*" errors hundreds of times. If visitors find them on your site, you are losing money.

They see that page and either click the 'Back' button or close the browser window. That doesn't have to be the case, however, if you design a customized 404 error page for your site. I use an .htacess file which is written as follows:

ErrorDocument 404 http://www.sage-hearts.com/dating services/404.html

What that page does is redirect visitors to a page that both apologizes for the inconvenience and offers them alternative options, all of which have my affiliate links embedded.

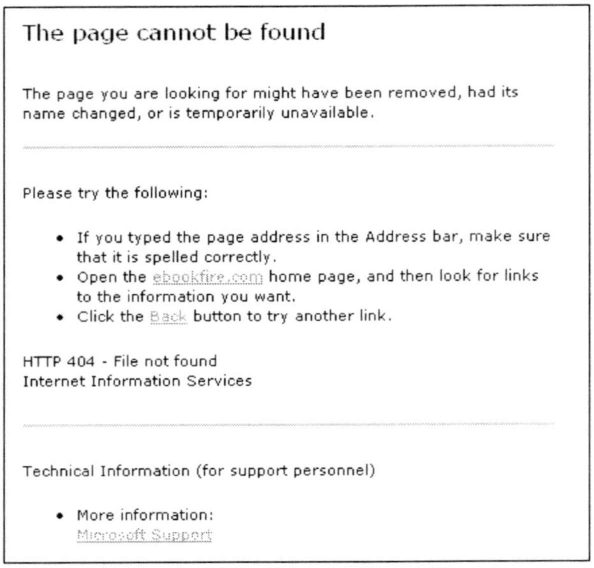

The page cannot be found

The page you are looking for might have been removed, had its name changed, or is temporarily unavailable.

Please try the following:

- If you typed the page address in the Address bar, make sure that it is spelled correctly.
- Open the ebookfire.com home page, and then look for links to the information you want.
- Click the Back button to try another link.

HTTP 404 - File not found
Internet Information Services

Technical Information (for support personnel)

- More information:
Microsoft Support

FIGURE 94 404 ERROR PAGE EXAMPLE

Take a minute of your time to create a custom 404 error page and reduce potential commission losses!

USE FOREIGN EXCHANGE TO YOUR ADVANTAGE

When I started affiliate marketing back in early 1998, getting paid in U.S. Dollars was a huge bonus to me as a Canadian resident.

At that time, one US dollar was valued at $1.43 Canadian. By late 2001, the greenback translated into $1.60 Canadian.

Woohoo!

Even if my merchants' product prices and commission rates remained the same, I got a raise simply by virtue of fluctuating foreign currency rates.

For example, let's say that one month I sold 100 dating service memberships at $29.95 for a 50% commission and earned $1497.50 US.

In January 1998 that $1497.50 was worth $2141.42 Canadian, and by November 2001, it was worth $2396.00 Canadian dollars, or almost $255.00 CAD more than in 1998!

Unfortunately, the U.S. greenback has been slipping steadily against other currencies since early 2002. As of **April 23rd, 2008** the US dollar is worth only $1.01126 Canadian --- and the drop shows no signs of letting up.

Using the example above, my $1497.50 USD commission check is worth a paltry $1,469.23 CAD in October 2007 - a whopping $926.77 LESS than it was worth in late 2001.

Affiliate marketers in many other parts of the world are facing the same scenario.

Here are some examples of how the US dollar has been performing against various currencies since early 2002.

Those are fairly sizeable drops across the board... and a pretty depressing situation for non-U.S.-based affiliates who earn their incomes in US dollars.

However, there are a couple of things affiliate marketers can do to protect their affiliate income from these disastrous declines.

British Pound
January 2002 - 0.69824 GBP
October 2007 - 0.48984 GBP

Australian Dollar
January 2002 - 1.93418 AUD
October 2007 - 1.11478 AUD

Euro
January 2002 - 1.13226 EUR
October 2007 - 0.70770 EUR

The first option is to work about 40% harder to bolster revenues to 2001 equivalent values. However, because I'm basically lazy, working harder is never my first choice.

The second option involves using foreign exchange rate changes to your advantage by selling products offered by merchants located in your own country, priced in your own currency.

The primary benefit of promoting 'local merchants' is to help your visitors save money by reducing shipping costs and eliminating customs duties on goods imported from the U.S. Basically, most of us prefer to shop locally if we can get the same product at the same or lower price.

Your task then is to find merchants that price products and pay their affiliates in your own currency. That unfortunately is still easier said than done.

The pickings were pretty slim when I searched Google for "Canadian" "affiliate programs."

A site that listed itself as a directory of Canadian affiliate programs - wasn't.

Furthermore, most Canadian merchants that set Canadian dollar prices on their sites, either pay their affiliates in U.S. dollars, or are affiliated with networks that pay affiliates in US dollars.

U.K. affiliates will have an easier time finding U.K.-based merchants that pay in Pounds Sterling.

Check out the the following UK affiliate networks and directories:

- Deal Group Media - http://www.ukaffiliates.com/
- Affiliate Window - http://affiliatewindow.com
- Trade Doubler - http://TradeDoubler.com

Here's something to watch for if you decide to affiliate with merchants who work in your own currency.

At Commission Junction I discovered that if you promote the Canadian Shopping Channel, which sells and pays commission in Canadian dollars, your commissions are first converted to U.S. dollars for CJ's purposes, then back into to Canadian dollars when they deposit the commissions in your Canadian dollar bank account.

You'd lose money each time the commission went through the exchange process.

To avoid being penalized by currency exchanges before the commission hits your bank, I suggest setting up a separate Commission Junction account just for affiliations with your 'local merchants.' Be sure to set the 'functional currency' on that account to your country's currency.

U.S. affiliates can also take advantage of drops in the U.S. dollar by selling for foreign-based merchants. When or if the U.S. dollar drops, you will actually get a raise on each of those promotions.

Expand your reach by taking advantage of any and all opportunities at home and abroad. It is the WORLD-WIDE web after all.

TRANSLATE YOUR SITE

There are substantial foreign markets ready and willing buy the products that you sell, but that won't happen unless they can read and understand your content!

Numerous online and professional translation services are available to translate the text of your site into virtually any language. The most popular online translation service is perhaps AltaVista's BabelFish at http://babelfish.altavista.com/

I wouldn't use the service to translate more than 2 or 3 words phrases unless you don't mind appearing truly weird. For example, I translated the first bit of the 'About Us' page on Roamsters.com from English into French.

The English version reads:

Ed and I have been friends since 1977, or almost 30 years at the time of writing.

When Ed retired in May 2006, I convinced him to get the hell out of the suburban Toronto rat race, and 'move west old man' to my little piece of paradise in the Okanagan Valley of British Columbia.

The French translation worked out to:

L'ED et moi ont été des amis depuis 1977, ou presque 30 ans à l'heure de l'écriture. Quand l'ED s'est retiré en mai 2006, j'ai convaincu lui d'obtenir l'enfer hors de la course suburbian de rat de Toronto, et homme occidental de mouvement de ` le vieil 'à mon petit morceau de paradis dans la vallée d'Okanagan de Colombie britannique.

When I translated that back into English I got:

The ED and I were friends since 1977, or almost 30 years per hour of the writing. When the ED was withdrawn in May 2006, I convinced him to obtain the hell out of the race suburbian of rat of Toronto, and Western man of movement of ` the old one ' with my small piece of paradise in the valley of Okanagan of British Columbia.

I'd suggest that it's perhaps best to pay for a real translation service. ☺

PUT AN AMAZON BOOKSTORE (ASTORE) ON YOUR SITE

When I built the original bookstore on Sage-Hearts.com, it seemed like it took days and days to cut and paste all the book titles and descriptions, download all the images and link all those books back to their appropriate pages on Amazon.

A few years later, I changed all those pages and placed Amazon category ads on them at http://www.sage-hearts.com/books.

However, they don't look that great (see the screenshot below) and I don't even link to them from the rest of the site now.

FIGURE 95 AMAZON ADS

Fortunately, building a bookstore using Amazon has gotten a whole lot easier over the years --- now that they have Amazon aStore.

To use the service you have to be an Amazon Associate, and then you can have up to 100 aStores per Associate account.

The referral fees paid for aStore sales are the same as for the general Amazon associates agreement – 4% under the Classic agreement. If you join now, you are automatically enrolled under the Performance Fee Structure which allows you to earn between 4% to 10%, based on your total number of shipped items from both Amazon and third-party sellers.

Building an aStore from inside the Associates interface is pretty straightforward. It's a step-by-step, page-by-page fill in the blanks system. You can hand pick products for each page, Amazon Listmania lists, and display products that belong to selected Amazon categories or sub-categories.

There are 3 ways to display your aStore. You can link to your store as a standalone site, embed your store using an inline frame or embed it using a frameset.

The screenshot below shows the standalone version of my aStore located at: http://astore.amazon.com/online-dating-20

FIGURE 96 AMAZON aSTORE

ADD A "READY-MADE" CLICKBANK PORTAL

I'm always on the lookout for new income streams that can generate profits without a lot of work.

Unfortunately, most of the 'ready-made' business sites that I've come across to date haven't impressed me as being particularly beneficial for affiliate marketers or visitor-friendly. Most are also much too expensive for what was being offered.

There is one ready-made affiliate marketing business that I do recommend however, and that is CBMall. The 'CB' in CBMall stands for ClickBank, and I love Clickbank! It primarily sells digitally downloadable products, which are the hottest selling products on the 'Net!

Clickbank's own Marketplace is somewhat difficult to sift through if you are looking for good products to sell. CBMall however makes all the best of Clickbank's products easy accessible in one place.

To learn more about CBMall, sign up for Jeff's free eCourse, '15 Powerful Ways CBMall Makes You Money' at http://www.CBMall.com/.

GOOGLE CASHING: AFFILIATE MARKETING WITHOUT A WEB SITE

OK, yes, you can set up an affiliate marketing business without a web site, using a method that has come to be known as "Google Cashing" and is taught by Chris Carpenter in his book "Google Cash." Although I neither teach the method, nor recommend it to affiliate marketers just starting out, I will provide you with a brief 3-point outline of how the strategy works.

1. Join an affiliate program.
2. Create a Google Adwords campaign for the product.
3. Send traffic from Google Adwords directly to the merchant's site with your affiliate link.

This strategy worked very well for thousands of affiliates until Google made changes to its Adwords program to improve the diversity of their search results.

Before the changes were made, multiple affiliates promoting the same product would all send traffic to the exact same page.

A search for the web hosting service 'HostGator' might have returned results similar to those portrayed in *the GOOGLE CASHING EXAMPLE #1* figure shown here to the right.

Surfers get confused when they see four, five and more results that come up all pointing to the same web site, and that makes Google look bad.

So Google changed the rules and now only allows two ads for the same web site to be displayed at any one time.

Sponsored Links

Host Gator - $9.95/mo.
Host Unlimited Sites at **HostGator** -
5GB, 75GB Transfer, Unlimited MySQL
www.HostGator.com ⟵

HostGator Discount Coupon
Save up to $25 on **HostGator**
Host unlimited websites.
www.HostGator.com ⟵

Hostgator Review
Compare **Hostgator** to the leading
web hosting providers. 20 Reviews.
www.HostGator.com ⟵

FIGURE 97 GOOGLE CASHING EXAMPLE #1

A search for "HostGator" returned the results shown in *the GOOGLE CASHING EXAMPLE #2* figure shown right. Notice that surfers are given more options.

Although affiliates may still create campaigns that send traffic to the same page, only those with the best clickthrough rate are displayed in the results.

This policy change posed a challenge for many affiliates who either had to improve their ad clickthrough rates, or drive traffic to a landing page on their site.

FIGURE 98 GOOGLE CASHING EXAMPLE #2

The change was a huge benefit to affiliates who sent their Adwords traffic to their own sites when Adwords prices decreased in most categories, because most of the 'Google Cashers' had their ads dropped from the results. Furthermore, because many also had no clue how to build a web site, they simply disappeared.

Even if you are the best copywriter in the world and can get your 'Google Cashing' ads displayed in the sponsored listings, there is another serious disadvantage to this method. When you send traffic directly to the merchant's site rather than your own, you give up the opportunity to build your list and profit from a relationship with your site's visitors.

Once you have experience selling products from your own web site, you may want to use the "Google Cash" method for testing new products and product categories.

Until then, send traffic to your own site first.

Problem-Solving and Avoidance

Sometimes 'stuff' happens.

Here are some examples of that 'stuff' and some suggestions on how to avoid problems with affiliate programs, your site.

Issues with Affiliate Programs

Rejected applications, terminated affiliations and not getting paid. These are just a few of the things that happen to affiliates from time to time.

Read the following section to find out how to handle (and prevent) issues with affiliate programs.

REJECTED APPLICATIONS

A letter like the one below is very disappointing to receive.

From: Some Merchant
Subject: Sorry, your application was not approved
Date: 2008-01-16 12:31:05.0
Dear Rosalind Gardner,

Thank you for applying to Some Merchant. We regret to inform you that your application was not approved for this program. This is not intended as disapproval of the quality or value of your Web site. Each advertiser determines how many and what types of publishers they will accept in their program for various reasons. You are welcome to apply to other advertiser programs in the Commission Junction network at any time. We apologize for any inconvenience this may cause you.

For assistance, please use the "Support" drop-down menu at the top of this page.

Best regards,
Client Services
Commission Junction

To avoid being on the receiving end of such a letter, be sure to read and understand all the ins and outs of the program you wish to join. Then dot your 'I's' and cross your 'T's' when submitting your application.

Of course, even affiliate managers make mistakes sometimes.

If you think you've received a letter like the one above in error, contact the affiliate program manager and very politely ask why your site was rejected. It's also a good idea to state why you feel your site is a good match for the program.

And now for the good news – I phoned Overture after receiving the above letter, and their program manager immediately reversed the decision.

Although she didn't give much credence to the fact that I spend a ton o' cash with Overture every month, she DID like the promotional methods I planned for their program.

Hey, whatever works.

TERMINATED AFFILIATIONS

Not getting accepted into an affiliate program, for whatever reason, is hard to take, but getting terminated once you are 'in' is even worse.

Dear Rosalind Gardner,

We regret to inform you that you have been dropped from the First PREMIER Bank advertiser program, and you will no longer be affiliated with this advertiser as of 1/23/03. This is not intended as disapproval of the quality or value of your Web site. Each CJ advertiser has the option to determine how many and what types of publishers they will approve to their program, and they may also make changes to their program which warrant removing some of their publishers. In this case, the advertiser has supplied the following reason for removal:

Website volume does not meet minimum requirement of 10,000 visitors/month.

You must remove any banners or links you are hosting on your Web site for this program at your earliest convenience. You are welcome to apply to and to host links from other Commission Junction advertisers at any time. Login to the member area at http://www.cj.com/login.jsp to find our current advertiser programs and to retrieve their links. Commission Junction values your participation in the CJ Network and we apologize for any inconvenience this may cause you.

Please be aware that this decision was not made by Commission Junction but by the advertiser. For assistance, please use the "Support" drop-down menu at the top of the Account Manager.

Best Regards,

Client Services
Commission Junction

OUCH!

That's what happens when you join an affiliate program too soon. When setting up my credit card offers site, I applied early to the best merchants. As luck would have it, Christmas, New Year's and life got in the way, and I did no work at all on the site for almost two months. First PREMIER Bank saw no traffic coming from my site to theirs, so they dropped me from their program.

To avoid having this happen to you, get 90% of your site together before applying to programs. In fact, I recommend that BEFORE applying to a program, write descriptions and endorsements for the products you plan to promote.

Once accepted, all you'll have to do is add your links and use pay-per-click to drive traffic to your site right away. Not only will you build revenue faster, you'll prevent nasty occurrences such as the one above.

5 GOOD REASONS TO DROP THAT PROGRAM!

Sometimes you can't tell until after you've joined a program that it's not going to work out. Here are 5 circumstances that are sufficient cause to drop an affiliate program.

1. PROGRAM SPAM

Although it may seem incredible that an affiliate program manager would spam his or her own affiliates, it does happen.

For that reason, I recommend that you create individual email addresses for the programs that you join and the services you use. For example, at the time you sign up to promote XYZ.com's product, create the address XYZ@mydomain.com.

Spam should never be condoned. If you start receiving spam to that address, drop the program.

2. INSUFFICIENT NOTICE OF PROGRAM CHANGES

Affiliate managers are busy people and everyone makes mistakes from time to time. However, it seems that affiliate managers fail to realize that affiliates too are busy people. Here is a real email that I received on August 28th.

URGENT: Change your links on August 29!

Dear XYZ Associate,

We're about to reveal some very exciting changes this week that will make it easier than ever for you to earn commissions with us! To take advantage of these changes, you must change all the XYZ links on your site on August 29. Please read below for details...

What's going on? We're updating our look and changing our name to better reflect the fun and excitement we know singles are looking for. On August 29, we will become XYZ2.com™!

What's " XYZ2.com™"? XYZ2.com™ will be everything that XYZ.com™ is, but better. We've improved our functionality and made the sign up process even easier. We believe these changes will encourage more of your visitors to become members...and that means higher commissions for you!

What do you have to do? You *MUST* change your banners, tiles and links on August 29, 2001. We will not be able to track or compensate you for members that are generated through old links after that date.

Please visit our Associates area now at http://associates.XYZ2.com and choose from the great new selection of banners, tiles and linking options.

Want to make the most of this exciting change? Since you're changing those old links anyway, we encourage you to review how and where you promote XYZ.com.com on your site. You may want to consider including news about the exciting upgrade from XYZ.com.com to XYZ2.com.com in any newsletters or on your website. This is just the kind of change that gets people interested, and that could translate into increased commissions for you!

Click below to log in to the Associates Program to choose your new links, but please note they will not be functional until August 29th!

See you soon!

XYZ2.com Associates Program.

In effect the program manager wanted his affiliates to change and upload all their new links at exactly midnight on August 29th.

No one goes on vacation during August, right?

Especially NOT in the Northern Hemisphere where this merchant is based. There was absolutely NO chance that affiliates might return from a week-long holiday to discover that they'd paid to send traffic to XYZ.com when their links were no longer valid.

No, not a chance.

This was more than just untimely. It was thoughtless and inconsiderate and more than sufficient cause to drop this program.

3. PROGRAM DOWNTIME

Merchant sites and affiliate tracking goes down from time to time.

However, for affiliates who pay to send traffic to those sites, there is a certain protocol most good affiliate merchants follow. First they tell their affiliates about the outage immediately and then they compensate for lost revenue on the basis of past performance.

Some programs don't play by the 'rules' as shown in the following example.

Hello [Affiliate Name],

The site is back to 100% normal capacity and fully operational. If you stopped sending traffic you can begin sending it heavily again! Thanks tremendously!

CHEERS TO MORE TRAFFIC AND MORE SUCCESS!

Thanks,
CEO XYZSite.com

Back to normal? Stopped sending traffic? Huh? There was NO prior notification sent to affiliates that any trouble existed with the site. Although the company apologized for their 'oversight,' they didn't offer to compensate affiliates who lost out when they couldn't change their links in the nick of time.

If you ever receive a notice such as the one above, contact the affiliate program manager and demand compensation on the basis of past performance. If he or she does not respond in your favor, drop the program.

4. CUSTOMER COMPLAINTS

Do you get repeated complaints about a specific product, service or merchant?

If you have a good relationship with the Affiliate Program manager, pass your visitors comments along. Good merchants and managers will listen and make the needed improvements.

If they don't, drop the program. It's your reputation that is at stake when you recommend poor products to your visitors.

5. LATE OR NON-PAYMENT

Keep track of your affiliate program earnings and the checks as they arrive.

If a check is slow to arrive, contact the affiliate program manager and let them know. If the payments are often slow to arrive, it may be best to drop the program.

It is very rare that you will come across a merchant who fails to pay his affiliates.

If you have been cheated out of commissions, contact the Better Business Bureau. Take screenshots of the affiliate interface that shows what you are owed. Then do other affiliates a favor and post your experience in the popular affiliate forums. Name names and put the 'bad guys' out of business.

In summary, I've joined, then dropped and later re-joined a program after improvements were made to either the product or the program. Don't hesitate to do the same. After all, it's YOUR money!

Issues with Webmasters & Other Affiliates

Thievery occurs on the web much as it does in 'real-world' retail stores, only perhaps more frequently and with fewer calls to justice --- unfortunately.

But knowledge is power, so in this section you'll learn how to catch thieves that will copy and steal your content and how to avoid commission theft.

HAS YOUR CONTENT BEEN COPIED (STOLEN)?

Sometimes you will find webmasters who like your web site SO much that they decide to copy the whole thing. For example, the figure below is a screen capture of a webmaster who requested a clone made of Sage-Hearts.com through Scriptlance.

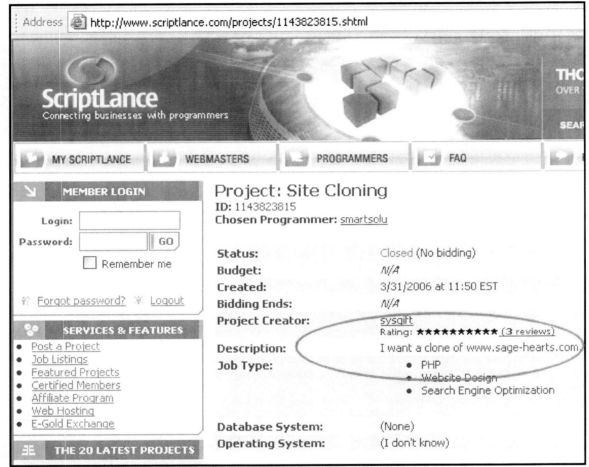

FIGURE 99 WEBMASTERS THAT STEAL

From time to time you'll stumble across a webmaster who has published an article of yours on his or her site without including the link to your site.

Cloning and copying sites and content is theft, pure and simple. You must be on the lookout for webmasters that steal your content and have them shut down as soon as possible. No one should be permitted to profit from your hard work. Furthermore, you don't want to suffer a duplicate content penalty by virtue of someone else's thievery.

If contact information is available on their site, I contact the webmaster and politely ask them to either include the URL to my site or to remove my article. Most, but not all, will comply with the request.

For those who don't, I sometimes trust karma to do its magic and chock it up as 'the cost of doing business.'

HOW TO CATCH A THIEF

The easiest way to catch thieves is to plant special words and phrases in your articles and on your site that only you would use. Then search for those phrases on Google.

For example, my 'About Us' page (http://sage-hearts.com/about_us.html) at Sage-Hearts.com begins with the paragraph:

"Our webmaster, site designer, writer, proof reader, editor, publisher, graphics and animation artist, site reviewer, 'feature sites' judge and jury, marketing specialist, traffic analyst; chief cook, bottle washer and keyboard duster all welcome you to our little corner of the World Wide Web."

That paragraph was written in 1998, and should be quite unique on the Web. Yet it is amazing how many other sites have that paragraph on their 'About Us' pages.

EXAMPLE OF STOLEN SITE CONTENT

The 'AFFILIATE THIEVES - MY SITE' *screenshot* to the right shows a corner of the 'About Us' page on Sage-Hearts.com with the cursor over the word 'here.'

You can see that the link to the 'Webmasters' page at http://sage-hearts.com/webmasters/ shows up in the status bar.

Now look at the *AFFILIATE THIEVES - THIEF'S SITE* screenshot, taken from the "About Us" page on meet-date-love.com.

When the cursor is over the word 'here' it also links to the 'Webmasters' page on Sage-Hearts.com!

THIEF!!!

It seems that Vesko - meet-date-love.com's webmaster – is also 'LOVIN' THE WEB' (all in CAPS). ☺

Actually, Vesko had stolen the entire site design from Sage-Hearts.com (an older version of the site) and in many cases, had forgotten to change my affiliate links to his own.

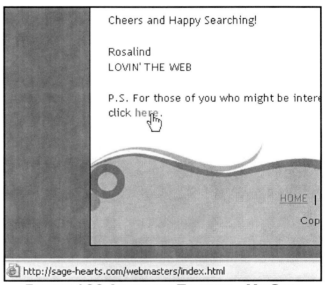

FIGURE 100 AFFILIATE THIEVES - MY SITE

FIGURE 101 AFFILIATE THIEF'S SITE

HOW TO STOP A THIEF

The AFFILIATE THIEF GETS SUSPENDED figure below shows what happened to an affiliate who cloned Sage-Hearts.com. Unfortunately for Vesko, I know the affiliate managers for all my dating site programs, so I just call them and tell them about the thief.

The affiliate managers are familiar with my site, so they can immediately see that the content and site design are copied.

Affiliate Suspended

You received this message because you were most likely directed to Adult FriendFinder by one of our affiliates who was using marketing or advertising methods that are in violation of our Terms of Use and Affiliate Agreement.

The person who directed you to our site has been banned from doing business with us. We apologize for any inconvenience that the offending activity may have caused.

FIGURE 102 AFFILIATE THIEF GETS SUSPENDED

They then cancel the thief's affiliation with their program.

What is more fun, however, is having the thief's site shut down completely. To get a thief's site shut down, first do a Whois Lookup at Whois.net.

The 'STOP A THIEF: WHOIS.NET LOOKUP' screenshot to the right shows Whois information for DatingFox.com, which was an exact clone of an older version of Sage-Hearts.com.

The Whois results lists the ISP that hosts the site.

In this case, the site was hosted by Yahoo!

Contact the ISP, and include information about your site, which will have an earlier domain registration date.

Include the links for pages on your site that have been copied, along with links to the copied pages on the thief's site.

```
WHOIS information for datingfox.com:

[whois.melbourneit.com]

Domain Name......... datingfox.com
  Creation Date........ 2005-12-18
  Registration Date.... 2005-12-18
  Expiry Date.......... 2006-12-18
  Organisation Name....
  Organisation Address.
  Organisation Address.
  Organisation Address.
  Organisation Address.
  Organisation Address.
  Organisation Address.

Admin Name..........
  Admin Address.......
  Admin Address.......
  Admin Address.......
  Admin Address.......
  Admin Address.......
  Admin Email.........
  Admin Phone.........
  Admin Fax...........

Tech Name............ YahooDomains TechContact
  Tech Address......... 701 First Ave.
  Tech Address.........
  Tech Address......... Sunnyvale
  Tech Address......... 94089
  Tech Address......... CA
  Tech Address......... UNITED STATES
```

FIGURE 103 WHOIS.NET LOOKUP

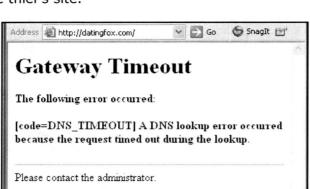

Address http://datingfox.com/ ▼ ⮞ Go ⓢ SnagIt 🔳

Gateway Timeout

The following error occurred:

[code=DNS_TIMEOUT] A DNS lookup error occurred because the request timed out during the lookup.

Please contact the administrator.

FIGURE 104 THIEF GETS SHUT DOWN

In most cases, a Gateway Timeout on the domain (see *the* THIEF GETS SHUT DOWN screenshot to the left) will be the happy result of your efforts.

3 WAYS TO PREVENT COMMISSION THEFT

There are two types of commission thieves - consumers and other affiliates.

Consumers steal affiliate commissions by removing an affiliate's ID from the URL prior to clicking through to the site. It baffles (and cheeses) me that consumers would deprive an affiliate of their rightful commission. As it costs them no more money to buy through the affiliate, I must assume that these folks are inherently mean-spirited.

How do they change the URL to cheat the affiliate?

Well, for example, my affiliate URL for the FriendFinder's dating site is http://friendfinder.com/go/g9517. Surfers see that URL in their browser status bar when they place their cursor over the link as shown in the figure on the right.

To prevent credit going to my link, a surfer could type FriendFinder's main URL, http://friendfinder.com directly into their browser's address window.

Or, they could right-click the link, then copy and paste it into the address window and remove the "*go/9517*" portion of the link before they clickthrough to the site.

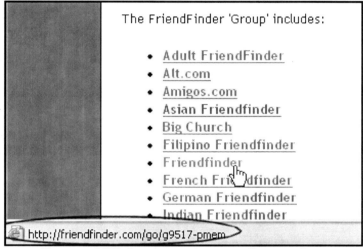

FIGURE 105 AFFILIATE LINK IN STATUS BAR

Other affiliate marketers use basically the same technique. However, they swap your affiliate ID for their own affiliate ID to get the commission when they buy the product. In effect, they are discounting their own purchase.

Responsible merchants have systems in place to prevent this type of commission theft. However, most merchants do not, so it's up to you as an affiliate to protect your commissions.

To overcome affiliate commission theft, here are 3 ways you can try to beat the cheats.

1. USE 'ONMOUSEOVER' CODE

The first method is to use an 'onMouseOver' script in your affiliate links. What this does is to show text of your choosing in the status bar when someone places his or her cursor over your link. Here's an example of the HTML:

FIGURE 106 ONMOUSEOVER LINKS

```
<a
href="http://friendfinder.com/go/
g9517-pmem"
onMouseOver="window.status='ht
tp://friendfinder.com'; return true
" onMouseOut="window.status='';
return true ">FriendFinder</a>
```

Now, when a visitor cursors over the link to FriendFinder, 'http://friendfinder.com" is displayed in the status bar without the affiliate ID attached.

Unfortunately, your affiliate link can still be seen when it's right-clicked, so in the next section you'll learn how to prevent visitors from seeing your affiliate ID when they right-click on your links.

2. DISABLE RIGHT-CLICK SCRIPT

Here's the script that that pops a message when a visitor tries to see your link coding by right-clicking on your links.

Put the following script in the Head of your page:

```
<script language="Javascript1.2">
// Set the message for the alert box
am = "This function is disabled!";

// do not edit below this line
// ===========================
bV  = parseInt(navigator.appVersion)
bNS = navigator.appName=="Netscape"
bIE = navigator.appName=="Microsoft Internet Explorer"

function nrc(e) {
if (bNS && e.which > 1){
    alert(am)
    return false
  } else if (bIE && (event.button >1)) {
    alert(am)
    return false;
  }
}
document.onmousedown = nrc;
if (document.layers) window.captureEvents(Event.MOUSEDOWN);
```

```
if (bNS && bV<5) window.onmousedown = nrc;

</script>
```

To change the message "This function is disabled!," simply replace it with whatever text you prefer in the script above.

Once again, this isn't a perfect method. To see the link coding on a right-click disabled page, all one needs to do is use "View Source" and look at the HTML page source.

3. USE AFFILIATE LINK CLOAKING SOFTWARE

None of these methods is foolproof, however. It doesn't take a rocket scientist to find the links hidden by redirection scripts or right-click disablers. A good solution is affiliate link cloaking software available at AffiliateLinkCloaker.com and it is very easy to use.

You simply input the affiliate link that you want to hide in the software, then name and save the page (i.e. cloaker.html), and upload it to your server.

Furthermore, when using other methods to try and hide affiliate links, your affiliate ID may still show up in the address window of the browser. With this software, it looks like you sent your visitor to a page on your site.

Avoid LONG Links in Email Messages

Sometimes, your affiliate links are so long that they may be 'broken' by the time they get to the recipient. For example, my '1ShoppingCart' affiliate link is:

http://www.1shoppingcart.com/app/default.asp?pr=1&id=63306

Some email programs may wrap the line and the second part of the URL is no longer linked as in the following example:

http://www.1shoppingcart.com/app/
default.asp?pr=1&id=63306

The recipient clicks on the first part of the link and gets a 'Page Cannot be Found' error, which diminishes their trust in you immediately and you may lose the sale.

In this case you may want to use the TinyUrl.com service. I turned my '1 Shopping Cart' link above into http://tinyurl.com/s6nd4. I recommend using this service sparingly however, i.e., don't plaster your site full of tiny URL's. If *their* site ever goes down, *your* site won't be making any money!

25 Mistakes to Avoid as an Affiliate

We all make mistakes, which is nothing to be ashamed of or worried about. But many mistakes can easily be avoided when we learn from the mistakes of others.

Here are the 25 most common mistakes made by affiliate marketers.

1. **Spamming** - Spam is unsolicited email. As well as not asking to receive it, the recipient has every right to contact the sender's ISP or the merchant involved in the offer, both of which will likely terminate their association immediately. Watch out for unrealistic email promotions that offer deals for 'leads,' i.e. $99.95 for 500M emails. Sending email to those addresses is spamming pure and simple.

2. **Posting Ads on Forums** – Forums and discussion boards can be good sources of information about Internet and affiliate marketing. Akin to spamming however, posting advertising on message boards gets the poster banned. Avoid acting in ways that upset the board owners.

3. **Not Doing Market Research** - Promoting products that people don't want is a futile endeavor. Test the waters before investing time and money into any new project.

4. **Overusing Merchant Ad Copy** - Successful affiliates set themselves apart from other affiliates promoting the same products. When you use advertising copy prepared by the merchants you're not giving your visitors any new information.

5. **Copyright Infringing** - How would you feel if you found an exact copy of your site on someone else's domain? With that reaction in mind, treat others' work with the same respect. Always ask permission to use graphic images or text found on another site.

6. **Submitting to FFA's** – Posting to FFA (Free for All) sites is a waste of time because your site will never get seen. Worse, because most FFA's have such low rankings, your own site's rankings may decrease by association.

7. **SHOUTING** - Other than using caps to give emphasis to a few words within an email or on a web page, refrain from using capital letters. Using all capital letters in text or correspondence is symbolic of shouting, and shouting at people just makes them leave.

8. **Not Responding to Visitor eMails** - If a visitor emails a question to an affiliate, and that affiliate doesn't reply in a timely manner, the visitor will go elsewhere for an answer and will become someone else's customer.

9. **Overusing Pop-Ups** - Getting hit by multiple pop-ups is annoying. Many surfers will close their browser completely rather than close 20 different windows and when they close your page, no sale is made.

10. **Using Free Hosting & Email Accounts** – Would you buy a car from a street vendor? Using free hosting and email accounts looks cheesy and impedes your ability to sell.

11. **Failure to Plan** - As the old saying goes, 'Fail to plan, plan to fail.' Without a map a journey into unknown territory takes much longer, costs more money and may get you lost. Simplify the project by having a plan.

12. **Not Having an Opt-in Newsletter** - Without an opt-in list, your visitors come, and then they go. You have no way to contact them again. Those who sign up to receive your newsletters or ads are telling you that they're interested in the products you offer. That's like having a license to print money!

13. **Keeping Poor or No Records** - Did that check from XYZ Company arrive? Was the amount correct? If your record keeping is less than accurate, you might never know. Don't get cheated - keep track of all your business activities.

14. **Building a Mall** - Mall sites don't get much search engine traffic, and they don't convert to sales. Highly focused theme sites attract traffic AND sales.

15. **Advertising Offline** - Most people don't jump off the couch and run to their computer to type in a URL that they see in the newspaper or magazines, so paying to advertise offline (as an affiliate) is generally a waste of money.

16. **Banner Ad Farming** - Informative text results in purchases. Lengthy pages of animated graphic banners ads simply soak up bandwidth.

17. **Competition Bashing** - Speaking ill of others only gives the basher a bad reputation. Mind your own business and do your own business.

18. **Advertising Product Prices** - Prices change all the time. With the exception of current price quotes placed in your newsletter, product prices do not belong on your site.

19. **Out-of-Date Advertising** - Banners or text links that expire are guaranteed to eventually send your visitor to a broken link or show a broken graphic on your page. Time sensitive advertising is best used only in email advertising campaigns.

20. **Using 'Leaky' Links** - Do you take money out of your wallet and throw it away? That's exactly what you are doing when you pay for traffic and then send visitors to another site through anything other than affiliate links.

21. **Placing Affiliate Links on the Homepage** – Putting affiliate links on your homepage is like showing visitors in the front door and immediately out the back. Give them a chance to browse, sign up for your newsletter and decide that they'd like to come back to your place before introducing them to your very attractive friends.

22. **Trying to Do it All** – Don't be a 'Jack-of-all-trades' and master of none. Hire an expert when required and save your time and money.

23. **Not Investing in Education** - Technology changes with amazing speed. Keep up on this rapidly evolving industry through research and education. Materials and courses are a tax write-off, and will pay you back many times over in additional revenue.

24. **Failing to Act** - The first step may be the hardest, but if you never act, you'll never enjoy the rewards!

25. **Giving Up** – Just as Rome wasn't built in a day, don't expect overnight riches from the 'Net. Enjoy the process, know that some days will be more challenging than others and keep going. Persistence is the single most important factor in determining success online or off. Be persistent and be successful!

Save yourself considerable frustration. Keep the 25 mistakes above in mind as you read this book and build your site and you'll be well on your way to becoming a successful affiliate marketer.

Bonus Tips, Scripts and Wrap-Up

How to Add Google Adsense Code to Your Blog

For the purposes of this example, we will be working with the Default Wordpress theme that was installed with your blog and installing the Adsense code to the Sidebar.

MAKE YOUR THEME FILES WRITEABLE

To place Google Adsense ad units on your site, first we'll have to make sure that your blog's theme files are writeable.

Login to your Wordpress administration panel and click on 'Presentation' then 'Theme Editor' in the sub-panel.

On the right side of the *Theme Editor* page, all the theme files are listed and linked.

Click on 'Sidebar.'

Scroll to the bottom of the page, and if you see the comment '*If this file were writable you could edit it*,' you will have to set file permissions on that file to **666** using either FTP or cPanel.

> 'WordPress Default' theme files
>
> Stylesheet
>
> rtl.css
>
> Footer
>
> 404 Template
>
> Search Results
>
> attachment.php
>
> Popup Comments

I recommend that you make all the main templates (e.g. Main Index Template, Single Post, Header, Footer, Page, Archives, Comments, etc.) writeable to save time later.

GOOGLE ADSENSE SIGNUP AND SETUP

One your template files are writeable, the next step is to sign up for a Google Adsense account at https://www.google.com/adsense.

Once you've signed up, login to your account and click on the 'Adsense Setup' tab.

Next, click the 'AdSense for Content' link on the resulting page.

FIGURE 107 ADSENSE SETUP

On the next page, find the 'Single page' link and click on that to display all the components on one page.

AD UNIT OR LINK UNIT?

Now, choose whether you want to display an ad unit or a link unit, each of which is shown below.

FIGURE 108 ADSENSE AD UNIT

FIGURE 109 ADSENSE LINK UNIT

CHOOSE YOUR AD FORMAT AND COLOR PALETTE

Ad formats include horizontal, vertical and square with sizes that range from 728 x 90 leaderboards to 125 X 125 pixel buttons.

To see what all the ad formats look like, go to:
https://www.google.com/adsense/static/en_US/AdFormats.html

Then choose from a variety of **color palettes** or create your own to match your site colors as I've done at http://roamsters.com/. Notice how the Google Adwords *ad units* displayed at both the top of the main content area and the *link units* displayed on the right sidebar near the bottom.

PUBLIC SERVICE ADS?

Now you will choose whether to display **Public Service Ads**, show non-Google ads from another URL or to fill the space with a solid color if no relevant ads are available. I personally always elect to show the Public Service Ads.

Next, you will choose your ad channel, or add an ad channel if this is your first time using the Google Adsense setup.

ADD A CHANNEL

To add a channel, click on '**Add a Channel**' and a pop-up window will appear into which you'll enter a name for your channel. In this case, I called the channel 'Test Blog.' If I plan to place more than one instance of Adsense on a site, then I will name the Channels according to their placement on the page, i.e. Test Blog Top, Test Blog Side, etc.

GET YOUR CODE

The last step is to **get your code**, which will appear in a box at the bottom of the page and look something as it appears in the *Your Adsense Code* screenshot shown here to the right.

Your AdSense code:

```
<script type="text/javascript"><!--
google_ad_client = "pub-                  ";
google_ad_width = 728;
google_ad_height = 90;
google_ad_format = "728x90_as";
google_ad_type = "text";
//2007-10-07: Roamsters - Bottom
google_ad_channel = "               ";
google_color_border = "CCCCCC";
google_color_bg = "F7F7F7";
google_color_link = "7F7F7F";
google_color_text = "333333";
```

<< Back to AdSense Setup

FIGURE 110 YOUR ADSENSE CODE

Will PPC Advertising be Profitable in YOUR Niche?

Determining whether pay-per-click advertising will prove profitable for certain categories with your niche is an inexact science, yet the following method gives me an indication of whether the topic has profit potential before I do any more work.

So, let's say you are interested in promoting online dating services for single parents.

In the following example, you'll see how I use an Excel spreadsheet to calculate profitability.

You can use a piece of paper and a calculator, but using a spreadsheet makes the job *so* much easier.

After collecting keywords and phrases relevant to your topic using Wordtracker, open a new spreadsheet and label Column A 'Keywords' and Column B 'Demand,' as shown in the next screenshot.

> **HELPFUL RESOURCE**
>
> If you are new to Excel and want more detailed instruction on its use than is offered below, I recommend Richard Kraneis' ebook, 'The World's Shortest Excel Book' at:
>
> http://www.TheWorldsShortestExcelBook.com/

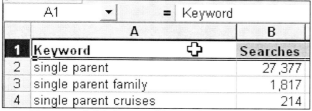

FIGURE 111 LABEL YOUR SPREADSHEET

Paste the keywords into Column A (under the heading 'Keywords') in your Spreadsheet.

Next, paste the predicted number of searches into Column B.

To get the predicted number of monthly searches, you'll have to multiply the results by 30.

FIGURE 112 CALCULATE TOTALS

Type the word 'Totals" at the bottom of the keyword list. I had 24 keywords in my list.

To calculate the total number of searches, I input the formula "=sum(b2:b24)" into the cell to the right of the cell containing the word "Totals", leaving out the quotations.

That tells the spreadsheet to add up all the numbers in the column from cell 'B2' to 'B24.' So if you had 399 keywords in your list, the formula would be "=sum(b2:b400)," which takes the row of headers into account.

If your totals don't show up correctly, you'll need to format the column of cells containing the number of searches.

To do that, select the cells to be formatted then right click and select 'Format Cells'.

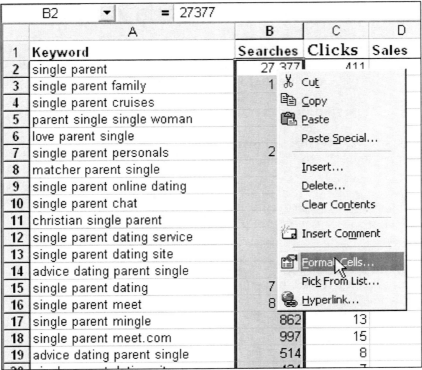

FIGURE 113 ADDING TOTAL SEARCHES

A new window like the one in the screenshot to the right will open.

Choose 'Number' and zero decimal places.

Likewise, when you are dealing with dollar figures, choose 'Currency' from the list, and set it to 2 decimal places.

When dealing with currency, you will also have the option to add the dollar sign ($), although I find that makes the sheet look over-crowded.

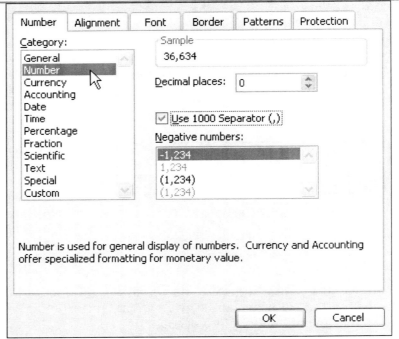

FIGURE 114 INPUT DOLLAR SIGNS

Next, label the following columns 'Clicks,' 'Sales,' 'Comm.,' 'PPC$' and 'Net' - in that order.

In the cell below each heading, input the formulae as shown in the table below. Hit 'Enter' when you are finished typing into each cell.

C	D	E	F	G
Clicks	Sales	Comm.	PPC$	Net
=Sum(b2*.01)	=Sum(c2*.015)	=Sum(d2*20)	=Sum(c*.06)	=Sum(e2-f2)

So, what the heck does all that mean?

Well, in the formulae above, I base my assumptions about sales and conversion rates on industry averages. Your own results may be much higher. Here are explanations for how I derive each formula.

	Formula	Excel Formula
Clicks (Clickthroughs) Assumes an average 1% clickthrough rate from pay per click search engines. My own rates vary from a low of 1% for keywords positioned very low in the listings to almost 30%.	Demand x .010	=Sum(b2*.010)
Sales Numbers Assumes a 1.5-percent conversion rate from clicks (visitors) from PPC engines to sales on the merchant site. Between 1 and 2 percent is a fairly typical conversion rate for affiliates. Super affiliates do MUCH better than one and a half percent however with highly targeted ads and relevant landing pages.	Clickthroughs x .015	=Sum(c2*.015)
Comm. (Commission) The number of sales x $20.00 per sale. (based on my own commission averages. At this point in your research, that number is still hypothetical. We'll find out later when we do research into affiliate programs and products how much average commissions are likely to be.	Number of Sales x $20.00	=Sum(d2*20)
PPC$ (PPC Cost) - The number of clickthroughs multiplied by 6 cents. This is an arbitrary number based on my own experience with PPC's, and is averaged across multiple pay per click search engine advertising campaigns.	Clickthroughs x $0.06	=Sum(c2*.06)
Net (Net Profit) The amount you can take to the bank.	Comm. minus PPC Cost	=Sum(e2-f2)

Once the formulae are entered, you'll have values in each column in Row 2 beside the first keyword. To get answers for all the other keywords, click in the cell under "Clicks."

	A	B	C	
	C2 ▾ = =SUM(B2*0.01)			
1	Keyword	Searches	Clicks	Sa
2	single parent	27,377	274	
3	single parent family	1,817		
4	single parent cruises	214		

FIGURE 115 CALCULATE CLICKS

Place your cursor over the little black square, then click and drag it all the way down to the row of 'Totals,' as shown in the screenshot below.

	A	B	C	
	C2 ▾ = =SUM(B2*0.01)			
1	Keyword	Searches	Clicks	Sal
2	single parent	27,377	274	
3	single parent family	1,817	18	
4	single parent cruises	214	2	
5	parent single single woman	234	2	
6	love parent single	241	2	
7	single parent personals	2,496	25	
8	matcher parent single	326	3	
9	single parent online dating	348	3	
10	single parent chat	359	4	
11	christian single parent	366	4	
12	single parent dating service	377	4	
13	single parent dating site	434	4	
14	advice dating parent single	514	5	
15	single parent dating	7,120	71	
16	single parent meet	8,374	84	
17	single parent mingle	862	9	
18	single parent meet.com	997	10	
19	advice dating parent single	514	5	
20	single parent dating site	434	4	
21	single parent dating service	377	4	
22	single parent online dating	348	3	
23	christian dating parent single	188	2	
24	single parent dating web site	188	2	
25	Totals	54,505	545	
26				

FIGURE 116 ADDING UP ALL THE CLICKS

Now do the same for each of the columns under 'Sales,' 'Comm.,' 'PPC$' and 'Net,' and end up with a table filled in like the one below.

	A	B	C	D	E	F	G
	A25 ▼ = Totals						
1	Keyword	Searches	Clicks	Sales	Comm.	PPC	Net
2	single parent	27,377	274	4	82.13	16.43	65.70
3	single parent family	1,817	18	0	5.45	1.09	4.36
4	single parent cruises	214	2	0	0.64	0.13	0.51
5	parent single single woman	234	2	0	0.70	0.14	0.56
6	love parent single	241	2	0	0.72	0.14	0.58
7	single parent personals	2,496	25	0	7.49	1.50	5.99
8	matcher parent single	326	3	0	0.98	0.20	0.78
9	single parent online dating	348	3	0	1.04	0.21	0.84
10	single parent chat	359	4	0	1.08	0.22	0.86
11	christian single parent	366	4	0	1.10	0.22	0.88
12	single parent dating service	377	4	0	1.13	0.23	0.90
13	single parent dating site	434	4	0	1.30	0.26	1.04
14	advice dating parent single	514	5	0	1.54	0.31	1.23
15	single parent dating	7,120	71	1	21.36	4.27	17.09
16	single parent meet	8,374	84	1	25.12	5.02	20.10
17	single parent mingle	862	9	0	2.59	0.52	2.07
18	single parent meet.com	997	10	0	2.99	0.60	2.39
19	advice dating parent single	514	5	0	1.54	0.31	1.23
20	single parent dating site	434	4	0	1.30	0.26	1.04
21	single parent dating service	377	4	0	1.13	0.23	0.90
22	single parent online dating	348	3	0	1.04	0.21	0.84
23	christian dating parent single	188	2	0	0.56	0.11	0.45
24	single parent dating web site	188	2	0	0.56	0.11	0.45
25	Totals	54,505	545	8	163.52	32.70	130.81

FIGURE 117 PROJECTING INCOME #1

Our projected net profit for one month would be $130.81, but don't be discouraged! Remember that that doesn't factor in traffic from free sources, such as free search engines, or sales from your newsletter.

Too, once your research is complete, you will have hundreds and hundreds, if not thousands, of keywords in your list, all contributing to increase your traffic.

Those projections are also based on industry averages, and as I've mentioned before, your results can be much higher than the industry averages – *especially* when you follow all the advice in the Super Affiliate Handbook. ☺

Actually, $174.09 per month for one little niche – based on only 24 keyword phrases - is looking pretty good.

As mentioned above, I felt that both the PPC clickthrough and conversion to sales rates were low. What happens when we increase those numbers?

If we increase our projected PPC clickthrough rate to 2%, (changing the formula in the 'Clicks' column to =SUM(B2*0.02), we come up with the following results:

37	Clicks 2%						
38	Keyword	Searches	Clicks	Sales	Comm.	PPC	Net
39	single parent	27,377	548	8	164.26	32.85	131.41
40	single parent family	1,817	36	1	10.90	2.18	8.72
41	single parent cruises	214	4	0	1.28	0.26	1.03
42	parent single single woman	234	5	0	1.40	0.28	1.12
43	love parent single	241	5	0	1.45	0.29	1.16
44	single parent personals	2,496	50	1	14.98	3.00	11.98
45	matcher parent single	326	7	0	1.96	0.39	1.56
46	single parent online dating	348	7	0	2.09	0.42	1.67
47	single parent chat	359	7	0	2.15	0.43	1.72
48	christian single parent	366	7	0	2.20	0.44	1.76
49	single parent dating service	377	8	0	2.26	0.45	1.81
50	single parent dating site	434	9	0	2.60	0.52	2.08
51	advice dating parent single	514	10	0	3.08	0.62	2.47
52	single parent dating	7,120	142	2	42.72	8.54	34.18
53	single parent meet	8,374	167	3	50.24	10.05	40.20
54	single parent mingle	862	17	0	5.17	1.03	4.14
55	single parent meet.com	997	20	0	5.98	1.20	4.79
56	advice dating parent single	514	10	0	3.08	0.62	2.47
57	single parent dating site	434	9	0	2.60	0.52	2.08
58	single parent dating service	377	8	0	2.26	0.45	1.81
59	single parent online dating	348	7	0	2.09	0.42	1.67
60	christian dating parent single	188	4	0	1.13	0.23	0.90
61	single parent dating web site	188	4	0	1.13	0.23	0.90
62	Totals	54,505	1090	16	327.03	65.41	261.62

FIGURE 118 PROJECTING INCOME #2

That's better! Now we're up to $261.62 in projected earnings for the month. Now let's see what happens if our conversion rate increases to 3%.

75	Conversion 3%						
76	Keyword	Searches	Clicks	Sales	Comm.	PPC	Net
77	single parent	27,377	548	16	328.52	32.85	295.67
78	single parent family	1,817	36	1	21.80	2.18	19.62
79	single parent cruises	214	4	0	2.57	0.26	2.31
80	parent single single woman	234	5	0	2.81	0.28	2.53
81	love parent single	241	5	0	2.89	0.29	2.60
82	single parent personals	2,496	50	1	29.95	3.00	26.96
83	matcher parent single	326	7	0	3.91	0.39	3.52
84	single parent online dating	348	7	0	4.18	0.42	3.76
85	single parent chat	359	7	0	4.31	0.43	3.88
86	christian single parent	366	7	0	4.39	0.44	3.95
87	single parent dating service	377	8	0	4.52	0.45	4.07
88	single parent dating site	434	9	0	5.21	0.52	4.69
89	advice dating parent single	514	10	0	6.17	0.62	5.55
90	single parent dating	7,120	142	4	85.44	8.54	76.90
91	single parent meet	8,374	167	5	100.49	10.05	90.44
92	single parent mingle	862	17	1	10.34	1.03	9.31
93	single parent meet.com	997	20	1	11.96	1.20	10.77
94	advice dating parent single	514	10	0	6.17	0.62	5.55
95	single parent dating site	434	9	0	5.21	0.52	4.69
96	single parent dating service	377	8	0	4.52	0.45	4.07
97	single parent online dating	348	7	0	4.18	0.42	3.76
98	christian dating parent single	188	4	0	2.26	0.23	2.03
99	single parent dating web site	188	4	0	2.26	0.23	2.03
100	Totals	54,505	1090	33	654.06	65.41	588.65

FIGURE 119 PROJECTING INCOME #3

Projected net profits of $588.65 for one tiny niche - now we're talking! Without factoring in free traffic, which will increase your earnings, that's very respectable.

Remember that we are considering only profit **POTENTIAL**. There are no guarantees that our actual results will be as successful. They may in fact be MORE successful.

Only real-world testing will prove if your projections are realistic.

"Limes are Greener" Google Adwords Keyword Strategy

Unlike Yahoo! Search Marketing, Google Adwords allows advertisers to bid on keywords for products that they don't sell.

For example, the *How Surfers are Misled* screenshot shows the Google Sponsored Link results for the term "eHarmony."

Notice how both PerfectMatch.com and AdultFriendFinder.com are at the top of the Sponsored Links. As a matter of fact, eHarmony.com wasn't listed in the Sponsored Links at all!

FIGURE 120 HOW SURFERS ARE MISLED

Here is another example.

The results shown in *More Misleading Ads on Google* screenshot were returned by a search for "FriendFinder."

Although AdultFriendFinder.com, one of the "Friendfinder" services shows up in the Sponsored Links, it is linked to PerfectMatch.com.

More importantly, notice how PerfectMatch.com uses the term "Friendfinder" in its ad title.

Although this tactic contravenes Google's editorial guidelines, repeated efforts by many advertisers have been unsuccessful in having this type of advertising changed or removed.

FIGURE 121 MORE MISLEADING ADS ON GOOGLE

The following table cites Google's editorial guidelines for advertisers as they apply to relevant keywords and ad text.

The full text is available at https://adwords.google.com/select/guidelines.html:

Your keywords and ad text must be relevant to your site, products, or services.

Write Accurate Ad Text

Your ad text and keywords must directly relate to the content on the landing page for your ad.

Distinguish your ad by including your company name, line of business, or product in your ad text or title.

If you offer a local service or product, clearly indicate your location in your ad text.

Example:

If your alterations business only services New York, you should include "New York" in your ad text, mention your company's particular specialty, "experts in reweaving fine garments," and link to a page that displays this service.

Target Specific Keywords

Use specific keywords that accurately reflect your site.
Use keywords that reflect your location if you offer a location-specific product or service.

Example:

A New York apartment rental agency would not be allowed to run on only the keyword "rentals." The agency would have to use keywords such as "New York rental agency" or "NY apartments."

Quite frankly, the fact that Google chooses to disregard their own guidelines cheeses me greatly.

However, as the old saying goes, "When you have lemons, make lemonade."

So, what is an affiliate to do?

First of all, I do NOT recommend that you use the keyword in the title (as shown in the second example above) if you do *not* in fact promote Friendfinder's product.

Someone looking for 'Friendfinder' may be surprised and disappointed to arrive 'by accident' at PerfectMatch.com instead.

Worse, while you may convince some visitors to buy a PerfectMatch.com membership, in all likelihood people who are looking for FriendFinder WANT Friendfinder, therefore you are just wasting money with this type of advertising.

What I DO recommend is a 'Limes are Greener' approach.

For example, if you promote limes, go ahead and bid on the term 'lemons.' Create an ad that explains why surfers should choose limes instead of lemons as shown in the sample below.

The other approach I recommend is to do an honest review of the product that you do *not* promote, i.e. Friendfinder.

At the end of the product review make a strong recommendation for an alternative, the product you do promote, i.e., PerfectMatch.com.

Lemons

Find the freshest lemons at LemonyLemon.com.
www.LemonyLemon.com

Greener than Lemons

Tastier and more nutritious than lemons. Eat limes for health.
www.LimesareGreener.com

FIGURE 122 'LIMES ARE GREENER' PPC TACTIC

In this case, it is perfectly acceptable to include the keyword in your Google Adwords ad as follows:

Using my 'Limes are Greener' approach in your Google Adwords campaigns will increase exposure to your merchants' products *and* increase your sales.

MAXIMIZE PPC PROFITS: "BEEF UP" YOUR KEYWORD LISTS

To use the 'Limes are Greener' approach and to maximize your pay-per-click advertising profits, you must think outside the box when you build your keyword lists.

For example, I run over 4000 keywords and keyword phrases, across several different pay-per-click search engines, in my dating niche.

Some keywords that I started advertising back in 1998 have never had a competitor and are still 'grand-fathered' at Yahoo! Search Marketing for just 5 cents per click. One of those phrases brings in more than 1000 visitors per month and there are several hundred that get 100's of clicks for rock-bottom prices.

When I first started building really big lists I used to jot notes on a yellow legal pad until my hand got tired. Luckily I discovered Wordtracker, which is discussed in more detail in the Do Keyword Research to Assess Market Demand section.

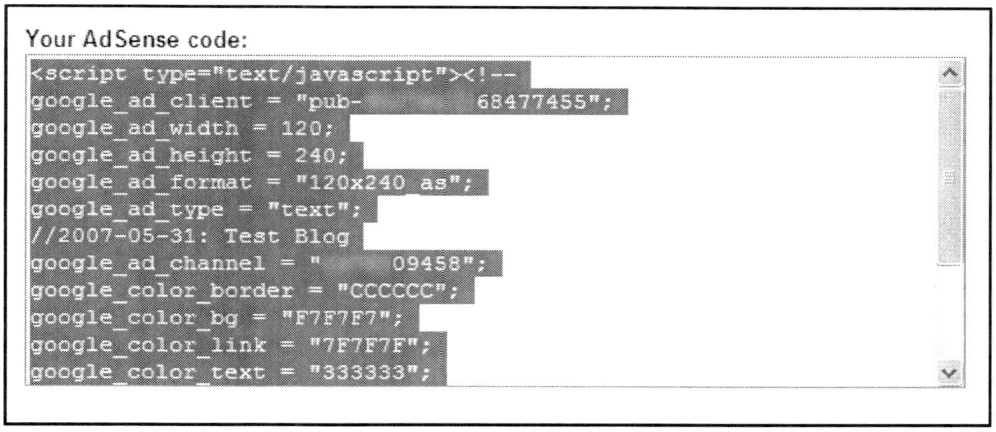

```
Your AdSense code:
<script type="text/javascript"><!--
google_ad_client = "pub-        68477455";
google_ad_width = 120;
google_ad_height = 240;
google_ad_format = "120x240_as";
google_ad_type = "text";
//2007-05-31: Test Blog
google_ad_channel = "        09458";
google_color_border = "CCCCCC";
google_color_bg = "F7F7F7";
google_color_link = "7F7F7F";
google_color_text = "333333";
```

FIGURE 123 ADSENSE CODE

If you look closely at the code above, you'll see that it is a 120X240 link unit with 'Test Blog' as its channel. Copy the code. Our next step is to paste the code into the sidebar.

PASTE CODE INTO SIDEBAR

Return to the Theme Editor page on your blog and select 'Sidebar' from the template choices shown on the right side of the page.

I've chosen to place the Adsense ad units right at the bottom of the sidebar.

So, I scrolled right to the bottom of the template file and inserted the Google Adsense code directly into the template file (see the screenshot to the right).

Note the highlighted section which shows the code positioned below the *<?php wp_meta(); ?> </ul></li>* code.

FIGURE 124 EDIT SIDEBAR

To add space between the 'Wordpress' link and the Google ad unit, I also put in the HTML code for 2 line feeds directly above the Google Adsense code, so the first part of my code looks like this:

```
<br><br>
<script type="text/javascript"><!--
google_ad_client = "pub-902...
```

Once you've inserted your code, click on 'Update File.' View your Adsense units in your browser by clicking on 'View Site' at the top of your Wordpress Administration panel.

Forum Etiquette

Below are some general guidelines that will help you from being banned from most forums.

- **Make sure your posts are placed in the correct category**.
  Many forums have many different topic sections. Be sure to post your messages and questions in the right section.

- **Do not post**:
  Questions or answers which have already been answered numerous times;
  Negative or aggressive remarks (i.e., Flames) directed towards other users;
  Anything not relating to the original topic;
  Any derogatory comments based on age, gender, race, ethnicity or nationality.

- **Have something to say**.
  A message such as, "anyone in here?" wastes time when the number of viewers who read the post is taken into consideration. Make intelligent posts that have a purpose.

- **Obey copyright rules**:
  Respect the law and do not post copyrighted work unless you have written permission from its owner.

- **Do not promote your own site, unless**:
  It is specifically permitted by the forum rules.

- **Don't Spam**.
  Spam includes advertisements, content deemed inappropriate or illegal, and flooding of the boards (repeated and/or multiple - read "unnecessary" - postings).

- **Ensure your signature file**:
  Remains a reasonable size and does not contain excessively large images or annoying animations, and follows all the rules applying to the posts themselves.

- **Respect others' privacy**:
  Don't post private addresses or phone numbers, including your own.

- **Do not make needless use of**:
  Emoticons;
  Line breaks or ALL-CAPS;
  Nested quotes;
  Giant fonts;
  Swearing, derogatory terms, hate-speech, obscene or vulgar comments. (Probably the most effective way to receive a permanent or temporary ban).

If you have problems, just make a post in the appropriate forum, and somebody will almost certainly be glad to help you.

10 Design Rules-of-Thumb

While it is not within the scope of the Super Affiliate Handbook to give detailed instruction on HTML Web design, here are 12 basic design rules that Super Affiliates generally follow.

1. HUH? WHAT DOES THAT SAY?

You may love the appearance of an unusual font, however there are a couple of problems with using fonts that aren't common to everyone's computer.

If the font you use isn't on your visitor's computer, your text won't appear as intended.

Do you know what the second problem is?

Legibility!

Script and unusual fonts should be used sparingly and in a larger size, so as to be legible.

The standard and best fonts for use on the web are Arial, Verdana and Tahoma.

Text should be large enough to read without the surfer having to adjust their browser's font size display - because they won't bother. They'll go elsewhere to find the information without the hassle of having to squint.

Text should always be dark on a light background.

I broke this rule when I was just starting out, by using white text on a black background. I received a couple of complaints and comments about how difficult the pages were to read but did nothing about it for the longest time. Sales were good and the site looked 'cool,' so why should I bother to change things?

"Why bother?" indeed! As soon as I changed over to black on white, my sales went up... way up!

There are two lessons here. First, if one person writes to complain, it's likely that one hundred more people feel the same way. Second, there are good reasons why practices become 'tried and true.'

2. IS THAT A LINK?

If visitors can't distinguish links from regular text, they won't click your links or buy your merchants' products, therefore it is best to use standard linking practices to avoid confusion.

I discovered the value of using standard linking practices through a test I did some time ago. The link colors at sage-hearts.com had been in keeping with the existing red and yellow color scheme.

As an experiment, I changed the link colors to the standard colors listed above, and it wasn't long before my conversion rates increased.

> **STANDARD LINK COLORS**
>
> <u>Underlined Blue</u> – Unvisited link.
> <u>Red</u> – Active link or 'hover'.
> <u>Purple</u> – Visited link.

Needless to say, I didn't change them back to their original colors!

By the way, changing all the link colors is super-simple to accomplish, when you use 'cascading style sheets' or 'CSS.'

CSS eliminates the need to 'hard code' the font face, size and color every time you wish to make a change to a word's appearance. Instead, all the different parameters are listed within a single file, or the cascading style sheet. All pages which link to the style sheet share the same font attributes.

Furthermore, when you use CSS to eliminate all that font coding, the size of your pages is reduced.

3. BABY BLUE AND OLIVE GREEN SHOULD NEVER BE SEEN

Different colors have different meanings and connotations. What would you think of if you saw a men's' site with pink as the primary color? Might it turn the average heterosexual guy off? You bet it would! They're terrified of pink.

I also can't imagine a health and fitness site succeeding with watery lavender and sickly olive green combination as well as it might with vibrant 'standard' colors.

Again, it's good to stick with the tried and true.

4. LEAVE 'BREATHING' SPACE

White space, or negative space, describes open space between design elements.

White space is an important layout technique often overlooked by inexperienced designers. Visually appealing design is easy on the eyes. Without adequate white space, text would be unreadable, graphics would lose their emphasis, and there would be no balance between the elements on a page.

White space takes on added importance on the Web because more of a strain is placed on the eyes than when reading printed material. White space gives our brains a break. Treat white space as more than just a background. Treat it as an integral part to your page design.

5. HOW WIDE IS TOO WIDE?

Having to scroll right to see all the text on a page is a symptom of poor design, or lack of knowledge of standard display sizes.

Standard screen resolutions are 1024 X 768 pixels, for those with good eyesight. However, many, many folks still use 800 X 600.

Given that knowledge, you have to design for the most common denominator, which in this case is 800 pixels wide by 600 pixels tall. That means that the 800, 1024, 1152, AND the 1280 pixel wide people can all see the whole page on their display.

You can also use percentage widths, i.e. width="100%," which then widens or narrows the page according to each surfer's screen resolution. However, this HTML coding technique leads to your pages being viewed differently on different computer displays and in different browsers. It's better therefore to design your pages so that they are consistent across various platforms and hard-code specific widths for your HTML pages.

6. DOWN WITH UGLY BACKGROUNDS!

I continue to be amazed by those who think that their visitors will waste time squinting to read text on a floral, striped or otherwise 'busy' background. It gives me a headache just to think about it!

Do the designers think those backgrounds are pretty? Well, they're half right. Those busy backgrounds are pretty UGLY!

7. BANDWIDTH HOGS

Bandwidth is an electronic resource that gets used up every time characters of information are downloaded from, or uploaded to, your Web site. As more bandwidth is used, data and information transmission times increase.

Surfers have short attention spans, and most don't have cable or fast ADSL connections. Therefore, page elements that slow down your pages may be reducing your income as impatient surfers click their 'Back' buttons.

Bandwidth hogs include large or animated graphics, Flash, and sound of any kind. If you need graphics on your pages, make sure they are compressed to their smallest size without affecting their appearance.

8. KILL THOSE POP-UPS!

I detest pop-up windows, so in keeping with my 'do unto others' approach; I try to limit my use of them as much as possible.

That story aside, popup windows might increase your conversion rates. Exit pops with your mailing list or newsletter subscription form are particularly effective.

Here's an experiment I did with pop-up windows.

Thinking that everyone hated pop-up windows as much as I do, I changed all of the links at Sage-Hearts.com so that they would no longer open new windows when clicked upon.

The new pages simply opened up in the same browser window. I didn't really notice too much of a difference in my conversion rate, and thought I'd done my visitors a favor.

However, a few months later, in another conversion rate experiment, I changed all the links so that they would open "new" windows when clicked. My conversions went up almost immediately.

In that instance however, I added the warning in the table below to each page of the site.

"Please note that links that leave Sage-Hearts.com **will open a new window**. That allows you to check out the service and come back to see more in the category."

It seems to work.

A POPUP HORROR STORY

One day I left the house for about an hour. On returning to my office, I was shocked to see about FIFTY browser windows open on my computer display.

How could that happen? Well, some unthinking and unkind webmaster programmed a pop-up script onto a page that I visited (and left open) that in turn opened a new browser window every minute or so. Each and every page was exactly the same.

What purpose did that serve other than to make me despise the dufus? Absolutely none other than his unscrupulous ways gave me a story to tell you.

9. I HATE PUNK ROCK!

Have you ever clicked through to a Web site and had your eardrums immediately assaulted by some Webmaster's "idea" of great music? Or how about a page that opens with a voice-over monologue?

In my opinion, this is always unacceptable.

Under *no circumstance* should a site broadcast noise and/or music without the visitors' permission. Even if your site is *about* music, your visitors should have the option as to what they want to hear, and when they want to hear it.

That's just basic courtesy. Consider the possibility that your visitors may be in an office or library environment while quietly surfing the 'Net. Any sudden unexpected noise will disrupt what they're doing and they are likely to retreat from your site in great haste.

That's bad for business.

Note: Audio is perfectly acceptable when the visitor can click a link to listen to the recording. Hearing a real person talk about the product can also increase your conversion rates substantially.

Case in point – my sales increased by about 33% after I added an audio link to one of my sales pages. The software I recommend for audio recording is Jay Jennings' 'Sonic Memo' (http://SonicMemo.com), and it's so easy to use, even I can do it! ☺

10. YOU'VE BEEN FRAMED

Frames are pretty cool, eh? Not! I became so obsessed with creating frames on one of my sites that one webmaster friend called me a recovering "frameaholic!" I am pleased that my obsession was limited to only one site.

Frames have one main page, and several 'secondary' pages. That feature saves the Web developer from having to add navigation to every page on the site.

What is doesn't do however, is allow you to link to individual pages and have your site design or layout appear on the framed page.

Also, if someone wants to link to a specific page on your site, they can't. The URL that appears in their browser's address bar remains the same the entire time they navigate your site. So if they choose to bookmark a page, what they are book marking is actually the main, or homepage - and NOT the page they expected and/or wanted to bookmark.

The biggest problem with frames is that search engine robots have a hard time spidering sites that are built in frames. Although there are ways to optimize your framed site to be attractive to search engines, the reasons above should quickly negate any compulsion you feel to use frames.

Follow the basic rules of Web site design above and you'll give your visitors an enjoyable site experience. You'll also enjoy improved conversion rates and more sales.

8 Ways to Make Your Site "Google" Friendly

Optimizing your pages for the search engines is absolutely essential if you want them to appear in the top 10 - 30 positions of results.

High-ranking pages are even more critical if you'll be starting your affiliate business with a very small or non-existent promotional budget and won't be using pay-per-clicks and other forms of advertising.

How do you get your pages to rank high in the search engine results? Here is a list of tips that will help.

1. PROVIDE RELEVANT CONTENT

Jill Whalen, a well-known search engine (SE) expert advises that you should work with at least 250 words on a page for search engine optimization purposes.

Having more or less words will also work, but Jill makes the point that you need at least 250 words to be able to repeat your keyword phrases a number of times throughout the page without seeming 'dopey.'

2. NAME PAGES ACCORDING TO PAGE CONTENT

Name HTML pages using keywords relevant to the product sold on that page, or the most relevant content. For example, if I were to write a review about *Proform Treadmills*, I would save the page as *'proform-treadmills.html.'*

You can take that a step further. If you write a review about the Proform 350 Treadmill, name the page *'proform-350-treadmill.html.'*

3. ELIMINATE CLUTTER

Search engines don't read graphics or javascript, and they get confused when they encounter nested tables. If graphics and javascript precede the first most important keyword phrases on your page, your ranking may be lowered as the search engine considers that phrase less relevant, due to its low placement on the page.

Search engine spiders prefer HTML text, loaded with keywords, placed 'high' on the page, and the left side is 'read' before the right side.

I therefore place my primary navigation on the right side of my pages so the spiders can get to their 'food' more quickly.

4. USE META TAGS OR 'META ELEMENTS'

Note to Bloggers: If you are doing a blog-only site, you may skip the Title, Description and Keyword portions of this section. However, you should make note of information in the Alt Tags portion.

A meta tag is an HTML tag that provides information about an individual web page or document. Unlike regular tags – such as font tags - meta tags do not format the way a page appears in a surfer's browser. Instead, meta tags provide a description of page content, the page title, the author, date of creation or latest update for the page, and keywords which relate to the subject matter.

Although Google does not currently use meta tag elements to index web sites, they do use text from the Title and Description meta tags in search results pages. Therefore, although I discuss 4 Meta tags or 'elements' in this section, the two tags that you need to be most concerned about are the Title and Description tags.

TITLE TAGS

The Title tag is perhaps one of the most crucial factors in how a search engine will rank your site. The text you use in the title tag must include your most relevant keyword phrases.

> <title>Proform Treadmills: Compare Proform Treadmills at MyTreadmillSite.com</title>
> <meta name="description" CONTENT="How do Proform Treadmills compare to other treadmills? Read our treadmill reviews.">
> <meta name="keywords" CONTENT="proform treadmills, proform, treadmills">

It must also make sense, as the title tag text is the wording that appears in the reverse bar of your browser. That's the blue bar right across the top of your browser window. It is also what the text that most of the search engines will display as the title for your listing.

DESCRIPTION TAGS

Some search engines will use the text contained in your meta description tag as your listing description. The meta Description tag may also influence your site's ranking in some search engines, so you should repeat the primary keyword phrase used in your Title tag at least once in the Description tag.

This is the Description meta tag for the Friendfinder review:

<meta name="description" content="How does FriendFinder dating service compare to other personal ads and dating sites?">

KEYWORD TAGS

Webmasters used to 'stuff' keyword meta tags with every keyword relevant to their site and then added some more.

Most search engine experts now advise that the keyword meta tag is no longer worth your time or trouble, and apparently only Inktomi, and perhaps Teoma, now index sites using the keyword meta tag.

However, I don't think that adding a couple of keywords to a meta tag is any trouble at all, so I continue to add them to my pages.

In the table below is an example of how you would structure the Meta Tags for a page selling *Proform Treadmills*.

ALT TAGS

The ALT tag, which stands for 'alternative text,' is primarily for use when the image is **not** being displayed. They were intended to make your site more accessible to visually impaired folks who use text readers. To solve this problem, you can enter the image description in the ALT tag, as in this example:

<img src="gifs/logo.gif" width="309" height="97" alt="Sage-Hearts.com Logo">

However, to achieve better page and site rankings, you could enter a keyword phrase relevant to that page, as in this example:

<img src="gifs/logo.gif" width="309" height="97" alt="Internet Dating Services">

Either way, don't let your ALT tags go to waste.

5. WRITE FOR YOUR VISITORS *NOT* THE SEARCH ENGINES

You must be extremely careful not to overuse keyword phrases on your web pages for fear that the search engines will consider you an engine spammer and penalize your site by having it de-ranked or de-listed.

Although you should still place your primary keywords in the meta tags and page titles, write in a natural way that is a pleasure for your visitors to read.

6. LINK DYNAMIC PAGES TO STATIC PAGES

Dynamic pages, which deliver content based on user input or other variables, can be more useful and responsive to visitor needs than regular static HTML pages. However, when indexing your site, if a search engine encounters a dynamically generated page - as distinguished by a question mark (?) in the URL -the SE stops indexing the site at that point.

So, here are a few tips to get your dynamic pages indexed.

The simplest and cheapest method to get your dynamic pages indexed is to link to them from a static page, preferably your site map. Although the SE can't index the whole page, it will index the majority of its content.

The other solutions involve software and scripting fixes that let search engines index their dynamic content. To learn more about these reconfigurations and rewrites, please consult your usual sources of information on the specific programming language.

Dynamic pages, which deliver content based on user input or other variables, can be more useful and responsive to visitor needs than regular static HTML pages.

7. CREATE A SITE MAP

Your site should have a site map (or blog archive) with links that point to all the important pages and sections of your site. If your site consists of one hundred or more pages, you may wish to break the site map into separate pages.

8. AVOID TRICKS AND DECEPTION

Google makes site quality recommendations to help you avoid having your site removed from their index. Once a site has been removed, it won't show up in Google.com or on Google's partner sites. The same suggestions hold true for all the major engines.

Don't deceive your users by presenting different content to search engines than is displayed on your pages. A common trick in the past was to include highly popular but irrelevant keywords in meta tags to get 'the click.' While that brought traffic to the site, the visitor was disappointed by results that had nothing to do with their search, and the engines appeared not to be able to produce relevant results. The search engines now pay attention to such tactics and will remove those using deceptive practices from their index.

Avoid tricks intended to improve search engine rankings. This includes using hidden text or links, sneaky redirects; pages loaded with irrelevant keywords and the use of 'doorway' pages. Google also recommends against creating subdomains and domains with essentially duplicate content.

When you follow the above guidelines you help the search engines find, index, and rank your site, which is the best way to ensure that you'll be included in their results.

Concentrate your energy on giving your visitors a good experience, rather than trying to manipulate the search engines. You'll be better rewarded with traffic and sales, and you'll also sleep better at night than your deceptive webmaster counterparts.

10 Scripts & Code Snippets

Here are 10 java scripts and code snippets for you to copy and use on your site.

1. BOOKMARK THIS PAGE

This script allows your visitors to bookmark your page with one click of your mouse. In the script below:

CHANGE 'var txt' from (Bookmark This Page!) to the text you wish to have appear on your page for the bookmark link. Onmouseover your text will also appear in the status bar.

CHANGE 'var url' from http://www.superaffiliatehandbook.com to the url you want to have bookmarked. Use the full address of the page!

CHANGE 'var who' from Super Affiliate Handbook to the title that you want the bookmark to show when the user bookmarks your site.

INSERT the script in your page where you want the Bookmark This Page! link to appear.

```
<SCRIPT LANGUAGE="JavaScript">
var txt = "Bookmark This Page!";
var url = "http://www.superaffiliatehandbook.com";
var who = "Super Affiliate Handbook";
var ver = navigator.appName;
var num = parseInt(navigator.appVersion);
if ((ver == "Microsoft Internet Explorer")&&(num >= 4)) {
document.write('<A HREF="javascript:window.external.AddFavorite(url,who);"
');
document.write('onMouseOver=" window.status=');
document.write("txt; return true ");
document.write('"onMouseOut=" window.status=');
document.write("' '; return true ");
document.write('">'+ txt + '</a>');
}else{
txt += "  (Ctrl+D)";
document.write(txt);
}
</script>
```

2. DATE & FUTURE DATE

Place this code on your page where you wish the current date to appear.

You can also change the bolded "0" below to another number to have a future date displayed. For example, if you wish to make a time-limited offer such as 'Buy before midnight (2 days from now)," you'd replace the "0" in the formula below with the number "2."

```
<script type="text/javascript">
var weekday=new
Array("Sunday","Monday","Tuesday","Wednesday","Thursday","Friday","Saturday")
var monthname=new
Array("Jan","Feb","Mar","Apr","May","Jun","Jul","Aug","Sep","Oct","Nov","Dec"
)
var today = new Date()
var todayInMS = today.getTime()
var inthreedays = todayInMS + (60 * 60 * 24 * 0 * 1000) // edit the 0 to
change the number of days
var newdate = new Date(inthreedays)
document.write(weekday[newdate.getDay()] + ", ")
document.write(monthname[newdate.getMonth()] + " ")
document.write(newdate.getDate() + " ")
document.write(newdate.getFullYear())
</script>
```

3. MAKE HOMEPAGE

Gives your visitors the option of making YOUR site THEIR homepage. Replace the bolded text with your own information and place the script where you wish the link to appear.

```
<SCRIPT LANGUAGE="JavaScript">
<!—Begin
// If Internet Explorer, use automatic link
if (document.all){
document.write('<A HREF="javascript:history.go(0);"
onClick="this.style.behavior=\'url(#default#homepage)\';this.setHomePage(\'ht
tp://superaffiliatehandbook.com\');">');
document.write('Click Here To Make Us Your Homepage</a>');
}

// If Netscape 6, tell user to drag link onto Home button
else if (document.getElementById){
document.write('<a href="http://superaffiliatehandbook.com">Drag this link
onto your Home button to make this your Home Page.</a>');
}
// For Netscape 4 or lower, give instructions to set Home Page
else if (document.layers){
document.write('<b>Make this site your home page:</b><br>- Go to
<b>Preferences</b> in the <B>Edit</B> Menu.<br>- Choose <b>Navigator</b> from
the list on the left.<br>- Click on the <b>"Use Current Page"</b> button.');
}
```

```
// For any other browser, display instructions
else {
document.write('<b>Make this site your home page:</b><br>- Go to
<b>Preferences</b> in the <B>Edit</B> Menu.<br>- Choose <b>Navigator</b> from
the list on the left.<br>- Click on the <b>"Use Current Page"</b> button.');
}
// End -->
</script>
```

4. *Hide Status Bar*

This is an inexpensive way to temporarily stop 'nosey-Parkers' from seeing your affiliate link coding. However, it's not very effective with savvy surfers and tends to upset visitors when their browser window suddenly changes appearance.

```
<script>
function hidestatus(){
window.status=''
return true
}

if (document.layers)
document.captureEvents(Event.MOUSEOVER | Event.MOUSEOUT)
document.onmouseover=hidestatus
document.onmouseout=hidestatus
</script>
```

5. ONMOUSEOVER

This code places text of your choosing in the status bar when visitors cursor over the link.

If text is placed between the quotations following onMouseOut="window.status=", the status bar will display that text until the visitor places his cursor over the next link.

```
<a href="http://www.one-and-only.com/index.htm?AssociateID=6486"
onMouseOver="window.status='One and Only'; return true "
onMouseOut="window.status=''; return true ">One and Only</a>
```

6. OPEN A NEW WINDOW

This snippet will open a "new" window without closing the current window when the link is clicked. So, when the visitor closes the "new" window, the current window (hopefully yours) will still be open underneath it.

```
<a href="http://sage-hearts.com" target="_blank">
```

7. POP-UP ON ENTRANCE

Opens the specified URL into a pop-up window when a visitor first enters a Web page.

PASTE the following bold script in between the <HEAD> </HEAD> tags on the page you want the pop up window to launch from. This particular script will open http://rosalindgardner.com, but you can change it to anything you like.

```
<script language="JavaScript" for="window" event="onload()">
<!--
window.open("http://rosalindgardner.com", "vb",
```

```
"scrollbars,resizable,height=600,width=800")
//-->

</script>
```

8. POP-UP ON EXIT

Opens the specified URL into a pop-up (pop-under) window when a visitor exits a Web page.

PASTE the following script in between the <HEAD> </HEAD> tags on the page you want the pop up window to launch from when your visitor leaves the page. This particular script opens a page named "popexit.html," but you can name it anything you like.

```
<script language="JavaScript" for="window" event="onunload()">
window.open("popexit.html" "scrollbars=no,resizable=no,height=300,width=300")
</script>
```

Next, paste the following bolded code into the **<body onunload="xit()">** tag on the same page.

9. TIMED POP-UP

The following pop-up script opens after a specified number of seconds and closes (if you want it to) after a specified amount of time.

Place the script between the <Head> </Head> on your web page.

To set the time delay before opening, change '40' in 'delay = 40' to the number of seconds of your choosing.

Likewise, if you wish the pop-up to close, change '600' in 'closetime = 600' to however many seconds you prefer.

```
<script language=JavaScript>

<!—Begin
closetime = 600; // Close window after 600 number of seconds?
// 0 = do not close, anything else = number of seconds

function Start(URL, WIDTH, HEIGHT) {
windowprops = "left=50,top=50,width=" + WIDTH + ",height=" + HEIGHT;
preview = window.open(URL, "preview", windowprops);
if (closetime) setTimeout("preview.close();", closetime*600);
}

function doPopup() {
url = "countdown.html";
width = 320;   // width of window in pixels
height = 650; // height of window in pixels
delay = 40;     // time in seconds before popup opens
timer = setTimeout("Start(url, width, height)", delay*1000);
}
//  End -->
</SCRIPT>
```

Add the following bolded code in the first <Body> tag to make the script above work properly.

```
<BODY onload=doPopup();>
```

10. DISABLE RIGHT-CLICK

This script is used to disable the right-click feature on your pages so that nosey webmasters won't be able to see the actual destination URL behind your link.

More knowledgeable webmasters will simply proceed from the "right click disabled" notice to "View Source," but the script may stop a few snoopers from removing your affiliate ID from the link.

To disable the right-click feature, place the following script in the Head of your page.

```
<script language="Javascript1.2">
// Set the message for the alert box
am = "This function is disabled!";
// do not edit below this line
// ============================

bV  = parseInt(navigator.appVersion)
bNS = navigator.appName=="Netscape"
bIE = navigator.appName=="Microsoft Internet Explorer"

function nrc(e) {
if (bNS && e.which > 1){
alert(am)
return false
} else if (bIE && (event.button >1)) {
alert(am)
return false;
}
}

document.onmousedown = nrc;
if (document.layers) window.captureEvents(Event.MOUSEDOWN);
if (bNS && bV<5) window.onmousedown = nrc;
</script>
```

I hope the foregoing scripts and code snippets make building your site just a little easier. You can find other scripts and codes at the sites listed below.

http://www.scriptsearch.com
http://javascript.internet.com/
http://cgi.resourceindex.com/
http://php.resourceindex.com/

Wrap Up: What it Takes to be a SUPER-Affiliate!

It has been reported many times that 2% of all affiliates are responsible for 90% of all affiliate program sales.

Why is that?

Well, here are the predominant factors that set Super Affiliates apart from their less productive counterparts.

1. **Super Affiliates treat Affiliate Marketing as a BUSINESS**. They don't slap up a site with a couple of banner ads. They invest in their businesses with time, money and effort. They are determined and persistent.

2. **Super Affiliates are Focused**. They find a niche with a huge market. They research, understand and sell to that market.

3. **Super Affiliates are Super Communicators**. They know and understand their merchants' products, and know how to sell the benefits of those products to their visitors.

4. **Super Affiliates Grow their Businesses**. After building one successful affiliate site, they look for opportunities to build new streams of income with affiliate programs.

5. **Super Affiliates are Constantly Learning**. They stay current with industry trends to stay on top of what they need to know about how to do business successfully. In other words, they educate themselves, just as you are doing now... you, the aspiring Super Affiliate!

Those are the basics of what it takes to be a Super Affiliate.

So, with those points in mind, Promote and Prosper!

Appendix A: Affiliate Networks

In this appendix you will find both a *list of 43 affiliate networks*, and a section that contains more detailed information about a selected number of affiliate networks including:

- Affiliate network URL
- Signup restrictions
- Program types
- Minimum payouts
- Payment processes
- Tracking
- Multi-tier programs availability
- Ability to use email marketing

For each network I've included a list of the program types available. The codes are as follows:

- CPA (cost-per-action/lead generation)
- CPC (cost-per-click)
- CPS (cost per sale)
- CPM (cost per impression)

I have listed networks that offer CPA, CPC and CPS programs, and left the CPM networks out of the equation.

CPM campaigns are usually low-paying sweepstakes or other 'freebie' types of offers whose merchants simply want to collect email addresses so that they can send out more promotional material for which you won't get paid.

Let's find programs and get paid! ☺

4 'Must-Join' Affiliate Networks

Although there are literally hundreds of affiliate networks, you will have ample access to merchants and millions of products through the following four affiliate networks.

1. COMMISSION JUNCTION

Commission Junction (CJ) is the largest affiliate network and refers to its affiliates as 'publishers.' There are no signup restrictions other than non-acceptance of sites that contain or link to sites that are libelous, defamatory, obscene, abusive, violent, bigoted, hate-oriented, illegal, cracking, hacking or warez, or offers any illegal goods or services. Turnaround time on the application is very quick. Commission Junction's merchant clients include eBay, Etronics, Frederick's of Hollywood, NetZero Platinum, Yahoo! Search Marketing and Yahoo! Personals.

URL	http://cj.com
Programs	CPA, CPC, CPS
Minimum Payout	$25/up to $75
Payments	Payments are made on the 20th of the month to Canadian and American publishers (i.e. CJ's name for affiliates), and on the last day of the month to publishers outside those countries. Advertiser payments are available in 16 different currencies and are consolidated into one monthly check. Direct bank deposits are available.
Tracking	Real-time
Multi-Tier	Yes, with restrictions. They allow only U.S. and U.K. publishers to earn commissions from introducing new publishers to their service.
Email Marketing	Yes

2. LINKSHARE

Linkshare reports over 10 million partnerships in the network and claims to be the most successful pay for performance (affiliate) network of its kind. Linkshare sends commission payment for some merchants while others process their own payments – sometimes in their own good time. Linkshare's clients include Coldwater Creek, Delta Airlines, FTD.com, Hallmark, Hickory Farms, Overtstock.com, Pitney Bowes, REI, and Sharper Image.

URL	http://linkshare.com
Programs	CPA, CPC, CPS
Minimum Payout	Variable
Payments	Variable depending on merchant
Tracking	Real-time
Multi-Tier	Yes
Email Marketing	Permitted

3. CLICKBANK

ClickBank distributes over 10,000 digital products and services through a network of over 100,000 affiliates and I can attest to the fact that the checks arrive like clockwork. ClickBank withholds 10% from each check to cover their risk of future returns. The holdbacks are credited back to your account after about 90 days.

You don't have to wait for acceptance from individual merchants. Simply browse the marketplace, get and post your link, and start making money.

ClickBank's clients and products include Yanik Silver and Jeff Ball's 'Get Fit While You Sit,' Jim Edwards' "How to Write Your Own eBook in 7 Days" ...and of course "The Super Affiliate Handbook: How I Made $436,797 in One Year Selling Other People's Stuff Online."

URL	Affiliate Signup - http://clickbank.com Marketplace - http://clickbank.com/marketplace/
Programs	Primarily CPS
Minimum Payout	$10, adjustable upwards. A $2.50 accounting fee is deducted from each check issued, so you may want to adjust your minimum payment upwards if your two-week earnings are low.
Payments	Checks are mailed within 15 days after the end of each pay period, and pay periods end at 12:00:01am on the 1st and 16th of each month. Checks over $5,000 are sent at Clickbank's expense by US Priority Mail (US) or Global Priority Mail (Europe, Canada, Australia, etc) wherever possible. Payment is by check only.
Tracking	Yes
Multi-Tier	Real-time
Email Marketing	Yes

4. SHAREASALE

Established in 2000, the smaller network, Shareasale.com has a huge reputation with both affiliates and merchants for being fair, honest, and proactive to customer concerns. ShareaSale's has a couple thousand offers and clients include Avitan Technologies Corp., Glamor Shades, DanceSavvy, World Speakers Association, Student Planner and Bonsai Boy of New York.

URL	http://shareasale.com
Restrictions	Must have a top-level domain, i.e., no Geocities sites.
Programs	CPA, CPC, CPS
Minimum Payout	$50.00
Payments	One consolidated monthly check. ShareaSale issues payments via check and PayPal on the 20th of each month for those affiliates who reach the $50 minimum before the end of the previous month.
Tracking	Real-time
Multi-Tier	$1 per signup as an affiliate, and 5% of their future earnings.
Email Marketing	Permitted

44 Affiliate Networks (A List)

Ad Reporting	http://AdReporting.com
Affiliate Bot	http://AffiliateBot.com
Affiliate Cop	http://AffiliateCop.com
Affiliate Crew	http://AffiliateCrew.com
Affiliate Fuel	http://AffiliateFuel.com
Affiliate Future	http://AffiliateFuture.co.uk
Affiliate Network	http://AffiliateNetwork.com
Affiliate Window	http://AffiliateWindow.com
BeFree	http://Reporting.net
BidClix	http://BidClix.com
Casino Coins	http://CasinoCoins.com
ClickBank	http://ClickBank.com
ClickxChange	http://ClickxChange.com
clixGalore	http://ClixGalore.com
Commission Junction	http://CJ.com
Commission Soup	http://CommissionSoup.com
CPA Empire	http://CPAEmpireAffiliate.com
Cyber Bounty	http://CyberBounty.com
DarkBlue	http://DarkBlue.com
eAdvertising	http://eAdvertising.com
FineClicks	http://FineClicks.com
Floppy Bank	http://FloppyBank.com
iCommissions	http://iCommissions.com
Income Access	http://IncomeAccess.com
iWhiz	http://iWhiz.com
Kolimbo	http://Kolimbo.com
LeadHound	http://LeadHound.com
Linkshare	http://LinkShare.com
MaxBounty	http://MaxBounty.com
Offer Fusion	http://OfferFusion.com
Offers Quest	http://OffersQuest.com
Paid on Results (U.K.)	http://PaidonResults.com
Partner Weekly	http://PartnerWeekly.com
Performics	http://Performics.com
Primary Ads	http://PrimaryAds.com
Quinstreet	http://members.Quinstreet.com
ReferBack	http://ReferBack.com
Revenue Pilot	http://RevenuePilot.com
Rewards Affiliates	http://Affiliate.CasinoRewards.com
Search4Clicks	http://Search4Clicks.com
Sell Shareware	http://SellShareware.com
ShareaSale	http://ShareaSale.com
ShareResults	http://ShareResults.com/
Traffic Doubler (Europe)	http://TrafficDoubler.com

Contextual Advertising Networks

The following is a partial list extracted from my "Google Adsense Alternatives" article posted
http://www.netprofitstoday.com/categories/Make-Money-Online/Contextual-Advertising/

That article lists 39 contextual advertising networks, while only the most popular are listed below.

- Affiliate Sensor (http://affiliatesensore.com) - Earn Clickbank revenue by signing up for Affiliate Sensor's free program. Choose from over 10,000 of Clickbank's products using Affiliate Sensor's context-relevant, text-link affiliate ads. You just have to paste a little javascipt on your pages. Ads are sorted to display the best performing products on top.

- Chitika eMiniMalls (http://chitika.com) - Although they serve up the most attractive contextual ads, the jury still seems to be out on the Chitika eMiniMalls network. With many affiliates reporting income audits with losses of 30 - 50% of their expected Chitika earnings, numerous publishers have pulled the plug on this fledgling contextual advertiser, still in beta.

- Clicksor (http://clicksor.com) - Pays up to 85% of the advertising revenues, net 15 terms on a bi-weekly schedule. Check (min. payout: $50), or PayPal (min. payout: $20). Media includes Text Banners, Graphic Banners, Pop-Under Advertisements, Search box and XML feed to host on websites or blogs.

- Kontera (http://www.kontera.com) - Payments via check in US Dollars on balances over $100 US. Who knows what percentage they actually pay?

- ValueClick (http://www.valueclick.com) - Commission Junction's parent company, use the "IAB" methodology for measuring impressions, clicks, leads and acquisitions, and payments are based upon delivery in accordance with these measurements and tracking data calculated by ValueClick. On the first day of each month, ValueClick will total all accumulated data for the previous month. Payments made Net 30 to Publishers who have earned more than $30.00 .

- Yahoo Publisher Network (http://publisher.yahoo.com/) - To be considered for the Yahoo! Publisher Network beta program, you must have a valid U.S. Social Security or Tax ID number, and web site content that is predominantly in English and targeted at a U.S. user base.

Appendix B: Additional Resources

Industry News

"Net Profits Today" Newsletter – I send information and news of importance to my affiliate marketing subscribers via my newsletter and post it to the NetProfitsToday.com blog at http://www.netprofitstoday.com/blog/.

Revenue Magazine (http://www.revenuetoday.com/) - As an affiliate marketer, one tool you shouldn't be without is a subscription to 'Revenue – The Performance Marketing Standard' magazine. Published bi-monthly, 'Revenue' is the ONLY magazine dedicated to the art of affiliate marketing.

Site Building Tutorials

MiniSiteCreator.net – This is Jim Edwards' step-by-step blow-by-blow Audio/Visual tutorial on how to build your own site. In a word, if you want to learn how to build your own site... it's great.

HTMLGoodies.com - HTMLGoodies may have started the site with just HTML tutorials, but now they offer 'primers' in ASP, CGI, Javascript and Perl to name just a few. The very best site I can suggest for anyone wanting to learn how to build his or her own Web site.

Hex and Word Colors Codes (http://www.htmlgoodies.com/tutors/colors.html) - Aquamarine and dark olive green should never together be seen. YUK! The colors AND my poetry. Visit the color code chart to find colors that pair nicely.

WebDeveloper.com Forums (http://forums.webdeveloper.com) - Visit this site when you have a programming question that your kids can't answer.

WebPagesthatSuck.com - Vincent Flanders' site 'Web Pages That Suck is where you learn good Web design by looking at bad Web design.' With an incredibly fine sense of humor, Mr. Flanders demonstrates by example all the evils of bad web design. It's a fun way to learn!

Improve Your Writing Skills

If you have no previous writing experience, or you want to brush up on your skills, here are books and tools that have helped me along the way. Read as much as you can on the subject, because the better you convey yourself in writing, the better your conversion rates will be.

Turn Words into Traffic by Jim and Dallas Edwards. Using the simple "*Turn Words into Traffic*" system, your articles will soon be all over the Internet attracting visitors to your web site like bees to honey... even if you think you can't write. Read my review at http://tinyurl.com/2ad6ao.

Make Your Content Pre-Sell (*http://webvista.sitesell.com/mycps/*) is a free ebook by Ken Evoy. Anyone familiar with either of Ken Evoy's work loves his easy-going style and generosity of spirit. Don't think you're a writer? Well you are, and Ken will prove it to you.

Net Writing Masters Course – Produced by Ken Evoy, the 'Net Writing Masters Course' is a **FREE email course**. Read it and become an effective 'e-persuader,' as Ken calls it. Send a blank email to *twmswebvista@sitesell.net* to access the course.

Ultimate Copywriting Workshop (http://ultimateinternetcopycourse.com/) by Yanik Silver. I love what Yanik says about the ability to put words on a computer screen and having people send you money. "It's the ultimate security in a very un-secure world... Your ability to produce cash on demand through the power of your pen or keyboard is truly the equivalent of modern day alchemy." He is *so* right! Visit the site to get access to a free 143-page PDF file and 1-hour audio presentation on the subject of copywriting.

OutSource Your Content Development

Private Label Rights Information (http://www.netprofitstoday.com/categories/Develop-Site-Content/Private-Label-Rights/) – Information about Private Label Rights along with a number of PLR distributors.

Public Domain GOLDMINE (http://www.publicdomaingoldmine.com) - This package produced by Yanik Silver and Michael Holland contains 35 different public domain works complete with market research, competitive analysis, keyword analysis, back-end affiliate revenue sources, and potential joint venture partners. *Limited quantities available*.

Elance.com, **Rentacoder.com** and **Scriptlance.com** are fabulous for finding programmers, designers and writers.

Instant Niche Emails (http://www.marketerschoice.com) – Great for those who hate writing, Lisa Preston's 'Instant Niche Emails' software creates one of a kind email messages for your autoresponder series.

Market and Trend Information Resources

Comscore Media (http://comscore.com/) – Claims to have 'the largest consumer measurement system of its kind' to deliver insight and expertise in the following industries; automotive, travel, pharmaceutical, retail, financial services, telecommunications, media, entertainment and consumer packaged goods.

Forrester Research (http://www.forrester.com/) - Surveys 250,000 consumers every year in 15 countries to uncover purchasing and spending habits, technology adoption trends, customer demand and buyer attitudes. Guest registration gives access to free research.

Jupiter Research (http://www.jupiterresearch.com/) - Provides unbiased research, analysis and advice, backed by proprietary data, to help companies profit from the impact of the Internet and emerging consumer technologies on their business. You may register as a guest for access to sample research and special features like personalized e-mail alerts and a personal research library.

Online Publishers Association (http://www.online-publishers.org/) - A not-for-profit industry trade organization produces research into online advertising and media consumption with the goal of advancing the online publishing industry.

PRWeb.com - one of the largest online press release newswires. Search news by category, country, MSA, day or trackbacks.

ClickZ Network (http://www.clickz.com/) – News, information, commentary, advice, opinion, research, and reference related to interactive marketing. You'll find In-depth profiles, interviews, case studies, and features on cutting-edge products, companies, and trends.

eBay Marketplace Research (http://pages.ebay.com/marketplace_research/) – This service was introduced in late 2005 and is designed to help buyers and sellers track transaction trends on eBay. The service provides average item prices, shows top keyword searches by category or related keywords, creates charts illustrating transaction trends and delivers data on completed sales over the past 90 days. Marketplace Research is subscription-based and comes in three tiers, starting at US$2.99 for two days of access.

Software and Services for Affiliates

This is a SHORT list of software tools and services discussed in the Super Affiliate Handbook.

For a much more COMPREHENSIVE list of tools for use in your affiliate marketing business, please go to http://www.netprofitstoday.com/marketing-tools

Affiliate Organizer, (OrganizedAffiliate.com) developed by Jon Mills (a Super Affiliate Handbook reader) lets you to store all your most important data from your day-to-day business.

Headline Creator Pro Software (ezHeadlines.com)- Headlines are what your visitors see first. It doesn't matter how great your copy is - if your headlines don't grab your visitors' attention, your message will not be read. Developed by Scott Britner, this software is based on the best headlines ever written and actually writes headlines for you.

Wordtracker.com - Check out the FREE trial and download the **FREE** Keyword Research guide.

Glossary of Terms

The Internet brings with it a language all its own. This glossary explains the meaning of the terms most commonly used. Many of these definitions rely on other terms for their explanation. Terms defined elsewhere are in italics.

A

Above the Fold: Once a web page has loaded, the part that is visible is said to be 'above the fold.'

Adware: Also known as "spyware," a program hidden within free downloaded software that transmits user information via the Internet to advertisers.

Affiliate: A web site owner that promotes a merchant's products and/or services earns a commission for referring clicks, leads, or sales.

Affiliate Agreement: Terms that govern the relationship between a merchant and an affiliate.

Affiliate Network: Acts as an intermediary between affiliates and merchants, allowing affiliates to source relevant programs quickly and often provide one-click application to new merchants.

Affiliate Program: Any arrangement through which a merchant pays a commission to an affiliate for generating clicks, leads, or sales from links located on the affiliate's site. Also know as associate, partner, referral, and revenue sharing programs.

Affiliate Program Directory: Information about a collection of affiliate programs. May include information about commission rate, number of affiliates, and commission structure.

Affiliate Program Manager: The person responsible for administering an affiliate program. Duties should include maintaining regular contact with affiliates, program marketing and responding to queries about the program.

Affiliate Solution Provider: Company that provides the software and services to administer an affiliate program.

Affiliate URL or Link: Special code in a graphic or text link that identifies a visitor as having arrived from a specific affiliate site.

Applet: A small Java program embedded in an HTML page.

Associate: Synonym for affiliate.

Autoresponder: An email robot that sends replies automatically, without human intervention. This is an important tool for conducting online commerce.

B

Bandwidth: How many bits-per-second are sent through a connection. A full page of text is about 16,000 bits.

Banner Ad: Advertising in the form of a graphic image.

Bit (Binary DigIT"): A bit is the smallest unit of computerized data. It is a single digit number, either a 1 or a zero.

Bits-Per-Second (bps): A measurement of how fast data is moved from one place to another. A 56.6 modem can move 56,600 bits per second...but usually doesn't!

Blog: Acronym for 'web log,' a blog is basically a journal that is published using an online content management system. The act of updating a blog is referred to as 'blogging' and those who keep blogs, are known as 'bloggers.'

Browser: A program that allows you to access and read hypertext documents on the World Wide Web.

C

CGI: Common Gateway Interface programs that perform certain functions in connection with your HTML documents.

Cgi-bin: A directory on a web server in which CGI programs are stored.

Chargeback: An incomplete or invalid sales transaction that results in an affiliate commission deduction.

Clickthrough: When a user clicks on a link and arrives at a Web site.

ClickThrough Ratio (CTR): Percentage of visitors who click through to a merchant's Web site.

Client: A software program used to contact and obtain data from a software program on another computer. For example, the email program Eudora is an email 'client.'

Cloaking: Hiding of page code content.

Commission: Also known as a bounty or referral fee, the income an affiliate is paid for generating a sale, lead or click-through to a merchant's web site.

Co-branding: Where affiliates are able include their own logo and/or colors on the merchant's site.

Contextual Link: Placement of affiliate links within related text.

Conversion: When one of your visitors makes a purchase on the merchant's site, i.e., converts from 'visitor' to 'buyer.'

Conversion Rate: The percentage of visits to your site that convert to a sale. For example, if 1 person in every hundred visitors to your site makes a purchase, then your conversion rate is 1:100 or 1 percent.

Comment Code: HTML tags used to hide text and code scripting from browsers.

Cookie: A cookie is a piece of information sent by a Web Server to a Web Browser that the Browser software is expected to save and to send back to the Server whenever the browser makes additional requests from the Server. You may set your browser to either accept or not accept cookies. Cookies can contain user preferences, login or registration information, and/or "shopping cart" information. When a cookied browser sends a request to a Server, the Server uses the information to return customized information.

Cost per Acquisition (CPA): The amount you pay to acquire a customer.

Cost per Click (CPC): The amount you pay when a surfer clicks on one of your listings.

Cost Per Thousand (CPM): The amount you pay per 1,000 impressions of a banner or button.

Creative: The promotional tools advertisers use to draw in users. Examples are text links, towers, buttons, badges, email copy, pop-ups, etc.

Cyberspace: William Gibson coined the term in his book, "Neuromancer." Cyberspace now describes the whole range of data available through computer networks.

D

Demographics: The physical characteristics of a population such as age, sex, marital status, family size, education, geographic location, and occupation.

Digital Subscriber Line (DSL): A much faster way to move data over phone lines.

Disclaimer: A disclaimer states the terms under which the site or work may be used and gives information relating to what the copyright owner believes to be a breach of his/her/their copyright. In some cases you may wish to permit certain activities, in others you may wish to withhold all rights, or require the user to apply for a license to carry out certain actions.

Disclosure Statement: A statement acknowledging that compensation is received for product endorsements and/or sales.

Domain Name: The unique name that identifies an Internet site; comprised of two or more parts and separated by dots.

Doorway Page: See Gateway page.

Download: Transferring a file from another computer to your own.

E

Email: Electronic mail, a message sent to another Internet user across the Internet. An email address looks like this jimsmith@bubblee.com, whereas, "jimsmith" is your user name, your unique identifier; "@" stands for "at;" " bubblee.com" is the name of your Internet Service Provider.

Email Link: An affiliate link to a merchant site contained in an email newsletter or signature file.

Email Signature (Sig File): A brief message embedded at the end of every email that a person sends.

EPC: Term used by the Commission Junction affiliate network, this is your average earnings per 100 clicks. This number is calculated by taking commissions earned divided by the total number of clicks times 100.

eZine: Short for 'electronic magazine.'

F

File Transfer Protocol (FTP): The most common method for moving files between computers, servers and Internet sites.

Fire Wall: Hardware and/or software used to separate a LAN into two or more parts for security purposes.

Flame: Derogatory comment.

Forum: An online discussion board.

Frequently Asked Questions (FAQ): Lists and answers the most common questions asked on a particular subject. Generally posted to avoid having to answer the same question repeatedly.

G

Gateway Page: Also known as bridge pages, doorway page, entry pages, portals or portal pages, these pages are used to improve search engine placement. **Caution:** some search engines will drop a site entirely if the existence of doorway/gateway pages is detected.

Graphic Interchange Format (GIF): An image file format, suitable for simple files. A JPEG is the preferred format for storing photographs.

H

Hit: A hit is a single request from for a single item on a web server. To load a page with 5 graphics would count as 6 'hits,' 1 for the page plus 1 for each of the graphics. Hits are therefore a poor measurement of traffic to a web site.

Home Page: Your primary HTML page, the first page anyone would see in your Web site. Also called a "landing page."

Hybrid Model: A commission model that combines different payment methods.

Hype (Hyperbole): A deliberate exaggeration for emotional effect. The addressee is not expected to have a literal understanding of the expression.

Hypertext Markup Language (HTML): The primary "language" that World Wide Web documents are created in.

Hypertext: A hypertext document has references to other documents sprinkled throughout. If you click on one of these references, you are transferred to an entirely different document. For example, if this report was a hypertext document, you could click on any italicized word, and you'd instantly be transported to the definition of that word.

I

Impression: An advertising metric that indicates how many times an advertising link is displayed.

In-house: Merchant that administers its own affiliate program.

Internet: Inter-connected networks that use TCP/IP protocols.

Intranet: A company or organization's private network that uses the same type of software found on the Internet, but that is only for internal use.

Internet Service Provider (ISP): The company you call from your computer to gain access to the Internet.

IP Address: A unique number consisting of 4 parts separated by dots, e.g. 165.115.245.2. Every machine on the Internet has a unique IP address.

J

Javascript: A programming language developed by Sun Microsystems designed for writing programs that can be safely downloaded to your computer through the Internet and immediately run without fear of viruses or other harm to your computer or files. Java requires a browser compatible with Java. Using small Java programs, Web pages can include animations, calculators, and other features.

Joint Venture: A general partnership typically formed to undertake a particular business transaction or project rather than one intended to continue indefinitely.

K

Keyword: The term that a surfer types into a search engine search box. For example, someone who wants to find a site that sells printer paper might enter 'printer paper' at Google.

Keyword Density: The ratio between the keyword being searched for and the total number of words appearing on your web page. If your keyword occurs only once in a page that has twenty thousand words, then it has a density of 0.005 percent.

L

Lifetime Value: The total amount that a customer will spend with a particular company during his or her lifetime.

Link: A link is a "clickable" object that, when clicked, will take the viewer to a particular page, place on a page, or start a new e-mail with an address you specify.

Link Popularity: The total number of qualified Web sites linking to your Web site.

Local Area Network (LAN): Computers linked together in a central location, such as a business or government organization.

M

Manual Approval: Process in which all applicants for an affiliate program are reviewed individually and manually approved.

Media Metrix: Measures traffic counts on all the web sites on the Net. They publish the Top 50 sites in the US, the Global Top 50, and the Media Metrix Top 500 web sites.

Merchant: A business that markets and sells goods or services.

Merchant Account: A commercial bank account established by contractual agreement between your business and a bank. A merchant account enables your business to accept credit card payments from your customers.

Meta Tags: Information placed in the header of an HTML page, which is not visible to site visitors.

Multipurpose Internet Mail Extensions (MIME): Allows an email message to contain non-text data, such as audio and video files.

Modulator/Demodulator (MODEM): The card that allows your computer to connect to the phone line and communicate with other computers.

Mosaic: The first major browser program.

Multi-Level Marketing (MLM): Also known as Network Marketing, MLM involves the sale of products through a group of independent distributors who buy wholesale, sell retail, and sponsor other people to do the same.

N

Newsgroup: A newsgroup is a discussion that takes place online, devoted to a particular topic. The discussion takes the form of electronic messages called "postings" that anyone with a newsreader (standard with most browsers) can post or read.
Netscape: Makers of the Netscape Navigator browser.

Newbie: Someone who is new to the Internet or Internet marketing.

P

Pay-Per-Sale (PPS): Programs in which the affiliate receives a commission for each sale of a product or service that they refer to a merchant's web site.

Pay-Per-Lead (PPL): An affiliate program in which an affiliate receives a commission for each sales lead that they generate for a merchant web site. Examples include completed surveys, contest or sweepstakes entries, downloaded software demos, or free trials.

Pay-Per-Click (PPC): An advertising payment model where the advertiser pays only when the advertisement is actually clicked. Also, an affiliate program where an affiliate receives a commission for each click (visitor) they refer to a merchant's web site.

Politeness Window: Most search engine spiders will not crawl an entire site in one session. Instead, they crawl a couple of pages and return after a day or two to crawl a couple more and so on until they have indexed the entire site. This is a self-imposed limit in order not to overburden a server. The time period between sessions are known as the politeness window.

Portable Document Format (PDF): PDF stands for Portable Document Format. It's a distribution format developed by Adobe Corporation to allow electronic information to be transferred between various types of computers. The software that allows this transfer is called Acrobat.

Post Office Protocol (POP): Refers to the way email software such as Eudora gets mail from a mail server.

Profit: The amount of money you earn from your sales. For example, if you sell 10 videos at $47.00 each, and each costs $10 to produce and ship, your profit would be $37.00 per video or $370.00 total.

Plugin: A small piece of software that adds features to a larger piece of software.

Portal: A term used to describe a Web site that is intended to be used as a main "point of entry" to the Web, i.e., MSN.com is a portal site.

Posting: A message entered into a newsgroup or message board.

Privacy Policy: A privacy policy establishes how a company collects and uses information about its customers' accounts and transactions.

Protocol: A method or language of communication.

Proxy Server: Computers, such as those belonging to Internet service providers that act as agents for multiple users, resulting in many users only having one IP address.

Publisher: Another term for 'affiliate.'

R

Real Simple Syndication (RSS): An XML-based format for syndicated content.

Referring URL: The URL a user came from to reach your site.

Residual Earnings: Programs that pay affiliates for each sale a shopper from their sites makes at the merchant's site over the life of the customer.

Return on Advertising Spend (ROAS): How much revenue is generated per amount spent on an advertising method.

Return on Investment (ROI): This is the amount derived from subtracting your net revenues from your total costs.

Revenue: Total income for your sales. For example, if you sell 50 ebooks at $27.00 each, your revenue would be $1350.00.

Robots: Any browser program not directly under human control that follows hypertext links and accesses Web pages. A search engine spider is a 'robot.'

S

Scumware: Software that contains additional 'features' for the purpose of displaying advertisements. This software will modify web pages from their original content to put ads on the user's computer screen. Examples of scumware propagators included: Gator, Ezula, Surf+ and Imesh.

Secure Server: A secure server allows a connection between itself and another secure server. Secured connections provide three essential things where online transactions are concerned: privacy, authentication, & message integrity. When viewing Web pages or posting information to a secure server, you'll notice that the "http://" that usually appears in the Web address bar changes to "https://." Also, on most Web browsers, the symbol of a closed padlock should appear somewhere in the browser's frame as an indicator that you are using a secure connection.

Server: The computer hardware that stores your homepage and sends and receives information through the World Wide Web.

Server Logs: Each time a user accesses a Web page, information is recorded on server logs. Server logs contain information about what pages where accessed, along with the date and time and computer's IP Address. Other statistics can also be tracked, including username, browser type, previous page, etc.

Shockwave: Co-developed by Netscape and Macromedia, software that allows animations and interactive programs to be embedded into HTML pages.

Sig (Signature File or Sig Line): Your signature at the end of an email or Usenet posting. Commonly consist of your email address and other contact information, very brief information about your business, and perhaps a favorite quotation or funny phrase.

Social Media Marketing (SMM): Using social media sites such as MySpace, YouTube and Facebook to promote products online.

SPAM: The term "spam" is Internet slang that refers to unsolicited commercial e-mail (UCE) or unsolicited bulk e-mail (UBE). Some people refer to this kind of communication as junk e-mail to equate it with the paper junk mail that comes through the US Mail. Unsolicited e-mail is e-mail that you did not request; it most often contains advertisements for services or products.

Spyware - Also known as "adware," a program hidden within free downloaded software that transmits user information via the Internet to advertisers.

SQL (Structured Query Language): A programming language for sending queries to databases.

SSL (Secure Sockets Layer): A protocol used to enable encrypted, authenticated communications across the Internet. URL's that begin with "https" indicate that an SSL connection will be used.

Super Affiliates: The top 1 or 2% of affiliates that generate approximately 90% of any affiliate programs earnings.

T

Targeted Marketing: The process of distinguishing the different groups that make up a market, and developing appropriate products and marketing mixes for each target market involved.

Text Link: A link not accompanied by a graphical image.

Third Party Credit Card Processing: A 'third party credit card processor' is a company that accepts credit card orders on behalf of another company, making a merchant account unnecessary.

Third Party Tracking Software: Software located on a server other than your own, that tracks and records visits to your Web site.

Tracking Method: The method by which an affiliate program tracks referred sales, leads or clicks.

Tracking URL: A web site URL, e.g., http://bluehost.com, with your special code attached to it, i.e. http://www.bluehost.com/track/rgardner/CODE5 (track/rgardner/CODE5 is the tracking code). Visitors arriving at the site are tracked back to you through your special code, or ID.

Two-tier: Affiliate program structure whereby affiliates earn commissions on their conversions as well as conversions of webmasters they refer to the program.

U

Unique User: A unique visitor to your Web site. Probably the best indicator of site traffic.

Upload: Transferring a file from your computer to another computer.

Uniform Resource Locator (URL): The address of a site on the World Wide Web. Here's an example URL:

http://www.netprofitstoday.com/articles/96/1/Buy-Content-for-Your-Site/Page1.html

The "http" stands for "hypertext transfer protocol"; "://" signals the beginning of the address; "www.netprofitstoday.com" is the domain name; "/articles/96/1/" are directories and subdirectories; and "Page1.html" is the name of the HTML file.

User Session: The session of activity for one user on a Web site.

V

Viral Marketing: Describes any strategy that encourages individuals to pass on a marketing message to others, creating the potential for exponential growth in the message's exposure and influence. Like viruses, such strategies take advantage of rapid multiplication to explode the message to thousands, and even millions.

Virtual Reality Markup Language (VRML): A language developed as a replacement for HTML. At a VRML web site, one can explore environments in three dimensions, and can interact with other people who are visiting the same site. VRML requires a special browser.

Virus: A computer virus is defined as a set of commands, created intentionally, that will do some level of damage to a computer. A computer virus does not float around in cyberspace, but is always attached to something. That 'something' could be a text file (MSWord document), an email, a photo, a music clip or a video clip. Your computer must receive one of these 'carriers' in order to get a computer virus.

W

Webmaster: The person at your Internet Service Provider who is responsible for maintaining the server. Also, any person who maintains a Web site.

Web 2.0: Web-based communities such as social-networking sites intended to facilitate user collaboration and sharing.

Web site: A collection of HTML pages.

World Wide Web (WWW, or Web): A section of the Internet containing "pages" of information, including text, photos, graphics, audio, and video. You can search for documents by using one of the many search databases. To access the Web, you must use a browser.

Y

Yahoo: The most popular and (perhaps) the most comprehensive of all search index databases on the World Wide Web. Yahoo's URL is http://www.yahoo.com.

Make Money with this Book!

FACT: Nobody sells a book better than someone who has already read it!

You know the strong selling points of the product and can endorse it without hesitation.

You can earn generous 50% commissions just by recommending "Super Affiliate Handbook" to people!

If you have a web site, an ezine or a customer list that would benefit from reading "Super Affiliate Handbook" – let them know about it!

I'll pay you 50% for every sale you make and my affiliate program, Clickbank, pays out twice a month! I also supply you with headlines, email teasers, pop-up scripts, graphic tools and more!

You'll find everything you need to quickly and efficiently promote for BIG profits on every sale.

http://SuperAffiliateHandbook.com/affiliates.php

About the Author

Rosalind Gardner's success with affiliate marketing on the Internet is proof positive that ANYONE can succeed in an Internet business.

After working as an air traffic controller for almost twenty years, the crazy schedules had started to seriously affect her health. She knew she had to leave the job before it killed her.

In 1997 after seeing a banner ad for the One and Only dating service offering webmasters a chance to make money with their web sites, she KNEW she had to give it a try.

The rest, as they say, is history.

In 2000, supported by her various online businesses, she quit her job. With nothing other than an intense desire to build a better life for herself, she proved that business or web design experience weren't necessary to succeed on the 'Net.

Since learning how relatively simple it is to make money online, Rosalind has been writing about affiliate and Internet marketing to encourage friends, colleagues and anyone who is interested, to join her on the path to Internet riches.

Her weekly *Net Profits Today* newsletter is freely available at http://NetProfitsToday.com and she writes the 'Affiliate's Corner' column for *Revenue* magazine, available at http://RevenueToday.com.

Her interviews have appeared in a multitude of online and offline venues, including *'Secrets to Their Success'* (http://secretstotheirsuccess.com) and *Small Business Opportunities* magazines.

Many of her Internet marketing colleagues have written about her success. Here is what Allan Gardyne of 'AssociatePrograms.com' had to say about Rosalind and the Super Affiliate Handbook:

"A perfect example is Rosalind Gardner, who earns $30,000 to $50,000 a month in affiliate commissions, with a very nice 40% to 50% profit margin... She explains how she attracts more than 4,500 unique visitors a day and has sales conversions that are 3 to 5 times higher than those of the average affiliate... This isn't vague theory or book learning, it's real-life, down-to-earth advice from real people like Rosalind."

Rosalind also offers one-on-one telephone consulting services at http://RosalindGardner.com/consultations/. She also speaks regularly at Internet and Affiliate marketing conferences.

You **too** can enjoy financial freedom with an online business. Whether you are just starting out or want to improve an existing site, Rosalind can help you achieve your dream.

After Word

You made it! Congratulations!

Now that you've read the whole 'Super Affiliate Handbook,' you're ready to begin your own affiliate marketing success story.

As the Nike slogan says, 'Just Do It!'

Take one step at a time and soon you'll have forged a new path in your life - the path to Internet riches.

Whatever you choose to do, I wish you Health, Happiness and great Success always!

Cheers,
Rosalind

Printed in the United States
126591LV00001B/31/P

9 780973 328738